Marriage After Mourning
The Secrets of Surviving Couples

Judy C. Pearson

KENDALL/HUNT PUBLISHING COMPANY
4050 Westmark Drive   Dubuque, Iowa 52002

Cover photo by Terry E. Eiler.
© Terry E. Eiler, 1994
One time rights available,
Mugwump Stock Agency
8611 Lavelle Road
Athens, OH 45701 (614)592-1280

Bronze statues designed and sculpted by Fred Glover, Athens, OH.

Library of Congress Catalog Card Number: 94-79689

ISBN 0-7872-0205-3

Printed in the United States of America
10 9 8 7 6 5 4 3 2 1

For everything there is a season, and a time for every matter under heaven; a time to be born, and a time to die . . . a time to kill, and a time to heal . . . a time to weep, and a time to laugh; a time to mourn, and a time to dance . . .
Ecclesiastes 3:1-4

Contents

PREFACE

In the past two decades, I have tried to understand and explain marital happiness. My efforts have been reported in both the popular media and in full-length books. In *Gender and Communication*, I explored how women and men communicate differently in their personal relationships. *Communication in the Family: Seeking Satisfaction in Changing Times* illustrated how communication could mediate between happy and unhappy marriages as marriages shift and change because of predictable and nonpredictable events. In *Lasting Love*, I provided the findings of interviews with couples in lasting and loving relationships. Individuals married forty to seventy years in creme de la creme marriages shared their previously undisclosed stories with me which formed the mosaic of the book.

As I have continued to try to explore the mysteries of marriage, I have considered other groups of people who might help me understand the increasingly rare phenomenon of lasting and loving relationships. I continue to seek out individuals who can instruct others about positive marital models.

When I was conducting the interviews for *Lasting Love*, I noticed, time and again, that these couples had almost invariably endured unimaginable difficulties. They told me about job loss, infidelity, near fatal accidents, and, most serious of all, the deaths of their own children.

Their words gave me hope that marriage was not an outdated institution. Their revelations suggested that just as iron becomes steel under heat and pressure, marriages become stronger when they are tested. I wanted to learn more about hardship and heartache in marriage. I wanted to know, from couples who had experienced the "worst of times," how they could survive and thrive in their marriages. The tenet that I operated under was that if people who had faced crises could make marriage work, their stories and inspiration would help us all.

When I began the research on this book, I interviewed couples who had experienced and survived the "slings and arrows of outrageous fortune" to learn more about marriages that happily endure. I talked to a couple in Wisconsin who were coping with the knowledge that they were HIV-infected. I spoke to another couple in which the husband, as sole supporter of the family, had lost his job as the CEO of a Fortune 500 company and then suffered an almost fatal heart attack. I talked to a woman who tearfully told me of a love affair she had that nearly ruined her marriage, but eventually strengthened it. Each time I explained to these couples that I was writing a book on marriages that had survived crisis, they looked puzzled and asked why I had chosen them to interview. They expressed their feelings by saying that they had some problems, but they were not really very significant.

The only exception to this patterned response was from couples who had lost children. These couples uniformly agreed that the loss of one's child is a true crisis in any marriage. I decided to focus my study on happily married couples who had lost children.

My investigation was limited, then, to understanding the mystery of marriage after mourning. My intent was not to deal with the child's death, although these stories of accidents, disease, homicide, and even, suicide, were inexorably intertwined with the love stories of the couples. My purpose was not to learn how couples cope with the death of the child, although again, the couples' stories could not be told without this detail. The goal was to explore, as I have done before, how couples could maintain loving and lasting relationships regardless of the experiences and the events that fate provided to them.

These couples are rare because most people who experience the loss of one or more of their children do not remain in stable or satisfying relationships. The statistics on how many couples who have lost children go on to divorce vary. Some earlier estimates suggest that 7 out of 10 such marriages result in divorce while more current figures gauge the divorce rate to be closer to 90%.

METHOD

My method in this investigation, as in *Lasting Love*, was to interview couples who had lost children. In the two years that I spent researching this book, I spoke with well-known people and ordinary people. I talked to couples who had taken advantage of self-help groups and to those who grieved more privately. I talked to those whose children had died of suicide, homicide, illness, and accidents. Bereaved parents of newborns, young children, teenagers, and adults shared their stories. Most interviews were done in people's homes, but a few were conducted on the telephone. All of the interviews were tape recorded and transcribed. A total of 58 in-depth interviews were conducted in the larger study; 31 people who had lost children were interviewed. In addition, pastors, ministers, physicians, and morticians were interviewed.

These interviews were among the most difficult, and yet most meaningful, of any I have conducted. In all interviews, the parents and I cried both for the lost child and for the amazing love that the couple expressed for each other. I felt that I could echo Ellen Goodman, who wrote in her moving book, *Turning Points*, "What began as an interview often ended up as a conversation, the kind in which you learn a lot about yourself by learning about others."[1] While I learned about others, I also learned about myself.

My goal in the interviews was not to gather informative statements nor even advice. Instead, I was looking for the stories that would reveal the hidden clues to happy relationships. Like Bernie Siegel, who observes, "The truth lies in people and their stories,"[2] I have learned that people's accounts and anecdotes reveal their truths.

Family happiness can not be prescribed universally. Each family is distinctive from every other family. Each family creates its own relational culture in which family members communicate uniquely and come to have shared understandings of specific events. Two authors suggest that, "Nobody who has not been in the interior of a family can say what the difficulties of any individual of that family may be."[3] Similarly we cannot understand the mysteries of family happiness without attempting to become close to the truths that each family holds.

In addition, although I have done my share of statistical studies, I have learned that people's stories rather than statistics about them speak to others. Hilaire Belloc observed that "Statistics are the triumph of the quantitative method, and the quantitative method is the victory of sterility and death." To which Bernard Lown, a medical doctor, added, "While science may help explain how a virus multiplies, it leaves unanswered why a tear is shed."[4] This book is less interested in the death of a body than in the emotion of love.

ACKNOWLEDGMENTS

Many people have been instrumental in the completion of this book. First, I want to thank Ohio University and the School of Interpersonal Communication for the time provided to me. Second, I wish to thank my students who spent time transcribing interviews, finding additional research materials, and offering their own thoughts on the effect of losing a child on marital happiness. They include Carol J. S. Bruess, Sharon Bernas, Laurie Manke, Jennifer Waldeck, Jennifer Cantlie, Jennifer Grey, Erin McCoy, Molly Kiser, Peggy Smith, Xin Xin Song, and David Klosterman. Most importantly, I want to thank the many individuals and couples I interviewed. They include:

Kay and Rodney Bevington
Harold Brisker
Don and Margie Brown
Debbie and Roger Cole
Sandra Collins
Michael and Chris Downard
Betty and Robert Eredics
Joe and Gerri Eszterhas
Miriam and Isaac Fife
Joseph and Mary (Bernie) Gluvna
Kittie Hartfelter
Marilyn and Glen Heavilin
Pamela Hinaman
Martha and Dick Johnson
Sherie and Michael Johnson
Mickie Mackabee

Les and Taffy Marks
Arline and Cliff McCarthy
Robert and Marilyn Merkel
Ferne and Harry Nelson
Max and Adrianna Norton
Steve and Barbara Ostrolenk
Mary and Eddie Poole
Eleanor and Roy Souders
Milly and Redgie Staskal
Connie Stevens
Marlene Stokes
George and Janet Voinovich
Jack and Louise Warner
Alice and Otto Weening
Sally and George Wenner
Kathleen Whitmer
Nancy and Steven Ziegenmeyer

Without their understanding, insight, and patience, this book would not be possible. I dedicate the book to them and to their families. I hope the wisdom that they have gained will help others to have meaningful marriages after mourning.

REFERENCES

1. Ellen Goodman, *Turning points* (New York: Fawcett Crest, 1979), p. xi.
2. Bernie S. Siegel, *Peace, Love, & Healing: Bodymind Communication and the Path to Self-Healing: An Exploration* (New York: HarperPerennial, 1990), p. 142.
3. Pesach Krauss and Morrie Goldfischer, *Why Me? Coping with Grief, Loss, and Change* (New York: Bantam Books, 1988), p. xv.
4. Repeated in *Reader's Digest*, December 1986, p. 207 and attributed to Bernard Lown, M.D., originally cited in Norman Cousins's *The Healing Heart* (Norton).

Marriage Ever After
An Introduction

"Hope" is the thing with feathers—
That perches in the soul—
And sings the tune without the words—
And never stops—at all—
Emily Dickinson[1]

"Chains do not hold a marriage together.
It is threads, hundreds of tiny threads
which sew people together through the years."
Simone Signoret.[2]

"And you learn. . .And you learn. . .
With every goodbye, you learn."
Anonymous[3]

This is not a book about death; it is a book about life. It is not about the loss of children; it is about enduring love. It is a celebration of the human spirit to overcome a couple's worst pain—the death of their child—to maintain their own love. Mary Tyler Moore, who is no stranger to pain, observed, "Pain nourishes courage. You can't be brave if you've only had wonderful things happen to you."[4]

MARITAL SATISFACTION AND STABILITY

Marital satisfaction—our assessment of our marriage—and marital stability—the endurance of our marriage—are both salient and important to people. Dr. Joyce Brothers states, "When you look at your life, the greatest happinesses are family happinesses." Sven Wahlroos, a family therapist, adds, "The greatest happiness and the deepest satisfaction in life, the most intense enthusiasm and the most profound inner peace, all come from being a member of a loving family."[5]

People seek marital and family relationships in order to attain a human connection. Graham Spanier, a marital researcher, remarked on a program entitled *Love and Marriage* on PBS, "Because we live in such an impersonal society, we are trying to personalize our lives through families." Mary Ann Glendon, a Harvard Law School professor specializing in family law, concurs, "After the loosening of legal and economic ties. . . the principal bonds which remain to unite the family may be the ties of human affection."[6]

Families form the most basic social unit. One speaker, discussing African American families, observed, "Strong and stable families are the first step to fuller participation in the American dream."[7] This sentiment is more than mere rhetoric. Psychiatric social worker Judith Wallerstein studied a sample of children, between the ages of nineteen and twenty–nine, of divorced parents, ten years after their parents' divorce. She found that many "are drifting through life with no set goals, limited educations, and a sense of helplessness. . . Although only a few have dropped out of high school, most have not seriously pursued higher education. . . They don't make long–term plans and are aiming below the intellectual and educational achievements of their fathers and mothers."[8] The study showed that children in divorced families may perceive a lack of personal attention, may not be able to give other people sustained attention, and may not be able to create a coherent life.

Americans value marriage and loving relationships. A survey completed in 1970 found that "96 percent of all Americans held to the ideal of two people sharing a life and a home together. When the same question was asked in 1980, the same percentage agreed."[9] A survey completed today would probably yield little difference in the findings.

While we romanticize marriage and hold high expectations for the role of love in our everyday lives, less than half of us are able to maintain long–term, loving relationships. Since 1975, one out of every two American marriages has ended in divorce. In the past two decades, those dire statistics have not been substantially altered.

Just as we value loving relationships, we recognize the difficulty of it. A national survey conducted in 1978 asked whether "most couples getting married today expect to remain married for the rest of their lives." Sixty percent said no. Commitment is desirable, but not easy.[10]

Why do Americans value marriage, but believe that most people will not be married for the rest of their lives? One explanation is the high expectations that people place on their relationships. Martin Seligman writes, "Marriage . . . now requires more than it used to. It's no longer just a matter of raising children. Our mate must be externally sexy, and thin, and interesting to talk to, and good at tennis."[11]

In addition to the many unstable or failing marriages, many marriages that do survive are not satisfying. Sociologist Andrew Greeley reports that, "The proportion of married people who said they were very happy had declined. . . Marriage . . . seemed to be responding less effectively to human needs in our hedonistic culture than it once had."[12] In addition, some of the marriages that do survive are riddled with problems; such as abuse, neglect, sexual disorder, and general dysfunction. As a society we seem unable to create and sustain our most basic social unit.

Robert Bellah and his associates conclude, "The family is in flux, and signs of trouble are widespread. . . divorce rates continue to rise, and the very meaning of the family as we have known it has become problematic. . . While there are practical and sometimes moral reasons for this decomposition of the family, it coincides neither with what most people in our society say they desire nor, especially in the case of children, with their best interests."[13]

CHANGING TIMES

We may be living in a time of unprecedented change. New forms of technology, communication, and transportation combine to create changes in both the social and personal realms. None of us are the same from birth to death. We individually meet challenges that call out for action. Ellen Goodman, in her book, *Turning Points*, writes, "There is, for all of us, a point at which not growing means diminishing. A point at which we can only choose between despair or change."[14]

Similarly, the structure and the meaning of the family has surely changed. New family forms replace traditional models, while the lifespan of the family is not nearly as long as it once was.

Families that do survive face individual changes. As the marital couple adds children to the family and as those children grow and develop, the family changes. When the last child leaves home and the couple retire from their occupations, major alterations will occur. The age of the couple—as they move from young adulthood to middle age and eventually older age—also affects their outlook on the marriage.

Unpredicted events can also affect the family. Financial problems, job distress, illness, and death all modify the stability and satisfaction of the family. Some families do not survive such stressors, while others take them in stride.

Each change that occurs may represent an exit or an entrance. While we are leaving one way of knowing the family behind, we are entering into another way of understanding our family. One set of authors noted, "When you walk out of something you do not walk into nothing unless that is what you choose. You walk into something else."[15] Philosopher Andre Gide offers a similar sentiment, "It is one of life's laws that as soon as one door closes, another opens. But the tragedy is that we look at the closed door and disregard the open one."[16]

ADVERSITY

We may be especially tempted to view negative events as ones that close doors rather than open them. Franklin D. Roosevelt is an individual who is often identified as an example of someone who was positively affected by a negative event. Krauss and Goldfischer write, "Before Franklin D. Roosevelt was afflicted with polio, he gave little evidence of greatness or even of sympathy for the ill and underprivileged. Viewed from the perspective of history, his affliction, however painful for him, may seem a small price to pay for producing a dedicated leader in the hour of world crisis."[17]

Viktor E. Frankl, a psychiatrist and Holocaust survivor, explored his understanding about the relationship between growth and adversity in his book *Man's Search for Meaning*.[18] One of the ways that he feels that we can discover the meaning of life is by transforming a personal tragedy into a triumph—turning one's predicament into a human achievement. Based on his experience, he believes that human potential, at its best, will allow people to turn their anguish into achievement.

The choice is ours. We can turn adversity to advantage. Krauss and Goldfischer suggest, "When someone or something bruises us, we can use the hurt to make our lives more radiant and more lovely. Despite its grim appearance, sorrow possesses vast potential power to deepen our understanding, sympathy, and courage, and to enlarge our visions."[19]

DEATH

Each person who faces adversity probably believes that his or hers is the worst anguish ever faced by anyone. The personal pain associated with a loss or a tragedy cannot be measured. Although some social scientists have attempted to place various stressful events on a rating scale, we cannot—with much meaning or accuracy—rate and rank pernicious circumstances as to their seriousness or potential detrimental effects.

Nonetheless, death is surely among the most difficult problems faced by human beings. Some people fear their own deaths. Elisabeth Kubler–Ross, Editor of *Death: The Final Stage of Growth*, and a foremost expert on death suggests that people who have not really lived are those who fear death the most. She writes, "those. . . who have left issues unsettled, dreams unfilled, hopes shattered, and who have let the real things in life (loving and being loved by others, contributing in a positive way to other people's happiness and welfare, finding out what things are really you) pass them by—who are most reluctant to die." She adds, "It is never too late to start living and growing."[20]

The idea that change presents both exits and entrances, doors that are closed as well as doors that are opened, may be especially relevant when considering death. Two wise men write, "That image, that every exit is also an entrance, gave me a partial answer... The concept of death as an experience of growth and transition and transformation rather than one of annihilation and destruction helped me to gain perspective. I felt as if I had awakened from a bad dream to a new day filled with promise and power and light."[21]

In one sense, we may all be viewed as terminal—that is, all of us will die. As one individual noted, the mortality rate for living things is 100 percent. None of us will escape death, but our feelings about death vary dramatically.

Jim McQuade, a medical student, observed that:

> It is important to come to an acceptance of death, not only as an absolute reality, but as part of the natural order of things. When the physician achieves this acceptance he no longer needs to avoid the people who have problems that he cannot solve. [He or she] is then able to remain in a partnership with the patient and to share the common bond of mortality and love that they have between them until the very end."[22]

THE SURVIVORS

Why does one person have the capacity to deal with death and the next person does not? Why does one marriage survive trial after trial while another marriage fails after the first test? What can we learn from those who have weathered the storms of severe stress and strain?

The International Committee for the Study of Victimization studied survivors of crises events. They found that people fell into one of three groups. Roughly one third of the trauma victims were "broken by their experiences, showing a lasting psychological impairment, reduced ability to function well in work and in relationships, or medical problems. Another third passed through a period of emotional difficulty and adjustment but eventually returned to their precrisis level of adaptation. The final third underwent an adjustment and healing period that resulted in great personal growth. Those in this last group eventually emerged wiser, stronger, psychologically healthier, and more productive than they had been before their ordeal."[23]

What distinguishes those who survive crises and those who do not? Professor Al Siebert of Portland State University has studied "the survivor personality." He has found a number of traits which characterize the survivor's personality: "getting smarter (wiser) and enjoying life more as one gets older; falling back to and successfully relying on inner resources in disruptive, chaotic circumstances; and having a talent for serendipity, being able to convert accidents or what others would regard as misfortune into good luck."[24] When these events are true calamities, such as the death of a friend or family member, the individual does not turn the event into "good luck," but instead changes the disaster into something that produces growth or somehow benefits others.[25]

LOVING AND LASTING RELATIONSHIPS

Maintaining a loving relationship in the face of adversity is not an easy task. One sage noted that "marriage is not for sissies." Lasting and caring relationships take great effort. They do not remain the same over time. Anne Morrow Lindberg noted that, "Marriage should, I think, always be a little hard and new and strange. It should be breaking your shell and going into another world, and a bigger one."[26] While Lindberg may have been referring to the new marriage, marriages tend to follow this pattern throughout the lifecourse. They continually require partners to break their shells and to go into a new and bigger world.

How do couples maintain their marriages? Robert Bellah and his associates discuss the Evangelical Christian perspective:

> ...chemistry may be a good start, but the only thing that makes it real love that will endure, and the kind of love that is taken into marriages, is that mental decision that you're going to force that chemical reaction to keep going with each other... Emotions can be sustained, or even created, by conscious choice. Reliance on that mental decision, in turn, guarantees a permanence or stability in relationships that would not be possible relying on feelings alone... The difficulty is that in any relationship there will be crises, and

> Christian faith allows you to 'weather' the storm until the
> calm comes back.[27]

Other studies have suggested that other considerations than selflessness may encourage satisfying and stable marriages. Marital researchers Lewis and Spanier provided a classic study which showed that three sets of factors were related to marital satisfaction. They included *premarital influences, social and economic elements,* and *interpersonal factors.*[28] Premarital influences included whether the two members of the couple were similar on such features as religion, ethnic group, family background, attitudes, and values; their resources including their education, social class, and physical health; their parental models; and their support from significant others. Generally, individuals who were more similar, rather than more dissimilar; had greater, rather than fewer, resources; had more positive parental role models; and received more support from significant others were more satisfied in their own marriages.

The social and economic elements included the couple's socioeconomic level, the wife's employment, the extent to which the union of the couple was approved by neighbors and friends, and who occupied the couple's home. Although these relationships are not easily generalizable, some conclusions can be offered. Couples are happier when they have fewer financial worries, when others approve of their marriage, and when fewer, rather than more, other family members share their home with them.

Interpersonal factors were identified as the expression of positive regard, the gratification of emotional needs, the effectiveness of communication, role fit, and the amount of interaction. Satisfied and stable couples appreciated being viewed positively and having their emotional needs met. They also named communication as a strong contributor to their marital happiness. To the extent that the couple agreed upon their roles and they matched each other's perceptions, they were happy. Finally, satisfied couples identified an optimum level of interaction as a contributor to their satisfaction.

This classic study has been complemented by more recent studies on marital satisfaction. The Lauers more recently studied the reasons provided by husbands and wives which account for their marital happiness. The top seven reasons that were provided were identical, and in the same order, for husbands and wives. They include; my spouse is my best friend, I like my spouse as a person, marriage is a long-term commitment, marriage is sacred, we agree on aims and goals, my spouse has grown more interesting, and I want the relationship to succeed.[29]

More recently, a study of happily married couples who had been married between 40 and 70 years provided provocative conclusions. The study used in–depth interviews to determine the underlying themes of those happily wed. Eight areas of agreement emerged from the studies. They included; lowered expectations, un– conditional acceptance, positive distortion, becoming one, remaining two, sexual satisfaction, coping with conflict, and persistence.[30]

Lowered expectations suggests that the couple did not hold each other or their marriage up to high standards that would be unobtainable and result in unhappiness. They were not unrealistic in their notions of what the other person or the relationship could do for them. The couples expected less than did others and therefore were almost always pleased with the comparatively high quality of the relationship.

Unconditional acceptance suggests that the couple loved each other just for being, not for doing. People always marry strangers and when these individuals learned about the surprising characteristics of their partners, they responded with humor or joy. The two members of the couple seemed not only to accept, but to appreciate, the idiosyncrasies of their partner.

Positive distortion means that the couple did not view each other objectively. Instead, they looked at each other through "rose–colored glasses." When they thought about their partner, they saw someone who was far more attractive, interesting, and generally better than others would see him or her. If love is not blind, this study suggests that it certainly evidences a strong astigmatism.

The couples described "becoming one" with each other. When one person became ill, the other hurt. One person said that they were essentially a "two-headed animal." Experiences, thoughts, and ideas held by one were often shared by the other—even without communicating it to him or her.

The couples also said that they were able to transcend their "oneness" to maintain separate identities. They participated in separate activities, had their own unique styles, and in other ways sustained themselves as individuals.

Sexual activity varies dramatically among couples. Some couples engage in coitus three or more times a week while others rarely, if ever, have intercourse. Happily married couples, regardless of frequency, express high levels of sexual satisfaction. They are pleased not only with actual copulation, but with all of the loving gestures that are related to sexuality including touching, kissing, and providing back rubs.

Couples do not all resolve their conflicts similarly, but they all learn methods to settle them. In addition, they seem generally satisfied with the techniques they use to manage conflict and feel that their approaches are constructive rather than destructive.

Finally, the couples were persistent in maintaining their marriage and their love. They stubbornly refused to allow anyone—including other family members—or anything—such as disagreements over money—to obstruct their happiness. Their belief in their marriage and their love superseded any other considerations.

MARRIAGE AFTER MOURNING

This book is another attempt to understand the mysteries of marriage. In this exploration, we go into the interior of several loving marriages to try to understand how marriages can be satisfying, even in the face of adversity. We will find that marital happiness cannot be achieved by following a simple formula.

Indeed, this study shows that happy couples often hold conflicting and competing beliefs and attitudes. Contented couples learn how to live with these contradictions. Satisfying marriages are marked by dialectics. The philosopher Hegel suggested that dialectics included an idea (or thesis) transformed into its opposite (or antithesis) and finally resolved in a truth that accommodates both (synthesis).

The couples in this book revealed several dialectics which help us to understand successful marriage. Their secrets include: embracing the world, but altering it; accepting yourself, but seeking to improve; expecting perfection, but accepting imperfection; being optimistic, but admitting reality; maintaining control, but relinquishing it; listening in order to be heard; staying as you are, but changing; and remembering the past, considering the future, but living in the present.

The couples whose words form the mosaic of this book are

remarkable. They have sustained long and strong marriages. They have also survived the most difficult test a marriage can be provided. They serve as role models for all who want to listen and learn about loving relationships.

Good marriages may be compared to the making of fine china: clay must be exposed to searing flame before it emerges as beautiful china. Similarly, in nature we see that trees, plants, and shrubs often need to be pruned and cut back in order to burst forward with greater growth. The individuals in the marriages in this book have been damaged and bruised, but they have emerged recovered and stronger.

When the dispirited soldiers retreated in Washington across the Delaware, Thomas Paine was inspired to write the words that have lived far longer than he: "These are the times that try men's souls. The summer soldier and the sunshine patriot will, in this crisis, shrink from the service of their country; but he that stands it *now*, deserves the love and thanks of man and woman."[31] Paine's declaration are often credited with inspiring the courage in the soldiers to eventually win the victory at Trenton.

Paine's insight was appropriate for fighting soldiers in another century. Today his message can be inspirational for those who desire good marriages. Marriages try people's souls. Many shrink away when times are tough. People in lasting marriages deserve our appreciation; more important, they deserve our study and understanding.

Marriage after Mourning: The Secrets of Survivors is not a book about death. It is a book about life. The focus of this book is not on the children who have died, but on the marriages that have survived. It is a book of hope, a book of love, a book of forgiveness. It is a book for anyone who truly wants to understand the secrets of surviving couples. We enter into the house of mourning to understand the house of rejoicing.

REFERENCES

1. No. 254, copyrighted 1861.
2. Reported in *Reader's Digest*, December 1987, p. 45.
3. From the poem "Comes the Dawn."
4. Mary Tyler Moore, quoted by Barbara Grizzute Harrison in *McCalls*, p. 101, and cited in *Reader's Digest*, February 1986, p. 137.
5. Sven Wahlroos, *Family Communication* (New York: Macmillan, 1983), p. xi.
6. Mary Ann Glendon, *The Transformation of Family Law: State, Law, and the Family in the United States and Western Europe* (Chicago: University of Chicago Press, 1989), p. 313.
7. "Straight Talk on Black Families," a speech by L. Douglas Wilder reported in *Reader's Digest*, July 1971, p. 99.
8. Judith S. Wallerstein and Sandra Blakeslee, *Second Chances: Men, Women, and Children a Decade after Divorce* (New York: Ticknor and Fields, 1989), pp. 148-149.
9. Reported in Robert N. Bellah, Richard Madsen, William M. Sullivan, Ann Swidler, and Steven M. Tipton, *Habits of the Heart: Individualism and Commitment in American Life* (New York: Harper & Row, 1985), p. 90.
10. Reported in Bellah, Madsen, Sullivan, Swidler, and Tipton, p. 90.
11. Martin E. P. Seligman, *Learned Optimism: How to Change Your Mind and Your Life* (New York: Pocket Books, 1990), p. 283.
12. This study conducted by Glenn and Weaver, 1988, was reported in Andrew M. Greeley, *Faithful Attraction* (New York: a Tom Doherty Associates Book, 1991), p. 3.
13. Bellah, Madsen, Sullivan, Swidler, and Tipton, p. 45.
14. Ellen Goodman, *Turning points* (New York: Fawcett Crest, 1979), p. 228.
15. Pesach Krauss and Morrie Goldfischer, *Why Me? Coping with Grief, Loss, and Change* (New York: Bantam Books, 1988), p. 110.
16. Krauss and Goldfischer, p. 102.
17. Krauss and Goldfischer, pp. 70-71.
18. Published by Touchstone and revised in 1984.
19. Krauss and Goldfischer, p. 108.
20. Cited in Krauss and Goldfischer, p. 113.
21. Krauss and Goldfischer, p. 110.
22. Reported by Krauss and Goldfischer, p. 233.
23. Sandy Banisky, "Experts Think Most Hostages Will Adjust Easily to Freedom," *Baltimore Sun*, November 6, 1980, reported in Ann Kaiser Stearns, *Coming Back: Rebuilding Lives after Crisis and Loss* (New York: Ballantine Books, 1988), p. 294.
24. Al Siebert, "The Survivor Personality," *Association for Humanistic Psychology Newsletter*, August-September 1983, p. 19.
25. Stearns, p. 193.
26. Anne Morrow Lindberg, quoted by James D. Newton, *Uncommon Friends*, and reported in *Reader's Digest*, February 1988, p. 56.
27. Bellah, Madsen, Sullivan, Swidler, and Tipton, p. 95.
28. Robert A. Lewis and Graham B. Spanier, "Theorizing about the Quality and Stability of Marriage," *Contemporary Theories About the Family: Research-Based Theories 1* (1979): 268-294.
29. Jeanette Lauer and Robert Lauer, "Marriages Made to Last," *Psychology Today* 7 (1985 July): 22-26.

30. Judy C. Pearson, *Lasting Love: What Keeps Couples Together* (Dubuque, IA: Wm. C. Brown, 1992).

31. Thomas Paine, "The Crisis," no. 1, *The Writings of Thomas Paine*, ed. Moncure D. Conway, 1 (1894), p. 170. Conway explains this quotation: "The first 'Crisis' is of especial historical interest. It was written during the retreat of Washington across the Delaware, and by order of the Commander was read to groups of his dispirited and suffering soldiers. Its opening sentence [above] was adopted as the watchword of the movement on Trenton, a few days after its publication, and is believed to have inspired much of the courage which won that victory, which, though not imposing in extent, was of great moral effect on Washington's little army" (p. 169).

The Loss of a Child

"To fear death. . . is nothing other than to think oneself wise when one is not; for it is to think one knows what one does not know. No man knows whether death may not even turn out to be the greatest of blessings for a human being; and yet people fear it as if they knew for certain that it is the greatest of evils."
                                        Socrates[1]

"The best of times, the worst of times"
            Charles Dickens, *Tale of Two Cities,*

"There's no tragedy like the death of a child. Things never go back to the way they were."
                    Dwight D. Eisenhower

Martha Hicks, the mother of serial killer Jeffrey Dahmer's first victim, Steven Hicks, continues to work to keep her son's memory alive. Her son disappeared on June 18, 1978, four days before his 19th birthday. Dahmer later admitted that he picked up Hicks, who was hitchhiking, took him to his home, beat him to death, and then dismembered his body.[2]

Dawn Marie Hendershot, seven years old, was abducted on her way home from Gorrell Elementary School, just four blocks from her home. Her mother called the police when she did not arrive home and a search for her began. The search continued until early Friday, October 2. Donald Lee Maurer, a neighbor of the Hendershots was arrested and charged with the murder, kidnapping, and rape of Dawn.[3] Ted and Patricia Hendershot of Massillon, Ohio, continue to mourn the loss of their daughter.

On June 17, 1985, college basketball star Len Bias captured national headlines when he became the top draft pick by the Boston Celtics. Two days later, Len died at his University of Maryland dormitory following an overdose of cocaine.[4] His mother, Lonise Bias, with no formal training, felt compelled to speak out on cocaine abuse. At high schools, colleges, and public auditoriums across the country, she delivers a stirring message of family togetherness, love, and mutual encouragement, and a stern warning about the realities of drug abuse.

Fame often arrives with a bang and departs with a whimper. Many would have said that was the fate of singer Eddie Rabbit. He scored two big hits, "Drivin' My Life Away" and "I Love a Rainy Night," and numerous No. 1 Country singles in the late '70s and early '80s, then dropped off the charts in 1983. His meteoric rise and fall was probably attributed to the normal rises and falls of success in the music industry. But Rabbit's downturn had a more serious origin: In August 1983 his second child, Timmy, was born with a debilitating disease that often affects the liver. Against the advice of his manger, Rabbitt prioritized his son over his career.

For two years, the singer, his wife, and their daughter visited Timmy almost daily at Vanderbilt University Hospital in Nashville where they live. In July 1985, Timmy appeared to be given a second chance when a liver became available to be transplanted into his body. However, his body rejected the new organ and the little boy went into a coma from which he never recovered.

The loss affected Rabbitt's song writing, which, by his estimation, glorifies home and family more than it did in the past.[5]

Jeff Dingus was a highly active sophomore in high school. He was a member of the football team, the wrestling team, the band and the pep band. In April of 1987, he turned sixteen and got his driver's license. In order to help pay for the expense of the car, and future college bills, Jeff took a part time job at Denny's Restaurant in Westerville, Ohio.

On the night of May 14, Jeff clocked out at 8:00 p.m. from his afternoon shift. At 8:45, he was found dead on a road about twenty–five minutes from Westerville. He had been shot in the back at point blank range.[6] Tom and Donna Dingus have never completely recovered from their son's death.

Ryan White was born a hemophiliac who could bleed to death from any minor injury. At the age of twelve, his health began to deteriorate. He was weak, had trouble breathing and had a constant cough. Ryan was rushed to the hospital and was diagnosed with the HIV infection. The doctors told his mother, Jeanne, that Ryan had contracted the disease from the numerous blood transfusions he needed to control his hemophilia. After a five and a half year battle, at the age of eighteen, in April 1990, Ryan died. Jeanne White continues to mourn her son.

On the night of February 24, 1993, Eric Clapton sat among fellow musicians and celebrities at the twenty–third annual Grammy awards. The rock legend had been nominated for nine awards; most were for the song "Tears in Heaven."

As a nominee for song of the year, Clapton performed the acoustic ballad live on stage. Dressed in a black tuxedo, the 47–year–old guitar legend began the song that he had written for his four–and–a–half–year–old son, Conor. The stage was dark, except for the soft light that was cast upon him and his guitar. The audience was completely silent. The solitary sound of the guitar hummed in the background. An emotional tribute was witnessed, by millions, as a father put his heart into the song he had written for his dead child.

On March 20, 1991, in a high–rise luxury condominium in midtown Manhattan, a housekeeper left a large picture window tilted open to dry. The window was located on the second floor bedroom of the fifty–third–floor duplex where Eric Clapton's son, Conor, was staying with his mother, Italian actress Lori Del Santo. Del Santo was in another room with the maid and a friend when the little boy wandered by himself into the room with the open window. He climbed out onto the ledge and fell forty–nine stories onto the roof of an adjacent four-story building. The superintendent of that building, Peter Goyco, found the body of Conor, dressed in red pajamas and blue slippers.[7]

The death of a child may seem like an unusual event in this time of improved health care, sophisticated developments in medicine, and the eradication of particularly pernicious diseases. Indeed, modern medicine and contemporary technology have reduced the number of infants' and children's deaths due to disease. However, the number of children who die from accidents, homicide, and suicide has increased steadily over the past twenty years. The leading cause of death among those from birth to age 34 is accidental death. For children under the age of 15, the second cause of death is malignant neoplasms and the third is heart disease. For those aged 15 to 34, however, homicide and suicide are the second and third causes.

Moreover, violent crimes involving children have sharply increased. Nearly one of every four victims of violent crimes is a child. In 1992, when the statistics were determined, about 6.6 million violent crimes were reported in the United States and approximately 23 percent of the victims were juveniles.[8]

An increased number of juveniles is involved in a violent crime. Out of every 13 juveniles, one was a victim of violent crime in 1992. This compares to 1987 when one out of every 17 juveniles was victimized by violent crime.[9]

GRIEVING

Author Nancy O'Connor observes, "We live in a death–defying society. We fight and resist death... This attitude makes the grieving process more difficult and confusing for the survivors because it denies the importance and depth of their feeling."[10] Many people are uncomfortable with the very idea of mourning or grief. They avoid being around those who are experiencing these feelings. As a consequence, people who are grieving and in desperate need of social support are often left wanting.

At the same time, everyone faces loss. No one escapes dealing with it. Grieving is also universal. At one time or another we all come to understand the meaning of the word "survival" which originates in two Latin words *super* which means "over," and *vivere*, which means "to live." We need to learn how to "over live" another person, and we need to come to know that losing someone creates a psychological wound which may take far longer to heal than any physical one.

Bereavement, mourning, and grieving are all involved when one loses a loved one. Bereavement occurs when a person experiences a loss or is deprived of something. It includes the behavior, as well as the attitudes and feelings, of someone who is "engaged in the severance of ties necessitated by death."[11] The closer we are to the person who is lost, the more bereavement we experience.

Mourning is the expression of the grief and bereavement that is felt. It involves "a process of extricating interest from that person (the deceased) and transferring it elsewhere."[12] Grieving refers to the feelings of mental distress that we experience. Grieving and our reactions to grief are largely learned.[13]

Grieving may appear to be a passive activity, but it is actually active. Several tasks need to be accomplished in the grief process including: (a) acknowledgment of the loss; (b) working ones way through the turmoil; (c) finding ways of living meaningfully; and (d) loosening ties with the deceased. Survivors ultimately choose how they will cope and where they will focus their attention.[14]

Many authors have attempted to identify the stages of grieving. The pioneer effort in this area was done by Dr. Elisabeth Kubler–Ross. She wrote a sensitive, yet controversial book, *On Death and Dying*, in 1969. In it, Kubler–Ross identified five stages of grieving: denial, anger, bargaining, depression, and acceptance. While more recent writers have offered slightly different schema, they basically agree with Kubler–Ross's original model.[15]

The denial stage occurs just after the death and generally lasts for four to six weeks when the survivor is both shocked and numb from the enormity of the event. The phase may take a physical toll on the individual. Several symptoms that resemble depression are present directly after the death. The most common are loss of appetite, sleeplessness, lethargy, withdrawal, loss of interest in life, anxiety attacks, depressed mood, and suicidal thoughts.[16] Generally, this is a protective state which buffers the individual from the insufferable circumstances he or she will eventually need to face. This period of disbelief sometimes results in guilt because the person does not "feel" anything.

The denial stage gives way to an anger stage. Individuals show their anger outwardly as they rail against God, if they have a religious belief; and as they show their fury with physicians, nurses, morticians, police officers, and anyone else who was involved with the individual who has died. They may also turn their anger inward and become depressed. Beneath this anger is an individual's fear. People fear that they will be unable to cope with their new circumstances.

After anger, the survivor begins to bargain. He or she may attempt to strike up a deal with a spiritual being. "If I do this, then you will give me my loved one back" is a basic message. The individual unrealistically believes that he or she can bring the loved one back to life with good works or with the possibility of trading his or her life for the lost person.

Depression, which includes feelings of helplessness, hopelessness, and powerlessness, generally follows. The survivor can no longer deny the event of the death. The anger that he or she has expressed is spent. Bargaining has been unsuccessful in bringing the deceased back to life. The individual begins to come to grips with the death and feels both sad and frustrated.   He or she may withdraw from people and activities, lose a capacity for pleasure and may avoid the enjoyable activities formerly experienced in life. This despair lasts for a long time in some people, particularly when the individual who is gone was very close to them.

Finally, the person moves into a stage of acceptance. He or she understands that the loved one will not return in physical form, but that he or she will be present in memories, personal possessions, and other memorabilia. The person knows that the death has occurred and that strong outbursts of emotion—whether anger or sadness—will not change events. While waves of anger or sadness may come and go, generally the individual understands and accepts the inevitability of the death.

While the stage models of grieving have been viewed as central to our understanding of the grieving process, it is crucial to iterate that no single model of grieving exists for people experiencing the loss of a loved one. Families and individuals respond differently to death because each provides a unique experience. Probably all people begin at a point of extreme grief and end in a state of relative recovery. Between these places, stages of suffering and re–organization occur.[17] They may occur in exactly the order that Kubler-Ross suggests or they may recur or go in reverse order.

Grief has no prescribed rules. One couple who lost their son in an automobile accident spoke to this point.   Eleanor and Roy Souders explained, "Every situation is different. Grief is personal. You should never judge someone and tell them how they should be feeling at this point, or that they should or shouldn't feel this or that. The timetable is different; nothing is standard. At the same time, the two emotions experienced most often, that are rarely ever missed, in the grieving process are anger and guilt."[18]

To be fair, Kubler–Ross has acknowledged that differences among people lead to differences in their stages of grieving. More information has been amassed in the last decade as two researchers and their colleagues have interviewed hundreds of people who have suffered serious traumas. They found that only 30 percent of people generally follow the patterns suggested in the stage approaches of grieving. By contrast, nearly half of all people who have suffered major traumas do not experience intense anxiety, depression, or grief after the loss. Weeks, months, or even years later, they remain psychologically well adjusted. Another 18 percent were identified as chronic grievers who have recurrent bouts with grief. Finally, about 2 percent of the people surveyed are known as delayed grievers; they appear well adjusted at first, but are distressed at least a year later.[19]

One of the questions about grieving that is often raised is about how long it should last. The answer, of course, is highly variable. Some people are essentially through with grieving in eight months while others remain in acute grief for two years or more. One study of parents who had lost children examined the parents two years and seven years later. The researchers found that parents were similarly depressed over the child's death at the two intervals, but there was a downward trend. They concluded that parental bereavement following the death of a child is an indefinite emotion.[20]

Grieving may take longer than most people recognize, particularly if the individual who has died is one's spouse or child. Normal grief has a beginning and an end, and gradually diminishes over the course of two or more years. However, the standard course of grief can be altered by a phenomenon referred to as an "anniversary reaction." The deceased's birth date, death date, graduation, or other more general holidays may elicit intense reactions.[21] Although acute grief may reappear only on relatively rare occasions, the death of a spouse or child may result in a feeling of "empty space" or emptiness forever.

One writer suggests that each loss an individual experiences leads to the development of a "new self." She suggests that this occurs as a person struggles to find a place for herself or himself in the midst of the anguish that is experienced. None of us want to experience loss, but we can evolve into better people. In speaking of her own losses, one woman writes, "Now I gaze in memory at all those scars, and I see reflected in them a map of our losses. But I also see a map of the journey we have taken to arrive where we are."[22]

Bereavement, mourning, and grieving are all natural, normal processes that are experienced after a loss. Although the ordeal is never positive, five life enhancing results may accrue. People may realize; (a) increased feelings of strength and security, (b) increased self-esteem and self-understanding, (c) better abilities to understand and respond sensitively to others, (d) an improved critical perspective on personal relationships, and (e) an enriched perspective on reality and the human condition.[23]

THE DEATH OF ONE'S CHILD

The death of a family member or friend is devastating. The death of one's child is probably the most stressful of any death. This death is one of the most tragic events that can happen to any family at any time. Bereaved parents generally experience more stress and anguish than even bereaved spouses.[24]

Former President Dwight D. Eisenhower, was thoughtful in a television program entitled, "*Ike*" that was aired on PBS television on October 15, 1986. In commenting on the death of his first son, cited at the beginning of this chapter, he observed that "things never go back to the way they were" after the death of a child.

Thomas H. Kean, Governor of New Jersey, was similarly quoted in the New York Times on March 20, 1985. He said, "The most painful death in all the world is the death of a child. When a child dies, when one child dies—not the 11 per 1000 we talk about statistically, but the one that a mother held in her arms— he leaves an empty place in a parents heart that will never heal." Kean, like Eisenhower, lost one of his children.

Indeed, most parents report that they learn to "adjust" to the death of the child rather than "recover" from it. They describe an integration of the loss into their lives rather than viewing it as an isolable event. They maintain that they are not able to return fully to the way they lived before the child's death. Most report feeling an empty space in their lives, years after the death.[25]

Why is this death so difficult to manage? The bond that exists between parent and child is unique. A parent's relationship with his or her child is different than his or her relationship with spouses, siblings, or friends. Parents bond with their children through both instinct and interaction. An individual's ability to parent results in feelings of competence which adds to his or her sense of self–worth.

Generally, parents feel a stronger connection to their children than they do to others. The special relationship between parent and child creates a unique type of grief when that tie is broken. The issues concerning the creation and development of the relationship come into play in response to the loss. The parent must deal with the child's death in the social realm of which he or she remains a part and the parent must deal with the death internally in his or her own representation of the child. The parent comes to realize that the world will never return to the way it was prior to the death.[26] He or she also learns that the grief after a child's death is one of the longest and most difficult types of loss.

A child's death is insufferable for other reasons. First, it is not in the natural order of things. Older people are expected to die before younger ones. Parents feel that it is unnatural for their children to precede them in death. One writer states, "The death of a child. . . seems to go against nature. The end of a life that is still forming or has just begun is an almost unthinkable cruelty."[27]

A child's death also apprises parents of the limits of their protective powers. Regardless of the child's age, the parents recognize their impotence in guarding the child. The loss threatens their sense of being an adequate parent because of their inability to protect their child.[28] The role of parent is to love, protect, teach, and nurture, and when the parents fail, they may come to "feel haunted by this realization."[29]

Since children are not expected to die before their parents, or even grandparents, no customs have been established for dealing with their deaths. The child in the family is the last person expected to die. Ronald Knapp writes, "Because a child's death is considered so rare and unnatural, few rules have been developed to guide loved ones—parents and others—in coping with the aftermath."[30]

Just as there are no rules to guide mourners in dealing with a child's death, no routine ways exist to describe the pain. Two authors write, "The nature of grief on the death of a child cannot be adequately described; no schema can contain it. Its breadth and depth defy description. Grieving is a continuous process, with peaks, valleys, and plateaus."[31]

The nature of the parent–child bond may also result in the parent's sense that they have lost some part of themselves. The parents experience both the loss of the child and a loss of part of their identity. They may feel less than whole. In *A Child Dies: A Portrait of Family Grief*, the authors write, "The parent's self-esteem is shattered, for the foundation of this significant role has been shaken. The longing for the child and the feeling of emptiness may last a lifetime. A parent grieves forever when a child dies."[32]

Related to the loss of self, the parents must bury not only the child, but the hopes and dreams he or she has had for the child. As a result, the parents may see little meaning to life. They may feel that their reason for living is gone. Two authors explain, "Parents may describe their profound emptiness or feeling of deadness inside. . . The injustice of losing one's child leads some parents to challenge beliefs and values. . . Expectations of what is reasonable, good, and just in life are changed.[33]

Surviving parents may be particularly stymied by the meaningfulness of the child's death. In *Psychology Today*, Knapp states, "There simply is no context within which such an event can be fitted."[34] Other writers add, "The questioning is endless. Self-blame, guilt, and feelings of failure can plague parents, who know that they must have been responsible in some way for the death. Self-accusations undermine all logical explanations. No reason is sufficient to explain the death of a child. There is no justice or justification in a child's death.[35] Parents cannot answer the "why" question, and they may blame themselves or others for the death.

Finally, parents may feel doubly wounded when they realize that they have little support from others. Some parents describe feelings of helplessness and abandonment by their acquaintances and friends. The parents of murdered children are even more likely to report being deserted by their peers. Parents who have lost children often feel that they are without social support.

Moreover, parents also report that their spouses are unable to provide them with support. Each parent is grieving so acutely that they cannot help the other. Rando explains, "The couple is forced to deal with the situation at the same time so they cannot be supportive of the other. Each must deal with his or her grief in an individual manner."[36] Parents feel abandoned not only by acquaintances and friends, but even by their own spouses.

An extensive study which focused on parents who had lost children identified six significant similarities among them. First, parents expressed a desire to never forget their child. They were afraid that they would forget the sight, sound, smell, and uniqueness of their children. Second, they all expressed a strong need to talk about their child and his or her death. Related to this similarity, many said they had been unable to talk about the loss when it would have benefited them the most, at the time of the death itself. Fourth, parents of deceased older children and of male children appeared to grieve more than did parents of younger children and of female children.[37] A fifth similarity was that few parents—mothers or fathers—never again feared death in the same way they did before the tragedy. Finally, the parents sought some cause or rationale for the death. Rarely did the family accept the loss as "fate."[38]

While parents who have lost children may show some similarities, they also evidence differences based on the nature of the death. Parents of children who have suddenly died are more likely to experience prolonged physical repercussions, guilt, and anger than are parents of deceased children who have had long terminal illnesses.[39] Parents of murdered children experience a different kind of grief than other types of deaths. These parents are angry, and often transform their anger into revenge and seek to lessen the power of the killer. They also report that they do not know where they fit into society or how to answer questions that come up about their children.[40]

GENDER DIFFERENCES AND MARITAL PROBLEMS FOLLOWING THE DEATH OF A CHILD

Most couples have problems in their marital relationships after the death of a child. Although they have shared the child's death, this common experience does not necessarily lead to a stronger bond. Each deals with the child's death in his or her own way. Grieving, even the grieving over one's child, is personal rather than shared. In addition, couples who lose children cannot comfort each other because each feels the pain of the child's death so acutely.[41]

Somewhere between 75 and 90 percent of people who lose children divorce; many others remain in unhappy unions.[42] If the couple was happily married before the child's death, they tend to remain together afterwards and may even become closer after the tragedy.[43] If they had difficulties before the death, including communicating with each other, their problems are magnified. In addition, if they experience unresolved mourning, they are also more likely to encounter marital discord and other negative outcomes.[44]

Couples who ranged in age from 27–60 and who had lost a child between one month and forty–eight months earlier were interviewed. The couples agreed that the death of their child was the most devastating thing that they had experienced. They reported withdrawal from each other at various points in their bereavement both because of their intense pain and in order to avoid increasing their spouses' pain. In addition, five major themes emerged: 1) the fathers' concern and/or frustration about their wives' grief; 2) wives' anger over the husbands' not sharing their grief; 3) the temporary halt in communication that occurred after the death of a child; 4) the loss of sexual intimacy; and 5) the general irritability between spouses. As a result, the marital relationship suffered.[45]

Women and men grieve and cope differently. For the most part, husbands keep their feelings to themselves while wives want to talk about both the child and his or her death. Consequently the couple is "out-of-sync," or not synchronized, with each other which adds to their inability to help the other.[46]

Marital partners have role differences imposed upon them from their wedding day. Husbands are expected to be the family protectors. They are assumed to control their emotions and to control the actions of others. One author outlined some of the roles that can impede the father's positive grief resolution. These include: 1) the role of being strong—a macho man who always controls his emotions; 2) the role of competing, of winning in a crisis, and of being the best; 3) the role of being the protector of family and possessions; 4) the role of being the family provider; 5) the role of being the problem solver—fixing things or finding someone who can; 6) the role of being the controller—controlling actions and the environment; and 7) the role of being self-sufficient—standing on your own two feet.[47]

These expectations are at odds with the circumstances of losing a child. Fathers are unable to express their grief; they feel that they have been irresponsible in protecting their family; and they cannot control life events or consequences. The father may feel that he has lost his sense of self and be both angry and guilty. If he holds the mother responsible for the child's death, which happens more often than may be realized, the couple is further divided.

The father's stoic behavior may lead the mother to believe that he does not love the child.[48] The father may avoid speaking about the child or even speaking the child's name because he believes that avoidance or denial will lead to better grief resolution. When the mother raises the topic, the father may thus fall silent. His intent is to ease the situation, while her conclusion is that he does not care.

One father expressed his pain: "When is it my turn to cry, I am afraid of the reaction and repercussion that might follow. I must be strong, I must support my wife because I am a man. I must be the cornerstone of our family because society says so, my family says so, and until I can reverse my learned nature, I say so."[49] In order to stay on the path of healing, the father must discard these stereotypes and articulate his emotions.

Fathers may be helped in their grief process if they are encouraged to talk about the lost child. They may be able to better deal with their feelings in active grief. In addition, they may be able to accept the reality of the child's death. Finally, they and other family members will be allowed to remember the child by discussing him or her.

Just like fathers, mothers are similarly expected to enact a specific role within the family. The mother is presumed to be the nurturer, the caregiver, and the initiator and manager of communication within the family. Generally, she carries the emotional burden of the family. When her child dies, grief encases her into a shell.

Mothers typically grieve more intensely than do fathers for the loss of a child.[50] They also are more likely to experience long term grief than are the fathers.[51] One author suggests that mothers grieve both for their children and for the loss of the delicately balanced family system.[52] In addition, maternal grandmothers grieve more than either maternal grandfathers or paternal grandmothers, who in turn grieve more than paternal grandfathers.[53] Finally, mothers' siblings grieve more than fathers' siblings.[54]

When a child dies, the mother needs to be provided nurturance while the expectations of other family members is that she will nurture them. Her husband is unable or unwilling to nurture as he withdraws and becomes uncommunicative. The mother interprets his behavior as a lack of love for their child, or worse, for herself. The mother may experience feelings of social isolation.[55]

Parents may grieve in sex role stereotypic ways which create misunderstanding or they may defy sex roles to grieve in a manner more similar to someone of the opposite sex. If one partner has unrealistic or heightened expectations, disappointment may follow. Consequently, the couple may experience additional stress and tension.

The couple may have been able to communicate in the past through sexual and sensual expression. Most couples find that this avenue is no longer viable. As many as 60 percent of the wives and 40 percent of the husbands expressed a lack of sexual satisfaction after the death of a child.[56] The lack of sexual happiness may be largely due to the women losing interest in sex due to personal grief, since men do not report the same loss of sexual desire.[57] Regardless of the cause, the couple cannot relate on this basic level because of their estrangement from each other.

Not only do couples grieve differently, they also cope with the situation in some very different ways. Mothers tend to share their grief with others. They cry, read, and write poetry or stories that deal with the issue of loss and grief. Mothers also tend to try to help others more than do fathers. Also, many mothers do not mind being alone with their thoughts. Fathers keep their grief to themselves. Many fathers pull away from their family and look for a more active lifestyle that does not center around the loss of a family member.[58] Differences in coping, like grieving, can pull the couple apart.

Coping with the Death of a Child and Saving the Marriage

The Book of Psalms 30:5 states, "Weeping may endure for a night, But joy cometh in the morning." For anyone who has lost a child, it is difficult to believe that a new day will dawn or that joy will ever be theirs again. How do couples who have been deprived of their child ever cope with the loss and experience joy again?

Many practical issues must be dealt with immediately after the death of a child. Parents who have dealt with these matters offer advice. They suggest that the first event that has to be faced is the funeral. If one parent handles the arrangements, the other parent can not feel left out or upset by the plans. Bereaved parents encourage others to view the child's body and to provide some last act for the deceased child such as bathing or clothing them.[59] When these events are past, people should not dwell on what might have been done differently.

The next concern that surviving parents may have is dealing with the child's belongings. Bereaved parents express a need to never forget the child, and they consequently encourage others to keep mementos of the child.[60] Those items that are left behind are what, at first, keeps the bereaved connected with their loss. Later they may serve to keep the memories alive. Another practical suggestion is to keep photographs of the child around the house which can serve as a constant reminder of the child. Sentimental belongings are vital to the survivor's grief.

Related to the child's belongings are special anniversaries and holidays that were significant to him or her. Holidays provide an opportunity to incorporate memories of the child into occasions that celebrate the continuity and richness of life. On the other hand, some typical family routines around the holidays may need to be changed. If the deceased child helped to set the table, or carve the turkey, for Thanksgiving or was in charge of lighting the sparklers, or barbecuing the meat, for the Fourth of July, someone else will have to do this now. Holidays may need to be adjusted.

In another study, surviving parents who had experienced the loss of their child in the past were asked how the death of their child was handled and how they might have had it handled differently. Nearly all of them wished to spend time with their child after death, even when the body had been mutilated. In addition, half of those who had seen the body said they had not had enough time to spend with the body. All felt that the process of identification was harshly handled.

Bereaved parents were most grateful for the support that came from professionals who were present at the time of the child's death. They named physicians, nurses, and police officers who played a role in the death of the child. The care and gentleness provided by such people were critical in the events surrounding the death.[61]

One researcher sought to determine how couples were able to cope after the immediate events of the child's death. He found ten categories of coping strategies. Examples of these categories include seeking a release of tension, such as taking part in a physical activity. Avoiding painful thoughts and feelings, or to simply not think of the death was also found to be useful. Others used a cognitive framework to understand and deal with the experience of loss. Many turned to helping others as a natural response. Another coping strategy was to turn to religion and religious beliefs.[62]

Many people cope with their loss by helping other people. When the bereaved parents realize that friends and family need them, they are strengthened.[63] One woman who lost her first child, a daughter named Gabrielle, in labor, explains, "After the death of a friend's child, I saw that one of the gifts I had been given by Gabrielle's death was that I was willing to talk about death and support the people who were left. I had been through it and so I didn't fall into the trap of trying to make it different or better, of offering homilies. I didn't shun people touched by death and would allow them to go through what they needed to go through. I knew my life had actually been enhanced by my child's death."[64]

Similarly, some couples decide to have another child. Five out of 24 mothers, in one study, became pregnant during, or immediately after, a child's fatal illness and two others were trying to conceive or adopt.[65] One problem for children conceived shortly after the death of another child is the possibility of becoming a replacement or substitute.[66] Since the new child cannot replace the deceased child, the parents may be frustrated in their attempts to cope with the first child's death and the new child may suffer, as well.

Many surviving parents identify talking with their spouse, their family, and their friends as instrumental to their coping.[67] Common sense might tell us that spouses should talk to each other, but many parents are so caught up in their own grief that they forget to share their feelings with their spouse. Indeed, the greatest problems in marriages arise when couples are unable or unwilling to share their feelings. When the surviving couple is unable to talk, needed compromises are impossible and resentments can grow. The assistance of the spouse in coping with the child's death cannot be overstated.[68]

The shared loss can lead to deeper levels of understanding and more compassion between the couple because the child belonged to both.[69] The child is both part of their bond and their history. Women, especially, identify husbands as very important sources of support.[70] Husbands and wives can both share the present pain and the past joys. Couple communication also allows couples to acknowledge and ventilate their feelings.[71]

Talking to friends and relatives can also help bereaved parents gain a new outlook;[72] however, friends and family may feel uncomfortable discussing the dead child. Bereaved couples must not feel that they have been abandoned by their friends. This loss added to the loss of their child can be devastating.

Friends and relatives can certainly offer a "sympathetic ear" to bereaved parents and this is sometimes all that is necessary. Beyond this, people outside the immediate family may need to be shown how to discuss the child.[73] The bereaved parents need to admit that they need help and comfort. Unfair as it may appear, the burden of relational maintenance often falls on the grieving couple.

Communication with others beyond one's spouse, family, and friends may be helpful, as well. Many couples report that social support groups have added to their physical and emotional well-being.[74] Some of the self-help groups that have been created for parents of deceased children include the following: Compassionate Friends; Parents of Murdered Children; Survivors of Suicide; Mothers Against Drunk Drivers; Support After Neonatal Death; Help After Neonatal Death; and Nautilus. Other people use support groups in which they are already a member. Eric Clapton, for example, used Alcoholics Anonymous after the death of his son, Conor.

The Compassionate Friends may be the most widely known support group for bereaved parents, and it includes parents who have lost children to disease, accident, homicide, and suicide. The organization was begun in England in 1969 and helps survivors to cope with their grief and to rediscover their relationships with the living.[75]

Compassionate Friends offers friendship and understanding to bereaved parents. The organization believes that bereaved parents can help each other toward a positive resolution of their grief. Compassionate Friends helps bereaved parents primarily through local chapters which belong to their members, but are coordinated nationally to extend help to each other.[76]

One of the advantages of a self-help group like the Compassionate Friends is that couples are encouraged to take a new approach to their life. It helps people to become more aware of their communication patterns and to get rid of the negative aspects of the relationship. The death of a child may lead parents to feel they have lost their sense of security and Compassionate Friends becomes helpful as it encourages parents to seek security in the marital relationship.[77]

Some couples find therapy to be useful in their coping with the death of a child.[78] Therapists can help the couple to clarify issues about their marital relationship as well as the child's death. They can help parents see that they are going through a normal grieving process. This type of third party intervention may provide parents an objective, or certainly a third, point of view of the situation. Similarly, psychotherapy can help a couple make the child into a memory instead of a ghost, and can provide individuals with new resources to confront their pain.[79] Therapy can show parents how to deal with the depression that occurred as a result of the death and how to control other situations in their lives so that future depression can be avoided.

No single model provides the answers. Each couple must cope in his or her own way. Each death is different and each person mourns differently for that person. Many times scholars attempt to write "how to grieve" books which include right and wrong ways to grieve. Generic grieving prescriptions and universal coping advice simply do not apply.

Some of the behaviors experienced by and exhibited by, people who are coping with the death of their child may appear dysfunctional. For example, one author writes, "It is not unusual to hear a bereaved mother discuss her fears of `going crazy,' `not being able to handle it,' `breaking down,' and `never coming back.'"[80] Many parents feel they are unable to tolerate the stress and intense emotions of the bereavement experience.

Other parents have death wishes. They may express the desire to "trade places" with the child. They may feel that their child's life is more valuable than their own. Or, they may feel that they have some command over the situation if they are allowed to exchange roles. Such illogical thought may suggest an identification with the dead child.[81] Others know that they cannot exchange the child's life for their own, but nonetheless they contemplate their own deaths.[82]

People who are able to cope with their children's deaths and to remain happily married seem to understand the importance of balance in their lives. First of all, they balance their own needs with the needs of other family members. They recognize that they cannot always grieve together; they may need to be alone. One psychologist observed, "The most loving thing for the two of you to do right now may be to respect each other's way of coping."[83]

Some couples find independent activities that help them cope. They may read, write poetry, or engage in creating art work. One of the most well–known examples of coping using a creative outlet is that provided by Eric Clapton. A year after his son's death, he created a hit single from his pain. "Tears in Heaven," was a stepping stone in Clapton's path to recovery.

Balance must also be established in the behaviors of the two members of the couple. In one study women who were successfully coping with the loss of a child reported that they were able to establish some emotional equilibrium with their husbands. The researcher explains, "If he cried, she showed less affect; if he did not acknowledge the loss, she reacted more intensely. . . Some marriages continued as they were, but the stress of the event caused other marriages to undergo changes. . . Several reversed traditional behaviors. Others modified the relationship, working out new compromises that facilitated adaptation."[84]

Therese Rando, a well–known author on coping with death, provides important advice for those who are coping with the loss of a loved one. She suggests, first, in the case of imminent death, that family members use the remaining time with a loved one to make the experiences matter. She encourages family members to express all of their feelings and to express their strong and painful emotions little by little. She warns against family members being overwhelmed by painful emotions. She also underlines the importance of reassurances to family members who are hurting. The personal limits of the family should also be acknowledged. Further that family members should know that what they are experiencing is normal. Finally, she states individuals should be encouraged to recall happier days and remind themselves that they will sometime experience them again.[85]

Successful coping often relies on individual reflection of the experience and a consideration of what has been learned from the death. Analyzing the pain is a constructive tool to deal with it. Many times this is the only way in which a bereaved family can construct any positive feelings towards the death. Some common lessons that include the ideas that life is precious, that suffering brings a depth of compassion and understanding that is unavailable to one who has not suffered, and that people, rather than possessions, are important may be useful to consider.[86]

A child's death is a tragedy. The death of the marriage of his or her parents after the death is further heartache. Most marriages end after the loss of a child. Married couples who have remained satisfactorily married after their child has died are unique. They are also special sources of information for people who desire good relationships. Why do some marriages survive while others fail?

What can surviving spouses tell others that will help them maintain stable and strong marriages?

In the next eight chapters we will explore eight case studies of people who have lost children and yet remained in long and satisfying marriages. You may never lose one of your children, but you may be interested in the creation and maintenance of happy marriages. You can learn about good marriages from those who have survived the toughest test. Singer Joan Baez observed, "You don't get to choose how you're going to die. Or when. You can only decide how you're going to live." *Marriage after Mourning* is not about death, but about the potential long and happy life of a marriage.

REFERENCES

1. Quoted in Nancy O'Connor, *Letting Go with Love: The Grieving Process* (Tucson, AZ: La Mariposa Press, 1984), p. xii.
2. T. M. Burnett, "Slain teen's mom seeking memorial for Dahmer victims," *Cleveland Plain Dealer*, July 11, 1992, p. 1B.
3. D. Bennett, "Mercy for Killers Spurs Public Rage," *The Independent*, January 12, 1991, pp. 1, 5; D. Bennett, "Hendershot Case Topic of 'Geraldo' Broadcast," *The Independent*, May 8, 1991, p. 3; R. Dreussi, "Slain Child's Mother: 'He's Killed us Again,'" *The Independent*, January 12, 1991, pp. 1, 5; D. Highben and M. Fox, "Dawn Found Slain: Neighbor Arrested," *The Evening Independent*, October 2, 1982, p. 1; T. Kaib, "300 Mourn Dawn Marie at funeral in Massillon," *The Cleveland Plain Dealer*, October 6, 1982, pp. 1, 10; L. Kay, "Massillon Girl, 7, Dead; Man Held," *The Cleveland Plain Dealer*, October 3, 1982, p. 1; J. Limbacher, "Mother Grieves over Celeste Act," *Akron Beacon Journal*, January 27, 1991, pp. 1, 10; R. Senften, "Jury Shows Dawn's killer No Mercy," *Canton Repository*, April 6, 1983, pp. 1, 3; A. Shyriver, "Maurer Sentenced to Death, "*The Evening Independent*, April 6, 1983, p. 1; T. Suddes and T. Kaib, "Searchers Hunt Massillon Girl," *The Cleveland Plain Dealer*, October 1, 1982, pp. 1, 16; M. Wallace, "Massillon Girl Kidnapped?" *The Evening Independent*, September 30, 1982, pp. 1, 8; M. Wallace, "Dawn Marie Still Missing," *The Evening Independent*, October 1, 1982, pp. 1, 14.
4. *News*, "One Mother's Crusade Against Drug Abuse," *Christianity Today*, May 15, 1987, pp. 50, 52.
5. Tim Allis and Bonnie Bell, "Still Grieving After the Death of His Young Son, Eddie Rabbitt Finds Solace in Country Music," *People Weekly*, *31* (April 17, 1989), p. 83.
6. D. Dingus, "In Memoriam," *The Sunbury News*, May 14, 1988; R. Edwards, "Killer Gets Life in Prison," *Columbus Dispatch*, December 16, 1987; F. Hinchey, S. Brooks, and B. Steiden, "Victim's Car is Found; 4 Arrested," *Columbus Dispatch*, May 16, 1987.
7. D. Fricke, "Clapton's Son Dies in Fall," *Rolling Stone*, May 2, 1991, p. 17; L. Y. Jones, Jr. (editor), "His Son's Freakish Death Brings New Pain to Guitarist Eric Clapton," *People Weekly*, *35* (April 1, 1991), p. 76; Charles Leerhsen with Marc Peyser, "His Saddest Song," *Newsweek*, March 23, 1992, pp. 52-53.
8. "Violent Crimes Against Children on Rise: Report," *The Messenger*, Athens, Ohio, July 18, 1994, p. 2.
9. "Violent Crimes Against Children on Rise: Report," *The Messenger*, Athens, Ohio, July 18, 1994, p. 2.
10. O'Connor, p. 1.
11. George Krupp, "Maladaptive Reactions to the Death of a Family Member," *Social Casework*, *13(3)* (1972): 426.
12. Krupp, p. 426.
13. Christine H. Littlefield, and J. Philippe Rushton, "When a Child Dies: The Sociobiology of Bereavement. *Journal of Personality and Social Psychology*, *51* (1986): 797-802.
14. Thomas Attig, "The importance of conceiving of grief as an active process," *Death Studies*, *15* (1991): 385-393.

15. See, for example, D. Carroll, *Living with Dying: A Loving Guide for Family and Close Friends* (New York: McGraw-Hill Book Company, 1985), and Lily Pincus, *Death and the Family: The Importance of Mourning* (New York: Random House, 1988).
16. S. Valeriote and M. Fine, "Bereavement following the death of a child: Implications for family therapy," *Contemporary Family Therapy, 9(3)* (Fall, 1987): 202-217.
17. Valeriote and Fine, 202-217.
18. All direct quotations are from a personal interview with Eleanor and Roy Souders, 1992.
19. See, for example, Geraldine Downey, Camille B. Wortman, and Roxane Cohen Silver, "Reconsidering the attribution-adjustment relationship following a major negative event: Coping with the loss of a child," *Journal of Personality and Social Psychology, 59* (1990): 925-940.
20. I. M. Martinson, B. Davies, and S. McClowry, "Parental depression following the death of a child," *Death Studies, 15* (1991): 259-267.
21. According to Sarah Bravant, "Old pain or new pain: A social psychological approach to recurrent grief," *Journal of death and dying: OMEGA 20* (1989-90): 273-279.
22. Diane Cole, "When you lose what you love the most," *McCall's*, February, 1992, pp. 68-72.
23. Thomas Attig, "The importance of conceiving of grief as an active process," *Death Studies, 15* (1991): 385-393.
24. Victor Floran, "Meaning and purpose in life of bereaved parents whose son fell during active military service," *Omega, 10* (1980): 92.
25. Martinson, Davies, and McClowry, 259-267.
26. Dennis Klass, "Toward a model of parental grief," *Omega, 19(1)* (1988): 49.
27. O'Connor, p. 79.
28. Paula P. Bernstein, S. Wayne Duncan, Leslie A. Gavin, Kristin M. Lindahl, and Sally Ozonoff, "Resistance to psychotherapy after a child dies: The effects of the death on parents and siblings,"*Psychotherapy, 26(2)* (1989): 227-232.
29. M. Osterweis, F. Solomon, and M. Green, *Bereavement: Reactions, Consequences, and Care* (Washington, DC: National Academy Press, 1984), p. 83.
30. Ronald J. Knapp, "When a child dies," *Psychology Today, 21* (July 1987), p. 60.
31. Joan Hagan Arnold and Penelope Buschman Gemma, *A Child Dies: A Portrait of Family Grief* (Rockville, MD: Aspen, 1983), p. 34.
32. Arnold and Gemma, p. 32.
33. Arnold and Gemma, p. 35.
34. Knapp, p. 60.
35. Arnold and Gemma, p. 35.
36. Therese A. Rando, "Bereaved parents: Particular difficulties, unique factors, and treatment issues," *Social Work, 30* (1985): 19-23.
37. The conclusion concerning male and female children was not reported in the overall conclusions discussed in the study featured in this paragraph. Knapp who is the author of that study found only that older children were grieved more than were younger children. For an example of one of many studies that demonstrates that boys are grieved more than girls, please see, Ann Hazzard, Jeannie Weston, and Cheryl Gutterres, "After a child's death: Factors related to parental bereavement," *Journal of Developmental and Behavioral Pediatrics, 13(1)* (1992): 24-30.
38. Knapp, p. 60.
39. Valeriote and Fine, pp. 202-217.

40. M. R. Peach, and D. Klass, "Special issues in the grief of parents of murdered children," *Death Studies, 11* (1987): 81-88.
41. C. M. Binger, A. R. Ablin, R. C. Feurerstein, J. H. Kushner, S. Zoger, and C. Mikkelsen, "Childhood leukemia: Emotional impact on patient and family." *New England Journal of Medicine, 280* (1969): 414-418; M. S. Miles and E. K. R. Crandell, "The search for meaning and its potential for affecting growth in bereaved parents," *Health Values: Achieving High Level Wellness, 7(1)* (1983): 19-23.
42. H. S. Sarnoff-Schiff, *The Bereaved Parent: A Book of Counsel for Those who Suffer this Heart-Breaking Experience* (New York: Crown Publishers, 1977); M. A. Simpson, *The Facts of Death* (Englewood Cliffs, NJ: Prentice-Hall, 1979).
43. Dennis Klass, "Marriage and divorce among bereaved parents in a self-help group," *Omega, 17* (1986): 237-249; Reiko Schwab, "Effects of a child's death on the marital relationship: A preliminary study," *Death-Studies, 15(2)* (1992): 141-154.
44. Krupp, pp. 425-434.
45. Schwab, pp. 141-154.
46. W. C. Fish, "Differences in grief intensity in bereaved parents," in T. A. Rando (Ed.), *Parental Loss of a Child.* (Champagne, IL: Research Press, 1986). These findings that women and men grieve differently have been disputed recently. A current study (J. E. H. M. Hoekstra-Weebers, J. L. Littlewood, C. M. J. Boon, "A comparison of parental coping styles following the death of adolescent and preadolescent children," *Death Studies, 15* (1991): 565-575) suggests that mothers and fathers grieve similarly. The authors suggest that this change is due to the expanding roles that fathers now have in raising their children.
47. W. H. Schatz, "Grief of fathers," in T. A. Rando (Ed.), *Parental loss of a child* (Champagne, IL: Research Press, 1986), p. 295.
48. Schatz, 1986.
49. John Defrain, "Learning about grief from normal families: Sids, stillbirth, and miscarriage," *Journal of marital and family therapy 17* (1991): 220.
50. Littlefield and Rushton, pp. 797-802.
51. E. J. Rosen, "Family therapy in cases of interminable grief for the loss of a child," *Omega, 19* (1988): 187-202.
52. Schatz, 1986.
53. Littlefield and Rushton, pp. 797-802.
54. Littlefield and Rushton, pp. 797-802.
55. Schatz, 1986.
56. Catherine M. Sanders, *Grief: The Mourning After: Dealing with Adult Bereavement* (New York: John Wiley & Sons, 1989), p. 171.
57. Schwab, 1992, pp. 141-154.
58. Reiko Schwab, "Paternal and maternal coping with the death of a child," *Death Studies, 14(5)* (1990): 407-422.
59. Sarnoff-Schiff, 1977.
60. Knapp, p. 60.
61. I. Finlay and D. Dallimore, "Your child is dead," *British Medical Journal, 302* (1991): 1524.
62. Schwab, 1990, 407-422.
63. Knapp, p. 60.
64. Joan Bordow, *The Ultimate Loss: Coping with the Death of a Child* (New York: Beaufort Books, Inc., 1982), p. 11.

65. Paul Chodoff, Stanford Friedman, and David Hamburg, "Stress, Defenses and Coping Behavior: Observations in Parents of Children with Malignant Disease," *American Journal of Psychiatry, 120(8)* (1964): 743-749.

66. For example, see Albert Cain and Barbara Cain, "On Replacing a Child," *Journal of Child Psychiatry, 13 (3)* (1964): 443-456.

67. See, for example, Knapp, 1987.

68. Morton Lieberman, "The Effects of Social Supports on Response to Stress," in L. Goldberger and S. Breznitz (eds.), *Handbook of stress* (New York: Free Press, 1981).

69. Klass, pp. 237-249.

70. Linda Edelstein, *Maternal Bereavement: Coping with the Unexpected Death of a Child* (New York: Praeger Special Studies, 1984).

71. Therese A. Rando, *Grief, dying and death: Clinical interventions for caregivers* (New York: Research Press, 1990).

72. Klass, 1986; Sarnoff-Schiff, 1977.

73. Sarnoff-Schiff, 1977.

74. Sidney Cobb, "Social Support as a Moderator of Life Stress," *Psychosomatic Medicine, 30 (5)* (1976): 300-313; and Sidney Cobb, "A Model for Life Events and Their Consequences," in *Stressful Life Events: Their Nature and Effects*, ed. B. S. Dohrnewend and B. P. Dorehnwend (New York: John Wiley & Sons, 1974).

75. R. Peterson, "The compassionate friends," *Death Education, 8(2-3)* (1984): 195-197.

76. S. Engram, *Mortal Matters: When a Loved One Dies* (Kansas City: Andrews and McMeel, 1990).

77. Klass, 1986.

78. Martinson, et al., 1991.

79. Paula P. Bernstein, S. Wayne Duncan, Leslie A. Gavin, Kristin M. Lindahl, and Sally Ozonoff, "Resistance to psychotherapy after a child dies: The effects of the death on parents and siblings," *Psychotherapy, 26(2)* (1989): 227-232.

80. Edelstein, 1984, p. 63.

81. David Peretz, "Reactions to Loss," in *Loss and Grief: Psychological Management in Medical Practice*, ed. Bernard Schoenberg et al. (New York: Columbia University Press, 1970).

82. Knapp, 1987.

83. Evelyn Bassoff, "My baby was stillborn," *Parents*, December, 1992, p. 35.

84. Edelstein, 1984, p. 89.

85. Rando, 1990.

86. Defrain, 1991, 215-232.

EMBRACE THE WORLD, BUT ALTER IT
Miriam and Isaac Fife

I gain strength, courage and confidence by every experience in which I must stop and look fear in the face. . . I say to myself, I've lived through this and can take the next thing that comes along. . . We must do the things we think we cannot do.
Eleanor Roosevelt[1]

Believe that life is worth living and your belief will help to create the fact.
William James[2]

Focus on making things better, not bigger.
Anonymous[3]

On September 10, 1985, 12–year–old Raymond Fife left for a Boy Scout meeting on his bicycle. Raymond never made his meeting. Hours after he left and family and friends had searched for him, his father, Isaac Fife, found his son's mutilated body. He had been raped and tortured, and his body was partially burned. Although he was still alive, he never gained consciousness. Two days later Raymond died.

MIRIAM FIFE

Miriam Fife was born in 1940 in Pittsburgh, Pennsylvania. She was the youngest of three children. Her parents were capable people, and Miriam says they were the kind of folks who said, "I can adjust to anything. Just send it my way, I can adjust to it".[4] Her father was calm and easygoing, and her mother was religious.

Miriam's mother's Baptist religion was intolerant of alcohol, but Miriam's father kept a bottle hidden outside. He would frequently have a nip and smoke a cigarette out of the watchful eyes of his wife. Miriam's mother knew his tactics, and while she did not approve, she did not stop him.

The mother was also a hypochondriac. Miriam recalls, "She likes pity. . . Every time I'd go up there, she'd have a whole list of things that were wrong with her. She would write things down, `I had this cold today,' and all this other stuff."

Miriam admitted that her mother was also resilient. "Yet she's strong. She's been through a lot herself. She was abused when she was young. Her mother died in childbirth when her fourth brother was born. She raised the brother for some years. He eventually died choking on a cracker. She had to deal with that. Her father saw the need for a mother, and he married again, but he married a hellion. She threw the one brother down the cellar steps and crippled him, and she would drag my mother home if she didn't rinse the dishtowels out in the morning before she went to school."

Miriam explained how the abuse was discovered. "My mother had an aunt who was wealthy and would visit and take her on trips. She bought my mother a nice coat, but the step mother took the coat and gave it to one of her own daughters. When the aunt stopped in unexpectedly one day, she saw the other girl with the coat. She began to keep watch. She learned what was going on and she went to my mother's father who was on the road a lot. He immediately divorced the woman, but not before she had done damage to his children."

Miriam is just the opposite of her mother. She never complains and she refuses to be sick. She explains, "I talk myself out of being sick. My mother used to make me sick when I was a child. I was the sickest kid in the world. She would start on me on Sunday night, `Oh your voice doesn't sound so good. Let me see your throat. Oh, your throat is red. Your voice sounds raspy.' Pretty soon, I'd have a sore throat and couldn't go to school. When I got older, I realized she had a compelling need to nurse and nurture. She wanted to take care of sick people, so she made me sick all the time."

In 1959, at 19 years of age, Miriam found herself pregnant. She had only two choices. She said, "It was `marry him or give the kid up.' I married him. And I had two more children with him, and I stuck around trying to change things. I thought he was going to change, that the children would change things. But he hasn't changed to this day. He wouldn't work; he assumed no responsibility. If he walked into the house and his child had no food but he has $10 in his pocket, he'd take the $10 and go out and buy beer. The child would go hungry and he would feel no guilt. He was around just long enough to get me pregnant. Eventually I saw the light."

Miriam was not single for long. "Then I married a man that was like almost the opposite. We're still friends. Even though I can't stand the man's personality—he's goofy—he's not the kind of person I want to be around very long. He was responsible to a certain degree, a lot more than the first one. He took responsibility for the kids."

Miriam was married for only three years to each man.

Today Miriam is a "petite, white–haired woman with a kind smile and gracious manner."[5] She has white hair and green eyes and large framed glasses. When she talks about her son Raymond, she rubs her eyes. Her dog, Lady, sits on the floor next to her.

ISAAC FIFE

Isaac Fife, like Miriam's mother, also grew up in a family loaded with problems. He was one of ten children, but three of his siblings died at, or shortly after, they were born. The first child to die was Michael, who was born a year after Isaac, in 1928. Michael lived only a few hours. The following year, a sister, Mary, was born but she died three days later.

Ike is most nostalgic about the last baby to die. "The last one she lost was in 1935. I was eight and my mother was 36 years old. I went to school in the morning and I came home at noon. My mother took me into the bedroom and opened the dresser drawer and showed me the baby. She had her all washed up and in a little dress, and she was dead. She was a beautiful little girl with long black hair and fingernails. Her name was Shirley Marie. She was stillborn at home at seven months, but she was complete."

Because all of the Fife children were born at home with a midwife, their lives were in more jeopardy than if they had been born in a hospital with incubators and other life-saving equipment. Even minor complications could result in death for the babies.

Ike's mother had another cross to bear. Her husband died when the children were young. She remarried, but the stepfather was a drunk and an abuser. Her efforts, alone, went into maintaining a home and helping the children to grow and develop. Ike recalls, "He'd be gone for months, and then he'd come back. I think that I got most of my strength from her." His mother was strong, but she died at the age of 63 from a cerebral hemorrhage.

Before Ike met Miriam, he had been married and had three children. His divorce was so bitter that he finally gave up even trying to see his three children—two of whom, Ike and Mike, were teenagers and one, Tim, who was in elementary school. He continued to financially support them, however, and worked at two different jobs in order to do so. He also drank heavily which sapped his money and his energy.

Although Ike has worked at many jobs during his lifetime, today he declares himself as retired. Nonetheless, he owns and operates a garage. Ike is a small, slender man who is 13 years older than his wife. He looks his age with his gray crew cut, gray beard, and skin roughened from working out of doors. He is never without a small cigar and a cup of coffee. His most noticeable feature is his bright blue eyes that are filled with warmth and concern.

EARLY MARRIAGE

Miriam's ex-husband introduced her to Ike, and she, in turn, introduced Ike to her girlfriend. The two women lived together for awhile and during that time, Ike and the friend dated and became intimate. Since Ike was a frequent visitor at their home and because both she and Ike were going through divorces, they became friends.

Miriam said, "We were crying in our beer together and then we started seeing each other."

Ike smiled, "She liked my blue eyes."

Miriam continued, "He and my girlfriend quit, and she wasn't upset. We're still friends with her."

Similarly, Miriam became friendly with Ike's first wife after the couple married. Although Ike gave up trying to see his children because of the hostile relationship he had with his ex–wife, Miriam began to see the boys. "I started seeing the kids over at the neighbors."

Miriam who had some of the nurturing qualities of her own mother began to care for his children as well as her own. She explained, "Ike's first wife didn't have time to bake cookies. I did, so I started sending cookies home to them."

"We were having a rough time. We weren't wealthy. He was working two jobs and, on top of that, he was a pretty heavy drinker. He wasn't an abuser, but he was a heavy drinker. With heavy drinking there is a certain amount of neglect of the family, neglect of the children. Mother does everything—in other words, I was doing everything. I also was boarding children and babysitting during the day. I was doing a lot of things to make extra money so I could be there with my kids. My ex–husband wasn't paying anything."

The Fifes first few years of marriage were tough. They had six previous children to support. Miriam's three children—Yvonne, Jim, and Regina, born within less than three years of each other and still in elementary school when they married lived with the couple. Not long after they married, their first child, Paula, was added to the crew. Less than three years later they had Raymond.

Miriam recalled, "Raymond was meant to be. He was the child that must've fought hard to get here. My father died just a couple of days before I had Paula. My husband was going to get fixed so we couldn't have any more children. Because of my father's death, he canceled. He never went back. When I became pregnant with Raymond, it was like `Oh, God, what do we do? One more child!' There was talk about abortion. Then the decision was made to have him. It was like he was meant to be here for some reason. I remember when he was murdered, one of the first things I said to my husband was `I wish I'd of had that abortion. Because this pain is terrible, and I can't stand to think that he went through such Hell to die.'"

Ike's wise comment to his wife was "But we had him for twelve beautiful years."

This wisdom is explained by Ray Grigg in *The Tao of Relationships*. He writes:

> Life isn't a matter of comparisons—my life in terms of someone else's life. Nor is it a series of measurements— the number of my years versus the number of somebody else's years. Nor is it a contrast in human values—my joys against another's—one way of death against another way of death. The judgment of God's justice and mercy is not in the mathematics of the years—nor in the sum of birthdays and anniversaries.
>
> Can we ask why wasn't Schubert's Unfinished Symphony drawn out into the longest symphony, or Lincoln's Gettys- burg address, only two minutes, expanded into a longer oration? Each is a masterpiece, complete in itself.
>
> So is each life and so is each moment of our life. So that, if we died, the next moment of our life would be complete in itself.[6]

Some parents distort their child's life by remembering only the positive features and discarding the negatives. The Fifes are more realistic and present a balanced picture. Ike smiled as he recollected, "He was a boy. He was ornery. He wasn't an angel, believe me. No, he was all boy. He was a Boy Scout. He played baseball. He bowled, fished, and went to camp. He got trophies for bowling. Pinewood derby, he won one year. I helped him with that."

Raymond's Death

A Yiddish saying suggests, "Never to have had pain is not to have been human."[7] If the connection between pain and humanness holds, Ike and Miriam Fife have demonstrated incredible humanness. On the other hand, no one should ever have to bear the pain experienced by them. The story of their son's death does not lose its horror over time.

On a September afternoon in 1985, in Warren, Ohio, 12–year–old Raymond Fife failed to meet a friend and then go on to his evening

Boy Scout meeting. Raymond left for the scout meeting at 5:15. His parents knew something was wrong when the friend came to their door at 6:00 p.m. asking for Raymond. Their son loved Boy Scouts and would not miss a meeting. Family members and friends began to search the neighborhood.

About 9:30 that night, Ike, Raymond's father, found the boy's mutilated body. He had been raped and tortured and his body was partially burned. Although he was still alive, he never gained consciousness. Two days later, Raymond died.

What had transpired between the time Raymond left the safety of his home and when his father found him? Miriam tells the story in her own words:

> Raymond was a Boy Scout and he loved attending all of his Boy Scout meetings. That's why we knew immediately when he disappeared that something was wrong. He would not cut scouting. He left our home at exactly 5:15 to go to his friends to go to a Boy Scout meeting. When the friend came to our home at about 6 o'clock, we realized that he had never gotten to the friend's house and we starting looking for him.

> The first place I went was the Boy Scout meeting and he was not there. So several people began looking. My husband, my daughter. My daughter rode her bicycle through the same path that they took Raymond off of. Raymond was on a bicycle.

> The boys all liked to go on this little path, it had like chilly bumps they called them. They liked to ride their bikes through there. It was like a one minute ride in back of a grocery store that would bring him out onto the street where his friend lived.

> He took the path that night and he was seen in the area by several witnesses coming to that path. This was broad daylight around 5:30. Evidently he was taken off his bike, slammed down hard onto his bike, and then they threw the bicycle off into a wooded area.

> They drug him off and they took turns raping him and beating him—two young men, one 17–year–old and one 18–year–old. Both of them had prior records for rape.

After one had finished with him, Raymond got away from him, and he went running out to the other boy. He thought he was a boy who was going to help him. This young man said that Raymond said to him, "Please take me to my mother. I have to be at my Boy Scout meeting. Please take me to my mother."

At this point, the boy just grabbed him and took him back into the woods and performed his sexual acts on him. Then they just beat him into hopefully an unconscious state because they took off his underwear and used his underwear as an accelerant to try to burn him.

They didn't want to leave any evidence there, and they thought that if they burned him then maybe nobody would recognize him and nobody would find him. After they got done with that, they heard him gurgling, breathing. They leaned over to see if he was still alive, put their hands up to his neck and he was still alive.

Their last and final act was that they found a broom handle with a point on it and they rammed it into his rectum and they impaled all his organs which, in turn, wiped out all of the evidence of rape that were there. When my husband found him. . . I can't tell you the Hell he has had to live with to have that picture in his mind, and he can tell you that himself. They found him about 9:30 that night.

He lived for two days, but he was unconscious. He never regained consciousness which is something to say, you never get a chance to say good–bye to these children. They are taken out of your life so fast that you don't get a chance like you do with a sick child. It was so terrifying. I can't tell you what a family lives through. And you keep wondering about it, but you are so engrossed in your own grief.[8]

Isaac added to his wife's description of their son's murder:

It never goes away. It's there continuously. But you have to go on. You have to live. You have to exist. You have to earn a living. It's with you everyday. It's just continuously, with you. The pain is always there. There's never a day goes by that I don't think about him. One of them had raped several boys and had been put away for it. The other one had raped a woman, broke into her house, raped her. She had a little child in the bedroom. And she told him, "Please, be quiet." I think the daughter was two years old. She said, "Please, be quiet. I don't want you to wake my daughter and frighten her." And he said, "Oh, you have a daughter. Well, she'll be next." This girl testified at our trial to this fact. This was one of them they had turned loose.

Because he was 18, they couldn't hold him as a juvenile any more. He was 18 years old, they had to turn him loose. I asked the prosecutor. He told me that the boy was on probation at the time, this one that was 18. This boy got the death penalty.

I said, "Why in the hell is this man walking around?"

He said, "It was the law. When he's 18. He's no longer a juvenile.

I wanted to go [to the trial]. I wanted to make sure there wasn't anything wrong, or any mistakes made at this trial.

Prior to the trial, I went to the police chief and I told him, "Don't make any mistakes that's going to let these guys off. Because 10 minutes after they're out, you're going to be arresting me for killing them."

He said, "There won't be any mistakes, believe me." They conducted the thing, they were very thorough and right.[9]

Miriam added her feelings:

I can't express the feeling that comes over you. You get nauseated. You get a feeling of crushing in your chest like these people are really here. These people are supposed to be human beings like me. And yet they did such a terrible thing. You see them standing there, but you can't believe they're really there.

We think it is important that people are aware that this happens even in small communities like ours. This can happen to you tomorrow. We're not unique. You can have someone in your family taken away just like we did. You can't rehabilitate them after they've committed murder like they did on my son.[10]

Thomas Paine, in *The American Crisis* wrote, "These are the times that try men's souls."[11] While he was writing about political problems, his statement could have been about the Fife's experience in losing their son. As we shall see in the next section, the Fife's quarter of a century marriage is strong. While they had three marriages between them when they met, they are unlikely to ever divorce again. They have been tested by the worst tragedy parents can ever know.

SUCCEEDING EVENTS

Raymond's death marked the end of his life, but it also marked the beginning of other events and new responses. Paula who was two years older than Raymond was devastated. Her parents became closer and more protective of her which is both natural and common.

Paula was not yet fifteen when her brother died. At first she blamed herself. "Why didn't I treat him better?"

Miriam said, "She was a typical bigger sister. So many times she'd say `Oh, I'm going to kill you, Raymond.' But that was just what kids do. She went to a couple counseling sessions, but she said she came to the realization when she went to these that she really had to do it herself."

The couple had to deal with a deluge of media interviews and requests. Miriam recalls, "The media invades you, but the media was kind to us."

Ike noted, "Because of the nature of the crime."

The greatest challenges in the aftermath of Raymond's death were probably the trials that were held. Danny Lee Hill, 18, was tried in the Trumbull County Common Pleas Court of aggravated murder, kidnapping, rape, aggravated arson, and felonious sexual penetration. He was convicted of the crime by a three judge panel here and sentenced to the electric chair.

Timothy A. Combs was tried separately in Portage County and was eventually convicted of the same crimes. Since he was only 17 years old when the crimes were committed, he was sentenced to life imprisonment. Ike explained, "He got seventy some years in prison without parole, without a chance. . . because the crime was committed while he was a juvenile he couldn't get the death penalty. This younger man was the aggressor and instigator."

The two tried repeatedly to have their sentences appealed. Each attempt at an appeal brought the tragedy to the forefront for the Fifes. They relived the acute pain of their sons horrendous death again and again. Ike said, "As long as there are appeals there's a possibility that they will get out of prison." The thought is chilling.

The trials brought out details about their son's death that were even more troubling than what they had originally known. Eighteen–year–old Hill first claimed that he was not involved, but only watched Combs. However, bite marks on Raymond's penis matched Hill's teeth. Hill was apparently attempting to cause Raymond to have an erection by biting him and bringing him closer and closer to death.

Two football players testified that they saw the defendants come out of the woods with a stick which had been used to impale Raymond's organs. The splinters in his rectum matched the stick they had.

HOW DID THE MARRIAGE SURVIVE?

Most marriages do not survive the loss of a child. Harold Kushner provides an explanation and analogy:

> The Talmud, the compilation of the teachings of the rabbis between the years 200 B.C. and A. D. 500, explains Abraham's test this way: If you go to the marketplace, you will see the potter hitting his clay pots with a stick to show how strong and solid they are. But the wise potter hits only the strongest pots, never the flawed ones. So too, God sends such tests and afflictions only to people He knows are capable of handling them, so that they and others can learn the extent of their spiritual strength.

> Does God "temper the wind to the shorn lamb"? Does He never ask more of us than we can endure?" My experience, alas, has been otherwise. I have seen people crack under the strain of unbearable tragedy. I have seen marriages break up after the death of a child, because parents blamed each other for not taking proper care or for carrying the defective gene, or simply because the memories they shared were unendurably painful.[12]

Why do some marriages endure while others break under the pressure of the loss of a child? The Fifes' marriage provides some important lessons. They accepted each other's differences, they were prepared for the worst, they remembered the positive aspects of their past, they did not blame each other, and they relied on religion.

Accept Differences

The success of the Fife marriage is largely because of their appreciation of differences between people. "Statistically, when a child is murdered there is a great strain placed on the parents," Miriam said. "We drew on each other's strength. We allowed one another to do what we had to do to deal with the loss."[13]

Ike said, "People are different. Some people withdraw; other people get angry. They have to get that anger out and get it in the open. Other people tell others and maybe it will help them in the future if the same thing happens to them. Everybody is different."

Miriam said, "Everything that I do is different from him. I went out and got active right away, and he supported me. And then he talks to me when he thinks I should calm down a little bit. I come home and I rant and rave. Sometimes I get so angry with everything that's going on."

Ike responded, "I understand. I let her vent. If she wants to get it out, let her get it out. I don't stop her."

Miriam said, "He's kind of quiet and then he blows up at something—not even at what bothers him."

Prepare for the Worst

Miriam and Ike are individuals who have experienced difficulties in their original families and in earlier marriages. Their lives have not been easy and, in some ways, these events may have helped them deal with their most tragic blow. They are matter of fact. Miriam said, "I've always prepared myself for the worst."

Miriam feels that she is a realist, but Ike labels her as a pessimist. Ike provides an example, "When the trials were going on, she went and listened to the testimony. She came home and I could tell that she was concerned about the outcome. I told her, 'You're foolish.'

Just from what I read in the paper, I knew this man was going to be convicted of first degree murder. There was no doubt about it. But she was worried."

Miriam said, "I don't trust juries."

Ike responded, "I trusted the jury."

Miriam added, "I'm not a worrier. I've always prepared myself for the worst so that I can really feel good when something good happens, something that I didn't expect."

In *Lasting Love: What Keeps Couples Together*, I interviewed over 40 couples who had been married between 40 and 71 years. One of the secrets for their success was lowered expectations. The couples did not have lofty expectations for their partner or the marriage and therefore they were not disappointed. Miriam's realism (or in her husband's words, pessimism) is akin to lowered expectations. Her preparation for the worst allows her to deal with terrible events when they occur and to rejoice in the positive features of her life.

Remember the Positive Past

In Chapter 12, we will highlight George and Barbara Bush and their secret of living in the precious present. While dwelling on the past is harmful to individuals and to marriages, particularly when a traumatic event has occurred, it is helpful to recall positive events. The Fifes are happy to talk about their son and to remember him to each other and to other people.

Although Ike had drunk heavily for most of his life, he quit drinking before Raymond died. Miriam said, "Two years before Raymond was killed, my husband had stopped drinking. As a result, he had spent so much time with Raymond. He helped him, they went fishing. There's this old bird feeder—it's falling apart now—but it's one that they built together. He really focused on him. When Raymond was killed, he was so happy that he had given him the last two years.

"Raymond had a great passion for fishing. He loved fishing," Ike said. "The Sunday before he got killed, we went fishing. I hadn't been fishing all year. I didn't even have a fishing license. It was in September. I had to pay $7.50 for a fishing license so I could take him fishing. Just that one day. A funny thing happened on the way back from fishing. I had an old truck we were riding in. He said that was the best day of his life. All we caught were a couple of little perch, but he ran up and down the lake. In September, the lake was down, way down, and I still have a bunch of the lures and hooks and sinkers and stuff that he picked up that day. That's all he did, was just run around and find those."

"They just loved that," Miriam said.

No Blame

The Fifes never blamed each other for Raymond's death. The author of *When Bad Things Happen to Good People*, writes, that such blame is common even when neither member of the couple was responsible in any way. The couples engages in "the trading of accusations by husband and wife after a child has died. `Why weren't you watching him more carefully?' `Why weren't you home so that I wouldn't have had my hands full with so many things all over the house?'"[14]

"Neither one of us blamed each other for his death," Miriam said firmly.

Importance of Religion

People may become drawn to religion or turned away from it when they face a tragedy in their life. Miriam's youngest daughter from her first marriage had real problems with Raymond's death. She became angry with God and quit going to church.

The Fifes were not overly religious, but their pastor met them at the hospital when Raymond was admitted. He was with them throughout the ensuing days, as well.

On the other hand, Miriam said they "never got angry at God." She did not believe that it was God who killed Raymond. "He did not guide Raymond over there. He did not want him to die then. That was a result of bad people, and I understood that, right from the beginning. There was no problem with me."

Philosopher Harold Kushner writes, "All the responses to tragedy [we are considering]. . .assume that God is the cause of our suffering, and they try to understand why God would want us to suffer. . . The psalmist writes, `I lift mine eyes to the hills; from where does my help come? My help comes from the Lord, maker of Heaven and earth.'

(Psalm 121: 1-2). He does not say, `My pain comes from the Lord,' or `My tragedy comes from the Lord.' He says `My *help* comes from the Lord.'

Could it be that God does not cause the bad things that happen to us?"[15]

Authors Krauss and Goldfischer offer an analogy:

> . . . life. . . [is] a game of cards in which we have no say over the hand dealt us. We do, however, have control over how we play the hand. There's no point in blaming the dealer for a bad hand. The trick is to play it out with all the skill and determination at our command. And that is where I focus the patient's attention when I say, "Take responsibility."[16]

Miriam said, "I think you get stronger, if you don't lose your religious beliefs altogether. You want to believe in the hereafter and that you're going see him again. You miss them now, but you have work to do here while you're here. You try to make things better for the next person."

One of the benefits of religion is the support provided by others. Harold Kushner writes about this notion. "In 1912, he [Emile Durkheim, one founder of the discipline of sociology] published his important book *Elementary Forms of the Religious Life*, in which he suggested that the primary purpose of religion at its earliest level was not to put people in touch with God, but to put them in touch with one another. Religious rituals taught people how to share with their neighbors the experiences of birth and bereavement, of children marrying and parents dying."[17]

Kushner shares a story which illustrates his point. "That wonderful storyteller Harry Golden makes this point in one of his stories. When he was young, he once asked his father, `If you don't believe in God, why do you go to synagogue so regularly?'  His father answered, `Jews go to synagogue for all sorts of reasons. My friend Garfinkle, who is Orthodox, goes to talk to God. I go to talk to Garfinkle.'"[18]

The Fifes' religious beliefs may have as much to do with the connection they feel with other people as it does with their connection to God. Since Raymond's death, they have given selflessly to others. They live their spiritual beliefs.

```
The Secret of Surviving Couples:
Embrace the World, but Change It
```

Couples in good marriages experience unpredicted stressful events just as do people in less satisfied marriages. The difference between those who are happily married and those who are not may be in how they define these events. The author of *When All You've Ever Wanted Isn't Enough*, observes, "Expecting the world to treat you fairly because you are a good person is like expecting the bull not to charge you because you are a vegetarian."[19] Happily married couples have no expectations that they would be free from problems and unexplainable stressful events.

Irwin Sarason, an important researcher on stress, explains that coping with stress requires people to set aside unproductive concerns, and to deal with problems. His advice is similar to the often quoted prayer, "Lord give me the courage to change the things I can, the serenity to accept the things I cannot, and the wisdom to know the difference."

Each of us needs to feel that we are in control of some aspects of our lives and that we can engage in some behaviors that will help us to improve the world. Victor Frankl, a Jewish psychiatrist, who was imprisoned in a Nazi concentration camp, authored the book, *Man's Search for Meaning*. Frankl's observations led him to "the realization that the most important life force for man is not the drive for sex, as Freud saw it, or the drive for power that Adler spoke about, but the search for meaning. He found a profound truth, in Nietzsche's words: `If you have a *why* to live for, you can bear with any *how*.'[20]

People in good marriages embrace the world with all of its flaws and they try to improve it. They accept pain and hurtful events as part of their lives, but they continually strive to ameliorate human suffering. Helen Keller, blind from birth, wrote, "Keep your face to the sunshine and you cannot see the shadows." The Fifes exemplify this trait in their lives.

One of the important contributions made by Miriam and Isaac Fife was their assistance in redefining the concept of being a victim. One reporter explained, "The couple applied for compensation because they believed Isaac become a direct victim by finding his son and helping in the investigation and trials. Application was made for work lost during the time of the court hearings. At first, the state Court of Claims rejected their request, but on appeal, the couple won. Ohio law and the court previously held that a victim is someone who suffers personal injury or death as a direct result of a crime. The couple received $2,624.43 for the ten days Isaac Fife was unable to work after Raymond's death."[21] The amount of the money received by the Fifes was negligible, but the contribution they made to others is immeasurable.

Being motivated to act based on anger toward a perpetrator is not uncommon. A similar story is told about Theresa Saldana, an actress, who "was nearly killed in a premeditated, violent stabbing attack that resulted in surgery, more than a thousand stitches in her body, and a long war with pain, rage, and terror. In her recent book, *Beyond Survival*, Saldana writes, `My rage gave me the drive to keep fighting death, pain, and the sick wishes of the person who harmed me.'[22] Too, it was her rage at the treatment victims receive."[23]

Miriam Fife has made many other contributions. She was initially inspired by John Walsh who spoke about the Adam Walsh Foundation in Cleveland. The two talked about testifying in front of the legislature and getting bills changed for juveniles. (Raymond was killed because the younger perpetrator was a juvenile and had consequently been let out of prison even though he had been convicted of rape.) Miriam empathized with John Walsh when she saw him again in Dayton, Ohio. "Even though it had been eight years since his son was killed, he still got choked up," she said.

John Walsh was a good role model for Miriam Fife. She has "expressed her grief by giving to others. She joined the Trumbull County chapter of Parents of Murdered Children and began volunteering at the county prosecutor's office, helping others who lost loved ones through violent crimes. Her volunteer efforts led her to being named court advocate of the prosecutor's Victim–Witness Assistance Division."[24]

Elie Wiesel, winner of the 1986 Peace Prize, was inspirational in his acceptance speech, "We know that every moment is a moment of grace, every hour a offering; not to share them would be to betray them. Our lives no longer belong to us alone; they belong to all who need us desperately."[25] When Raymond died, the Fifes dedicated themselves to the many other victims who reach out to them.

Miriam continues to help the "survivors of hideous crimes. She defends their rights to privacy and counsels them in their grief."

"'Seeing good things happen to victims can give you hope,' she said. 'I share their pain and their joy when something good happens to them. I found that sharing makes things better.'

"Fife believes that she has become a stronger, more capable person since the death of her son.

"'I am more compassionate,' she said. 'I have become more educated. I can help people today, where before my son's death, I didn't believe I could.'"[26]

As the court advocate in the prosecutor's office, Miriam does just about everything. "I go with the victims. I send out parole notices. I do some office work. When you work in a prosecutor's office, you work as a team. Whatever is left there for you to do, you do it."

Miriam began her work almost immediately after Raymond's death. It has probably been highly therapeutic for her. She said, "You can sit back and feel sorry for yourself, but you always find somebody who's worse than you."

Ike added, "Not necessarily worse off than you, but someone who handles it worse than you. It's harder for them. They don't cope as well as you do. When you help them, you make some difference. That's the whole thing."

No one has a life free of pain. An increasing number of parents are experiencing the loss of one of their children. Other people face other crises, sometimes unknown to acquaintances and even friends. Kushner observes, "Anguish and heartbreak may not be distributed evenly throughout the world, but they are distributed very widely. Everyone gets his share. If we knew the facts, we would very rarely find someone whose life was to be envied."[27]

One way to cope with our own crises is to help others deal with their problems. The Fifes' recognition of this notion is reflected in a story that is told in the book, *When Bad Things Happen to Good People:*

> There is an old Chinese tale about the woman whose only son died. In her grief, she went to the holy man and said, "What prayers, what magical incantations do you have to bring my son back to life?" Instead of sending her away or reasoning with her, he said to her, "Fetch me a mustard seed from a home that has never known sorrow. We will use it to drive the sorrow out of your life." The woman set

off at once in search of that magical mustard seed. She came first to a splendid mansion, knocked at the door, and said, "I am looking for a home that has never known sorrow. Is this such a place? It is very important to me." They told her, "You've certainly come to the wrong place," and began to describe all the tragic things that had recently befallen them. The woman said to herself, "Who is better able to help these poor unfortunate people than I, who have had misfortune of my own?" She stayed to comfort them, then went on in her search for a home that had never known sorrow. But wherever she turned, in hovels and in palaces, she found one tale after another of sadness and misfortune. Ultimately, she became so involved in ministering to other people's grief that she forgot about her quest for the magical mustard seed, never realizing that it had in fact driven the sorrow out of her life.[28]

Ike and Miriam Fife have provided countless hours of service to others. They have appeared on national and regional television and have presented programs throughout the state of Ohio. They also help create and print a newsletter for Parents of Murdered Children. In many ways, Raymond's life is honored through their work. Harold Kushner observes, "All we can do is try to rise beyond the question 'why did it happen?' and begin to ask the question 'what do I do now that it has happened?'"[29] The Fifes clearly moved to the second question.

People who are experiencing loss may find comfort in helping others. They also need to communicate their pain. Kushner writes, "We need to share our joys with other people, and we need even more to share our fears and our grief. . . When we feel so terribly alone, singled out by the hand of fate, when we are tempted to crawl off in a dark corner and feel sorry for ourselves, we need to be reminded that we are part of a community, that there are people around who care about us and that we are still part of the stream of life."[30]

Perhaps the most well-known person who shared his grief over his son's death in a creative project is Eric Clapton. He was not married to his son's mother when the boy fell to his death from an apartment window in New York City. Nonetheless, he turned his pain into the Grammy-winning song, "Tears in Heaven." Clapton is a survivor of drug addiction, alcoholism, the death of friends such as Jimi Hendrix and Stevie Ray Vaughan. His biggest loss, however, was his 4–year–old son, Conor. "Loss and emotional trauma are almost like everyday feelings," he said recently on Westwood One radio. "You become. . .not happy *with* that but happy *despite* that."[31]

Young people who marry may believe that love is about champagne and caviar, satin sheets and moonlit walks. Lasting love is not about such delicacies or romantic notions. Author Harden writes about an older couple who understand the meaning of love.

> In sickness and in health, I thought. They were supposed to be preparing for a Florida vacation, not holding on to one another in cardiac care unit at Mount Carmel East Hospital.
>
> "Help me sit up," he whispered hoarsely.
>
> In the end, love comes down to this; not Gable's devilish first appraisal of Leigh, not Lancaster and Kerr rolling in the surf. But, "Help me sit up."
>
> In the end, love is not the smoldering glance across the dance floor, the clink of crystal, a leisurely picnic spread upon summer's clover. It is the squeeze of a hand. I'm here. I'll be here, no matter how long the fight, even when what you want most is to close your eyes and be done with it all.
>
> "Water? You need water? Here. Drink. Let me straighten your pillow."
>
> When all is said and done, love is not rapture and fire. It is a hand steadier than one's own squeezing harder than a heartbeat. Wine changes back to water. Roses no longer come with love messages, but best wishes for a quick recovery. Endearment is exhibited by what once might have been considered insignificant kindnesses, but which, in the end, become the tenderest of ministrations.[32]

The Fifes are not movie stars. They do not live in a mansion. Ike does not bring Miriam flowers every night. She does not greet him at the door in a sheer negligee. They are an ordinary couple who have been touched by an extraordinary loss.

The Fifes' love for each other is evident to the most casual observer. They accept each other for all of their mysterious differences. They do not blame each other for what goes wrong in their lives. They have lowered their expectations of what life and marriage can bring. Finally, they are working together to both embrace their world and to change it. Theirs is a real love story.

REFERENCES

1. Quoted in *Great Quotes from Great Women*.
2. Quoted in Sol Gordon, *When living hurts* (New York: Dell Publishing, 1988).
3. H. Jackson Brown, Jr., *Life's Little Instruction Book* (Nashville, TN: Rutledge Hill Press, 1991), #399.
4. The direct quotations are from an interview with the Fifes in 1992 in their home in Warren, Ohio, unless otherwise noted.
5. R. L. Smith, "High court won't hear appeal by Hill," *The Tribune Chronicle*, Warren, Ohio, April 2, 1983.
6. Ray Grigg, *The Tao of Relationships* (New York: Bantam Books, 1982), pp. 52-53.
7. p. 114.
8. Miriam provided this version of her story on The Sally Jesse Raphael Program. She is directly quoted.
9. Isaac shared these remarks on The Sally Jesse Raphael Program. He is directly quoted.
10. Miriam shared these feelings on The Sally Jesse Raphael Program. She is directly quoted.
11. Reprinted in *Reader's Digest*, July 1991, p. 70.
12. Harold Kushner, *When All You've Ever Wanted Isn't Enough* (New York: Summit Books, 1986), pp. 25-26.
13. R. L. Smith, April 2, 1993.
14. Kushner, 1986, p. 106.
15. Kushner, 1986, pp. 29-30.
16. Pesach Krauss and Morrie Goldfischer, *Why Me? Coping with Grief, Loss, and Change* (New York: Bantam Books, 1988), pp. 47-48.
17. Kushner, 1986, page 119.
18. Kushner, 1986, p. 122.
19. Kushner, 1986, p. 63.
20. Krauss and Goldfischer, pp. 72-73.
21. R. L. Smith, April 2, 1993.
22. Theresa Saldana, *Beyond Survival* (New York: Bantam Books, 1986), pp. 81-82.
23. Ann Kaiser Stearns, *Coming back: Rebuilding lives after crisis and loss.* (New York: Ballantine Books, 1988), p. 296.
24. R. L. Smith, April 2, 1993.
25. Krauss and Goldfischer, p. xii.
26. R. L. Smith, April 2, 1993.
27. Harold S. Kushner, *When Bad Things Happen to Good People* (New York: Avon Books, 1981), p. 112.
28. Kushner, 1981, pp. 110-111.
29. Kushner, 1981, p. 71.
30. Kushner, 1981, pp. 119-120.
31. Charles Leerhsen with Marc Peyser, "His Saddest Song," *Newsweek*, March 23, 1992, p. 52.
32. M. Harden, *Heartland Journal* (Columbus, OH: Wing & Prayer, 1988), pp. 3-4.

4

ACCEPT YOURSELF, BUT SEEK TO IMPROVE
Melly and Redgie Staskal

"Let me listen to me and not to them."
Gertrude Stein

". . . there are only two emotions, love and fear. The first is our natural inheritance, and the other our mind manufactures. . . .we can learn to let go of fear by practicing forgiveness and seeing everyone, including ourselves, as blameless and guiltless."[1]
Gerald G. Jampolsky

"In the midst of winter
I find in myself at last
Invincible Summer."
Haiku by Albert Camus

Melly and Redgie Staskal have lived their entire lives in a small town in Wisconsin. They had two children, a son, and four years later, a daughter. Melly and Redgie were given tickets to a dinner theater in a nearby town when their children were twenty and sixteen years old. Mark called just before they left to say that he had had car trouble and needed a ride home. Although Melly was willing to go, Marcy urged her mother to go on to the dinner theater and offered to pick up her brother. When Melly and Redgie returned home hours later, they learned from one of the officers that their son had stabbed their daughter to death.

63

REDGIE STASKAL

Redgie Staskal was born in 1940 in Lancaster County to Mr. and Mrs. Jefferson Staskal. He was the oldest of five children. In the sixth grade his family moved to Maquoketa, Iowa. The move was important since it was the hometown of his wife–to–be.

MELLY STASKAL

Melly was born in 1943 in Missouri to Mr. and Mrs. William Hayward, but her family soon moved to Maquoketa, Iowa. She was eventually the oldest of three children with two younger brothers.

MEETING AND COURTING

Redgie and Melly attended the same high school, but because she was three years younger than her husband, she began high school just after he had graduated. The couple dated for two years, and it was certainly not love at first sight. Melly said, "I thought he was good looking, but real arrogant. I went out with him because I was upset with another boyfriend. He was a fill–in until someone real came along." She acknowledges, "I think he liked me right away."

MARRIAGE

The Staskals married in November of 1962. Melly had been raised a Baptist, but shortly after they were married she joined her husband's Methodist faith. Redgie had attended two years of school in Chicago at DeVry Technical before they married. The school helped him to get a job in Wheaton, Illinois, after their wedding so Melly moved away from her family in Iowa. She said, "To me it didn't matter. All that was important was to be where he was."

CHILDREN

The couple became pregnant almost right away. Just over a year after they were married, their son Mark was born. Melly recalled, "He was never a happy baby. He had colic the first three months and he did a lot of crying. He was a thin and tall baby."

Four years later, on February 11, 1968, Marcy was born in Janesville. Melly noticed a sharp difference between her children. "When you'd hold him, he'd be real rigid, and Marcy would conform to you. They say babies can't see, but from the very beginning, it seemed she would give you facial and eye contact. At the time, I just felt the differences were boy/girl."

As the children grew and developed, their differences were more pronounced. Mark had nightmares and was obsessed with prehistoric animals. In kindergarten, Mark saw "Peter and the Wolf" and he was terrified. "He had nightmares almost that whole year after seeing that. We took him to a psychiatrist who said that he was as scared as you and I would be if somebody was going to shoot us."

Mark declared on the last day of kindergarten, "That wolf isn't going to bother me anymore, because I killed it last night." However, other problems ensued. Melly said, "Mark seemed to like other kids, and he tried to play with them. But all of the kids would just separate and leave him. Kids teased him all through school. Now they would call him a nerd."

Marcy, on the other hand, was an open and trusting person who made friends more easily. Two communication experts write that "Trusting behaviors are those that... deliberately increase a person's vulnerability to another person."[2] Marcy's lack of skepticism left her open to others.

During their younger years, the children got along very well. Melly said, "I wrote in her baby book that I never saw so much love between two kids."

"I have pictures of them as they were growing up, playing in the swimming pool, having a good time. As they got older, it might have been in the teenage years, they started bickering a lot. I did not see it as abnormal because other kids do that."

Mark had difficulty in school, although he graduated from high school in 1982. During his last few years, he received below average grades. He also attended some special classes for reading and language through eighth grade and again as a junior and senior.

His high school principal, Tom Kemppainen, "described him as a `quiet individual' who appeared to be a loner. Kemppainen said Staskal was not a discipline problem and had a good attendance record."[3]

Learning disabilities in language and an inability to hold a job led to psychological and physical testing after Mark graduated from high school. On February 4, 1983, a psychological report was filed by Mental Health Consultants. Melly and Redgie said they did not learn of the report until sometime in August of 1984, after their daughter's death.

The report stated that Mark was referred for psychological evaluation by the Division of Vocational Rehabilitation, and he was to be evaluated "as a candidate for a work training program." Mark was apparently given the Minnesota Multiphasic Personality Inventory and was interviewed by the consultants.

The consultants wrote, "As the interview progressed Mark described a history of severe family conflict. He reported that he disowned his sister since she was nine or ten saying `she's not my sister.' He described his mother as extremely moody fluctuating between being nice and becoming totally angry for no apparent reason. He states he has been involved in physical altercations with his father."

They added, "He elaborated at some length upon what he called `premonitions.' He said that he has had these premonitions or precognitions of future events for many years and that they include both visions and voices. He said they occur usually in dreams but have occurred on at least one occasion when he was awake. He says that the visions often involve a murder, sometimes of himself, and he feels compelled to act on the premonition in order to prevent it from coming true."

The consultants concluded, "In summary, Mark Staskal is a nineteen–year–old who demonstrates significant psychopathology at the present time. He demonstrates several cardinal clinical symptoms of a schizophrenic disorder, and it is suggested that he is in need of referral for further psychological and psychiatric evaluation. Mark does not appear capable at present of coping successfully with the stresses of a work or work training program, but he may be able to function successfully in such areas if provided with psychotherapeutic support."[4]

Marcy, by contrast, was a happy high school student who spent many hours babysitting for children in her neighborhood. She was described by school officials as "more outgoing" than her brother, and a popular student who was involved in school activities and programs.

Before Marcy's death, Melly saw herself as a woman who had everything. "I just felt as though I was lucky. I had everything I wanted, the son, the daughter, a million dollar family, everything I would ever want. Anything above that was icing on the cake."

THE DEATH

The Staskals had no forewarning about the terrible events that laid ahead. Indeed, in February of 1984, they went on a three–week trip and left the kids home alone. Mark was 20 and Marcy turned 16 while they were gone. Melly said, "We trusted both our kids. My husband's sister and her husband lived here, so they drove over and checked on them. We gave them a lot of space because they had earned it."

One shadow fell on the incident. "When we came back, the chief of police here in town told us that our son had tried to buy a hand gun. We were concerned about that and we asked him about it, and he said `I just want that like a kid wants a hot car or a motorcycle.' We didn't think that was really why, but we found it believable."

What happened a few months later, on June 16, was unbelievable. At the same time, it could have occurred in any family's home. Two years earlier, Redgie had been given a gift certificate for a dinner theater. Melly said, "We tried giving it away, but no one would take it. So we decided to use it that night."

After work Melly came home to get ready to go out. She found only Marcy at home. She learned that Mark had gone over to Edgerton, a town about ten miles away. According to a news report, Mark had been in Edgerton to view the scene of a recent homicide. Mark called to say that his car had stalled and that he needed a ride. She and Marcy talked about who would retrieve him. Marcy encouraged her mother to keep her dinner theater date and promised to get him. Before she left to get Mark, she dropped her mother off at the restaurant where Redgie and another couple held their reservation. When Marcy arrived, Mark was not where he had told her he would be. She told him she was angry. Melly said, "Marcy could kind of come on a little strong, forget that he was the older brother. And that irritated him."

Melly tried to understand her son's motivations. "My thoughts are that he had a half dozen thoughts running around in his mind. It was her, it was us, and classmates that had given him a hard time. Probably anyone he blamed for things not working out for him. He didn't know he had a mental illness, and even though he's got one today, he will not admit that he has one."

When Mark and Marcy arrived home, Marcy went to her room. A news report stated that Mark "went to his bedroom where he had a shot of brandy before he went for a knife. He then invited his sister to the basement on the pretense of looking at a Father's Day gift."[5]

When Marcy began to come down the basement steps, Mark began to stab her. A news report reconstructed the event. "His sister attempted to fight him off and asked why he was attacking her, but he kept stabbing her until the knife broke and she fell to the floor bleeding, according to reports."

"Staskal then went upstairs, retrieved his father's new fishing filet knife, unwrapped it, took it from its sheath, sharpened it on a can–opener knife sharpener, and returned to the basement, where he found his sister still breathing, reports said."

"He then stabbed her 10 to 17 more times until he was sure she was dead, dragged her body into a closet and cleaned up the blood, according to reports. Witt said Staskal told him he then changed clothes and made plans to kill his parents, but they did not return home."

"Staskal also told Witt he thought about killing his high school classmates, reports said."

"Rock County Coroner Richard McCaul said he was called to the Staskal residence about 10:25 p.m. An autopsy was conducted in Madison on Sunday. It showed that Marcy bled to death from multiple stab wounds. McCaul said she had been stabbed more than 20 times."[6] Marcy's death was estimated at 7 p.m.

Robert Block, crime lab photographer, said "the victim suffered a total of 39 stab wounds."[7] The wounds covered Marcy's arms, hands, chest, back, and hip.

Mark must have waited only a short time for his parents to return home because one hour later, at 8:07 p. m., he was stopped in

Janesville by a police officer, Douglas F. Johnson. The officer stopped young Staskal because he was going the wrong way on a one–way street.[8]

The Janesville Police Chief, Ray Voelker, explained that Johnson questioned him in detail because Staskal "appeared `fidgety and nervous'" and he was also "sweating profusely."[9]

During the questioning, the officer asked him to show him the contents of his pockets. An empty, leather knife sheath was discovered. Johnson asked Staskal where the knife was, and he asked to look in the trunk of the car. A blood–stained knife was found in the car's trunk. When he asked Staskal about the knife, Mark said, it came from "fishing...no I mean hunting...I mean fishing."[10]

Mark tried to convince the officer that he had been fishing the week before, but Johnson observed that the blood appeared too fresh to be a week old. Staskal changed his story to say that he may have been fishing more recently. Johnson then told Staskal to put the knife in the trunk, and he released him since he had no charges.

Melly detailed the events after Mark was released. "Mark tried to turn himself in to a Catholic church in Janesville. He said he wanted to talk to a nun, but they were having a wedding. He left and came back to Milton, and turned himself into the St. Mary Catholic Church here in Milton. He knew the priest, Fr. James McEnery, from Boy Scouts and he felt safe with him. He walked in the church and said, `I've killed my sister.' The priest said, `Did you really kill your sister?' Mark said, `Yes,' and the priest asked him if there was any chance she was still alive. When Mark said `No,' the priest asked if he should call the ambulance. When he did so, the call also alerted the police who picked Mark up at St. Mary's.

Not long afterwards, Melly and Redgie returned from their evening out. Melly said, "We came home after the play, and we thought we'd go over to the other couple's house, but we were going to stop by the house to see if Mark dealt with the car. It was around 10:00, and when we turned our corner, the whole street was full of vehicles. It's such a quiet little street, nothing is ever going on. My husband got out at the corner, and said, `I'm going to see what's wrong.'"

"I don't know what he was thinking, and I remember saying, `Well, I think I should go, too.' I couldn't tell if the problem was at our house, or where it was. And as we walked up close, we knew almost all of the people on the ambulance squad, and many of the people from the sheriff's department, and they just encircled both of us. And then, they told us separately."

"One of the women on the ambulance squad said, 'Marcy is dead, and Mark is being held.' I almost fainted, I went all the way down. All of the energy drained out of me and it just refueled in an instant before I completely fell. It was the adrenaline coming back. Then I felt so strong, I've never felt so strong. I said, `Take me to her.' The sheriff shook his head, and said `No.' They were putting up this yellow ribbon around the yard, and I said `I'm her mother, take me to her.' He shook his head. I remember looking over my shoulder at my husband's face. I knew that he knew, that they had told him."

Mark Staskal was held without bond in the Rock County jail for thirty days. Marcy's death occurred on a Saturday night and on Monday morning, he was arraigned in Rock County Circuit Court, Branch I, by Judge Mark Farnum. He was represented by public defender John Bergstrom.[11]

The Staskal parents stood behind their son even though he had killed their daughter. Melly said, "The DA and the Public Defender both said we should just talk to the public defender. They said we should support our son. We said, `We're here, we're both kids' parents. We feel that the truth is what is needed, we're going to talk to both of you, and if we find anything, the first one we see is going to get it, we're not going to play favorites. We lost one kid, we don't want anything to happen to the other that is unnecessary. I think because of that, the situation was kept more quiet, less sensationalized. It was the public defender's job to get our son a place that was suitable for him."

Marcy Staskal's memorial service was conducted in the Faith United Methodist Church in Milton, Wisconsin, on June 20, 1984, at 11:00 a.m. Her pastor, Virgil Holmes, officiated and a poem "Footprints" which was found on Marcy's bulletin board in her room was incorporated into the service. Her body was buried in Milton West Cemetery. The family asked that memorials would be made to the Milton Recreation Department for playground equipment.

Originally, Mark pleaded not guilty to the killing because of his mental state. Later he changed his plea, admitting that he killed his sister, but that he was not responsible because of mental disease.

"A psychiatric examination of Staskal July 21 by Dr. Leigh M. Roberts of Madison concluded that at the time of the murder Staskal `had a mental disease that caused him to lack substantial capacity to conform his conduct to the requirements of the law, though he was able to appreciate the wrongness of his conduct.'"

Dr. Roberts' report included the comments that Staskal suffered "social isolation," that he related "feelings of inferiority and rejection" and showed "symptoms of a schizophrenic disorder."[12] Staskal was committed to the Mendota State Health Institute where he remains confined.[13]

Redgie acknowledges that the relationship between the district attorney, the public defender, and he and his wife was crucial to the positive outcome in the case. He said, "We all agreed that my son was ill. They mutually agreed to go for commitment and that was what happened. There was no trial."

Redgie made an unusual disclosure. "Probably a lot of people didn't understand, but I made a statement that if the state of Wisconsin had the death penalty, I would have pushed for it. The reason is not that I am uncaring about my son, but death is a cure for mental illness. It would prevent another person from being killed by him again."

How Did the Couple Cope?

How could any couple cope with the loss of one child at the hands of another? The immediate events provided both opportunities to heal and tragedies to survive. The couple was taken to their minister's house soon after arriving home. They entreated the authorities to be present when Marcy's body was removed from the house. Redgie said, "We drove down in the squad car and just sat in the car and watched her being carried out to the hearse and then they drove away. Why that was important, I have no idea. Also, I told the undertaker that my wife and I wanted to be the last two people to see her and that we would close the lid on her coffin. I don't know why I felt we just had to do that."

The couple also busied themselves with the plans for the funeral. Melly recalled, "At first, we were really close. The shock protected us from the pain. I felt good about making the funeral arrangements. It almost seemed enjoyable because it was something we could do for her." Redgie agreed that planning the service was a "good experience."

As time passed, the shock wore off and the couple began to experience problems. Melly remembered, "We tried to continue our lives. He went back to work and I went back to work. We would visit our son. There wasn't a time when we lost contact with our son."

Differences in Grieving

While they tried to live in harmony with the normalcy of everyday life, the couple responded differently to their loss. Melly said, "We lived in the same house, but we lived separately because we grieved so differently. You'd like to think that you just hold each other through this. Our experience was that you don't. It's a miracle that we survived."

One difference in their grieving was how they responded to religion. Redgie became more religious, and Melly became less so. The congregational song, in Marcy's memorial service was "Because He Lives, I Can Face Tomorrow." The song clearly had less relevance for Melly than for Redgie.

Melly said, "I was very religious before this happened. Since then, it just blew my spiritual life. I was one of these people who almost felt like I had a direct line to the Holy Spirit. This happened right under the chair where I prayed for my kids everyday. I just felt that God ran out on me. It is one of the things I'm not sure I'll ever overcome."

"One thing," said Melly, "that did help me be less concerned with my own spiritual life is a book called *Steps of a Fellow Struggler* and it was written by a rabbi. He had an eleven–year–old daughter who had leukemia, for whom he prayed. She asked him, 'You're praying for me, why aren't I getting better?' He said he didn't have an answer for her. He said the only answer I have for anybody is that maybe God will give the answer. I don't expect to find answers in this life; he just had to let go. I guess that's just what I had to do. There were just so many things that had to be done right now, and if God was all that I thought he was, he would understand that I just had to let go for survival."

"I learned that there was not a God as I had come to understand him. Redgie was not as actively religious, but it made him strengthen his religion. His religion is based on hoping to get where she is."

Another difference that the couple expressed was their need to see the crime lab pictures. Melly said, "I don't ever want to see them. I've never seen any need. My husband did."

She added, "He didn't see the crime lab picture until this year. It gnawed away at him, `Was she really dead?' I think it was good that he did that, I wish he had done it sooner."

"He had always seemed to have more anger with our son. He wondered whether he was really mentally ill, but after seeing the pictures, he was convinced. He said, `Only a crazy person could have done that.' It did hurt him, and it's taken him months to recover from that new hurt of it. It was hard on him, but he had to do that for his own healing process, to come to grips with all of it."

Redgie's impressions are similar to Melly's perspective. "I asked If I could see the pictures. The authorities were reluctant because they were gruesome, but I explained why I needed to see them. My wife did not want to see them. I looked at the pictures as the best thing I have ever did; it was a hard thing to do. It did answer my questions. My daughter probably felt no pain after the first 10 or 12 seconds; she probably lost consciousness in a minute and she was dead within two. I needed to know that she wasn't slowing bleeding to death while I was sitting outside in the squad car."

While Redgie wanted to see pictures of his daughter after death and Melly did not, Melly wanted all of the details of the murder while her husband did not.

"I had to know every detail of what happened. Visit after visit [with Mark], I had to get all of my questions answered. I asked him a lot of questions. I believe he was very honest with me. I believe he understood my need and seemed to want to help give me the answers to the questions I had."

"My husband's need was different from mine. He may have been more protective of Mark. I'll bet he didn't ask him any detailed questions. But when I did, I would share what I learned with my husband."

Another difference was that Redgie became introspective while Melly wanted to be more verbal. She said, "He had been in a depression, and he insisted on putting Marcy's picture right across the room. He later admitted that all those hours he pretended to watch television and ignore me, he was looking at her picture. He just shut everything out except her, including me. It was very lonely. I felt as though I had lost all three of them."

Melly elaborated, "Many people have told Reg and I that we don't belong together, we ought to be divorced. We are very different. Reg is a very committed person. I can remember when we were going together, and I said, `I love you,' he'd say, `Don't say it unless you really mean it.' He would have done anything to hold this marriage together when I was thinking of ending it. I felt so uncared for, because of his depression, and because of the isolation. I couldn't believe that the marriage really meant that much to him based on his behavior."

Friends and Family offered support

The Staskals received support from others. Melly said, "I joined a support group, but not to make a life out of it. I went to Compassionate Friends. It was helpful in the beginning stages because I learned about the technical part of grieving. I had grieved before, but nothing compared to this. I needed to learn about it."

Melly and Redgie were eventually dissuaded from seeking help in a support group because a ritual in the meeting is to disclose your own loss. She said, "Redgie said it was like killing her every time. If you could just introduce yourself. After a while, part of you screams, `Yes, I am part of this tragedy, but that is only a part of who I am. It is not my complete self. I am not identified solely with this tragedy.'"

Marcy's friends provided the couple with support. Melly said, "My daughter must have had a knack for picking wonderful friends. Her friends were a constant support. She had a boyfriend and a friend who came and sat in the swing with me in the backyard; they walked me to the car to go to the funeral; they came so many times."

"She had girlfriends that came and insisted in having an overnight in her room after she died. Three girls came here and slept in her bedroom."

"These kids stuck around for the longest time. They would bring flowers on the appropriate dates. They would remember her death date, her birth date."

Even strangers offered support to the Staskals. "I ran across a customer at work that hadn't known either of us, but she knew our names. She said, `Oh, your daughter is a legend. I've heard about her from so many people.'"

Friends and family members wrote tributes, essays, and poems in Marcy's memory. A cousin, Tina Staskal, who was about the same age as Marcy, wrote, in part:

> "Marcy was taken from us still a kid,
> > but Marcy had a meaning in life and anything she
> > could do for people she did.
> I'll never forget what she meant to me,
> > we grew up together and yet we had so much
> > more to see.
> I'm not quite sure how I'll make it without you,
> > it seems without you, the things I did just aren't as
> > easy to do."

A fellow classmate, Paul Elliott, wrote an essay entitled "Remember Marcy." Coincidentally, Paul was killed in an auto accident shortly after Marcy's death. His essay read, in part:

> "She was a sweet person when you got to know her, as I did. She cared about others, much like her mother. Marcy did what was asked of her from anyone she knew, without a gripe.

But what Marcy cared about most were kids. She babysat for any family that asked her, including my own. She's done one–time "stints" and a couple of full–time jobs where she had to live there during the school year. Marcy was like a parent to a lot of kids. She cared so much about a certain two that she bought and wore mother's rings with the kids' birthstones in them."

These tributes were no doubt comforting to the Staskals. As George Vaillant wrote in *Adaptation to Life*, "Support from others is important to all people." Vaillant adds, "But there is much that humans must do for themselves."[14] In the next section we will see how the Staskals helped themselves in the grieving process.

Expressing Themselves

Immediately after the murder, the Staskals were unable to express themselves. Perhaps as a result, Redgie became ill. Woody Allen, in one of his movies, says somewhat tongue–in–cheek, "I can't express anger. I internalize it and grow a tumor instead."[15] Redgie did not grow a tumor, but chronic jaw pain became even more severe. Melly said, "The jaw pain was undiagnosed."

When people are unable or unwilling to discuss their pain with others, they often internalize. Bernie Siegel notes that "Internalizing is exactly what you don't want to do. When someone asks you how you are and you say "Fine" even though you feel terrible, that's internalizing."[16]

James Pennebaker did a project on the healing properties of sharing one's pain and grief. He writes, ". . . actively holding back or inhibiting our thoughts and feelings can be hard work. Over time, the work of inhibition gradually undermines the body's defenses."[17]

He notes, ". . . confronting our deepest thoughts and feelings can have remarkable short–and long–term health benefits. Confession, whether by writing or talking, can neutralize many of the problems of inhibition."[18] As time progressed, Melly and Redgie were able to confront their feelings through both writing and talking.

Melly kept a journal which allowed her to regularly express herself. In one entry, she eulogized her daughter. The entry read, in part:

"I have never known anyone who was so alive. She had a capacity for love of children that was well beyond her age. . . She seemed to make the best of both situations and never complained. When things didn't go as she wanted them to she would try to change them but in a way so as not to hurt or offend someone else."

Redgie added, one day she and I had an argument and a few minutes later I asked her if she was still mad at me to which she said `I don't waste my time being mad.' And that was right, she didn't. She really got the most of every day. . . She often enjoyed and shared other people's good moments with them. She never felt that she had to be first or the best, but rather willing to be part of good things. . . I told a lot of other people how proud of her I was but I regret that I never really told her."

Redgie wrote about Marcy, too, to help with his grieving. In one essay, he wrote both to God and to Marcy. "Living was easy when she was there to care and share. . . .God I miss her so. We had so little precious time back when she was mine. When my time comes to meet thee, O God, please send Marcy for me. Good night punkin, know I love you."

The Staskals also learned of a way to allow others to express their feelings in writing. Melly talked to a woman at Compassionate

Friends who had lost her child and had had her cremated. This woman put a note jar in her daughter's room and placed within it all of the notes that the daughter had written in her lifetime as well as the notes that others wrote after her death.

Melly said, "I put a note jar at Marcy's grave. It was set beside her marker. I did it about a year after Marcy's death. The jar is full. The kids will write serious stuff like "I'm not afraid to die because I know you're there with me." They write funny things, too. The one says, "Today, I thought about you. . . I got my bra. You said that you were going to be the first one to snap it. . . I snapped it for you."

Potential Infidelity

All of the Staskal's behaviors were not so healthy. The couple came close to divorce because Melly, in her desperation to have another child, sought outside relationships. She said, "This is real painful to my husband. I did go out on him with the intention of having a baby. I couldn't cross that line. I'd go to motels, I'd take my clothes off, but I couldn't do it. It happened over a period of four to six weeks, with several men."

Melly recognizes that her motivation was not exclusively a sexual one. "I was somehow attracted to people like me, in that they were having crises in their relationships. I think we had lost being able to have intimacy. The relationships were based on the lack of intimacy and an ability to work out big problems. We were confused by the world we live in. I was searching for my identity."

Having a relationship with another person is a fairly common response to grief. Sometimes the spouse feels that he or she is not understood by the partner and seeks understanding from someone else. Sometimes the reason for the infidelity is the seeking of intimacy—both verbal and sexual. Finally, partners sometimes seek others to take flight from their pain—to seek escape.

Unique Problems

The Staskals also had some unique problems because of the nature of their loss. The first problem they confronted was that neither person knew that Mark had been diagnosed with a mental illness. Melly said, "After it happened, the public defender came here and he was trying to piece together Mark's defense. He said something about our son being diagnosed with a mental illness. We said `What?' It made me distrust my husband because I thought that they couldn't possibly have had that information and not given it to one of us. I finally realized that he didn't know either."

A second unique problem was that the couple has had to endure decisions and hearings about their son. Mark's case can be reviewed and his mental condition can be re–examined for the rest of his life. In August 1990, such a hearing occurred. A Rock County Circuit Court jury heard testimony regarding Mark's mental condition. The state public defender, Barbara Due, told the jurors that the state had to prove that he was dangerous.[19]

Psychiatrist Vincent Giannattasio interviewed Mark and testified that he was "not well enough to be released from the secure setting of the hospital." He added that Mark was "seclusive and dangerous to others." He concluded that Mark "suffers from a mental disorder affecting his thought process and includes a personality disorder, an anti–social disorder and paranoid schizophrenic."[20]

Eugene McCarney, a social worker who worked with Mark for five years, also recommended against a release. He said his condition had not changed since he had been first committed to Mendota in 1984. He added that Mark's only show of remorse was over his own life. "He was only sorry because of his own difficulty," he said.[21]

The jury deliberated less then ten minutes and returned a verdict for recommittal. Redgie was surprised.

"I'm upset about the fact the jury wasn't back there long enough to read the instructions. They couldn't even have been seated," he said.[22]

Finally, the Staskal's experienced attorney malpractice. Melly said, "Our attorney didn't file some papers. As a result, they put a lean against our house. We didn't know this until we went to borrow some money about six years later. It was a lean for their expenses because we lost the law suit. This lawyer didn't even tell us about it. Otherwise, we would have taken care of it six years ago. So since then, he ran out of his law firm in the middle of the night. My husband feels very strongly about it. He says he doesn't want to pay people for killing his daughter."

The Secret of Surviving Couples:
Accept Yourself, but Seek to Improve

Couples who lose children often blame themselves or each other for the death. People in satisfying relationships do not turn on themselves or each other. Instead, they externalize their problems, they become self–reliant, they exercise personal control, and they become survivors.

Externalizing Problems

One psychologist explains, "When bad things happen, we can blame ourselves (internalize) or we can blame other people or circumstances (externalize). People who blame themselves when they fail have low self–esteem as a consequence. They think they are worthless, talentless, and unlovable. People who blame external events do not lose self–esteem when bad events strike. On the whole, they like themselves better than people who blame themselves do."[23]

The Staskals found outside sources to blame. They blamed a system which did not tell them about Mark's psychological evaluation and his danger to others. Melly said, "We were at a meeting and we were told that the psychological report was not in yet. They had a doctor come from the other side of the state, so they wanted to go on with the meeting. We all agreed. We feel we were probably lied to. If we weren't lied to, then somebody had misplaced the report. Something went wrong and somebody was negligent. The psychologist's report appears to me as if its been tampered with."

They also view mental health as being outside a parent's control. Melly said, "Mental illness is a terrible thing, but it is something that could happen to anyone, touch any family. What happened to my daughter is a terrible thing, a bizarre thing, but if it happened to our family, it could happen to any family. People need to be educated about this."

"My son is mentally ill. It was hard for me to be able to say that. I don't want my son released. I love him dearly, and I feel badly that he has been afflicted with this disease. I didn't cause it; I can't do anything about it. But I don't want anyone else hurt by it. I don't want him to be hurt."

Becoming Self-Reliant

Melly's background made her particularly vulnerable to self–blame. She said, "My anger at myself would be for being so gullible. As a kid, I was taught to believe that I was dumb. I let people's education or their intellect have power over me."

Each of us have self–doubts. Kraus and Goldfischer note, "All of us are crippled in the sense that we have unresolved internal conflicts that prevent us from functioning at our top levels... Even the most outwardly successful people in our society—writers, composers, scientists, captains of industry—experience soul–searching periods when they question their accomplishments, their self–worth, and consider themselves failures and inferior to others... no one is immune to feeling inferior."[24]

Melly's biological parents were divorced when she was just three months old. Her mother was only 18 years old when Melly was born. Consequently, she was raised the first six years by her grandmother who had ten children of her own plus Melly.

Melly said, "My mother remarried when I was six. She's more of a sister than a mother to me. I feel a lot like I do toward my aunts with her. She wasn't grown up enough to be a mother at the time that I needed a mother. I believe that she's given me the best mothering that she is capable of. My grandmother and other people filled in when she couldn't. She has helped me understand and accept the limitations of myself."

Melly shows the wisdom of accepting herself and taking responsibility for what is properly hers. "I have learned that it's my job to take care of me."

Before Marcy's death, Melly identified herself only, or at least primarily, as a mother. Afterwards, she began to see herself as a separate person, complete in herself. One author explains:

> At the opposite pole from evangelical Christianity, there is something we might call the therapeutic attitude, based on self–knowledge and self–realization ... [It] begins with the self, rather than with a set of external obligations. The individual must find and assert his or her true self because

this self is the only source of genuine relationships to other people. External obligations, whether they come from religion, parents, or social conventions, can only interfere with the capacity for love and relatedness. Only by knowing and ultimately accepting one's self can one enter into valid relationships with other people...

But this search for a perfect relationship cannot succeed because it comes from a self that is not full and self-sustaining. The desire for relatedness is really a reflection of incompleteness, of one's own dependent needs.

Becoming a more autonomous person means learning self-acceptance... To be able to enjoy the full benefits of a love relationship, one must stop needing another's love to feel complete."[25]

Today Melly is a self-reliant person who believes in herself. In some ways she is like the boxer Muhammad Ali who exclaimed, "I am the greatest," and meant it. Melly, too, has come to feel that she is special. Two authors write, "No one is perfect. And until I learned the basic truth of my own uniqueness and concentrated on it, I suffered a lot of unnecessary sorrow and anger and guilt."[26] They add, "That's a hard lesson to learn."[27] Melly Staskal has learned to accept herself.

Author Ann Stearns explains, "One characteristic of people who have achieved peace of mind is their independence. They trust their instincts. Nobody can tell them what to think if their inner voices say otherwise."[28]

Exercising Personal Control

The couple turned a corner after Melly's attempts to have an affair. Before that time they were dwelling in a land of helplessness. Afterwards, they began to take positive action. Martin Seligman writes, "At the core of the phenomenon of pessimism is another phenomenon—that of helplessness. Helplessness is the state of affairs in which nothing you choose to do affects what happens to you. Personal control means the ability to change things by one's voluntary actions; it is the opposite of helplessness."[29]

Melly said, "We put things back together. We bought a new bedroom suit. We started all over. We created a new life and a new marriage. Reg was as much into this as I was. Maybe he was even the creator of that. It was almost like another courtship."

One author who examined people who rebuilt their lives after crisis and loss observed that those who stayed healthy "in the face of stressful life circumstances felt in *control* of their lives (as opposed to helpless/hopeless), *committed* to lives in which they found meaning both at home and at work, and *challenged* by events that other people might find threatening.[30] The Staskals clearly gained control, commitment, and challenges.

They have also enriched their lives by taking foster children. Melly said, "In the last fifteen months, we've had five kids here. Two of them have stayed, two boys, ten and eleven, and they have just really helped this marriage a lot. Reg and I are parenting together again. We're probably more sensitive to each other's feelings than we ever were."

The couple thought a number of times about leaving their house which contains the memories of their particular tragedy. Melly said, "At times we thought about leaving this house. Yet we've stayed."

Reg added, "I've come to the realization that there are no safe places. I thought this was the one place she was safe."

Becoming Survivors

The Staskals, it must be concluded, are survivors. Melly said, " We're both really just two strong people. We're survivors. I think that probably being the first born has helped."

Everyone does not have the survivor's instinct. Ann Stearns summarizes research on the survivor's personality. She writes, "It is said that fighter pilots have an extra amount of self–confidence. `If a hundred go up and ninety–nine get shot down, I'm the guy coming back,' confirmed POW Robbie Risner, explaining his mental set and that of most of the other fighter pilots he has known."[31]

Stearms summarizes the conclusions about those who are survivors.

- [Survivors] seem to like happy endings, good completions.
- They try to set things right, to clean up bad situations.
- They manage somehow simultaneously to love the world as it is and try to improve it.

- [They have] some hope that people and nature and society [can] be improved.
- They change to improve the situation. . . They enjoy improving things.
- They enjoy bringing about law and order in the chaotic situation, or in the messy or confused situation, or in the dirty and unclean situation.
- They like doing things well, "doing a good job," "to do well what needs doing."
- They enjoy greater efficiency, making [things] more neat, compact, simple, faster, more foolproof, safer, more "legant," less laborious.[32]

SUMMARY

The Staskals have surely experienced the worst pain a couple can know. They have lost both their daughter and their son. They nearly divorced. Melly tried to commit adultery. Today they are happily married and living in peace.

Eli Wiesel, in his book *Souls on Fire,* tells us: "When we die and we go to heaven, and we meet our Maker, our Maker is not going to say to us, why didn't you become a messiah? Why didn't you discover the cure for such and such? The only thing we're going to be asked at that precious moment is why didn't you become *you?*[33]

The Staskals might not have become who they were to be without the tragedies of the past decade. They have learned to accept themselves even though they try each day to improve who they can become. They have learned not to blame themselves, they have developed self–reliance, they exercise personal control, and they have become survivors. Eudora Welty said that "All serious daring starts from within." They Staskals have demonstrated their courage.

Ann Stearns provides their benediction, "Parents need to be forgiven for their mistakes and to forgive themselves. . . My heart goes out to all imperfect parents, which is what we all are."[34]

REFERENCES

1. Gerald G. Jampolsky, *Love is Letting Go of Fear* (Berkeley, CA: Celestial Arts, 1979), p. 2.
2. C. Rossiter and B. Pearce, *Communicating Personally* (Indianapolis: Bobbs-Merill, 1975).
3. J. Dowd, Man charged in sister's murder. *The Janesvile Gazette*, June 18, 1984.
4. This report was dated February 4, 1983 and was signed by Christine J. Kuchler, M. Ed., Psychological Assistant, and Nicholas J. Bisenius, Ph. D., Consulting Psychologist.
5. J. Dowd, Don't release Staskal, say psychiatrists. *The Janesville Gazette*, August 28, 1990, p. 1B.
6. J. Dowd, "Man charged in sister's murder," *The Janesvile Gazette*, June 18, 1984, p. 1A.
7. J. Dowd, "Don't release Staskal, say psychiatrists," *The Janesville Gazette*, August 28, 1990, p. 1B.
8. This account was provided by D. Riemar, "Officer stopped suspect after killing," *The Janesville Gazette*, June 19, 1984, p. 1.
9. D. Riemar, "Officer stopped suspect after killing," *The Janesville Gazette*, June 19, 1984, p. 1.
10. D. Riemar, Officer stopped suspect after killing. *The Janesville Gazette*, June 19, 1984, pp. 1A, 8A.
11. This information was summarized in a newspaper article, entitled, "Staskal charged with sister's murder," *The Milton Courier*, June 21, 1984, p. 1.
12. D. Riemar, Officer stopped suspect after killing. *The Janesville Gazette*, June 19, 1984, p. 1.
13. Staff, "Mental re-exam of Staskal expected," *The Janesville Gazette*, June 1, 1990, p. 1B.
14. Cited in Ann Kaiser Stearns, *Coming Back: Rebuilding Lives after Crisis and Loss* (New York: Ballantine Books, 1988), p. 179.
15. Cited in Bernie S. Siegel, *Peace, Love, & Healing: Bodymind Communication and the Path to Self-Healing: An Exploration* (New York: HarperPerennial, 1990), p. 33.
16. Siegel, p. 33.
17. James W. Pennebaker, *Opening up: The Healing Power of Confiding in Others* (New York: Avon Books, 1990), p. 13.
18. Pennebaker, p. 14.
19. Summarized by J. Dowd, "Jury picked to decide Staskal's mental state," *The Janesville Gazette*, August 27, 1990, p. 1B.
20. Direct quotations are taken from J. Dowd, "Don't release Staskal, say psychiatrists," *The Janesville Gazette*, August 28, 1990, p. 1B.
21. Direct quotations are taken from J. Dowd, "Don't release Staskal, say psychiatrists," *The Janesville Gazette*, August 28, 1990, p. 1B.
22. Direct quotations are taken from J. Dowd, "Staskal to stay at mental hospital," *The Janesville Gazette*, August 29, 1990, p. 1B.
23. Martin E. P. Seligman, *Learned Optimism: How to Change your Mind and your Life* (New York: Pocket Books, 1990), p. 49.
24. Pesach Krauss and Morrie Goldfischer, *Why Me? Coping with Grief, Loss, and Change* (New York: Bantam Books, 1988), p. 63.
25. Pennebaker, pp. 98-99.

26. Krauss and Goldfischer, p. 62.
27. Krauss and Goldfischer, p. 62.
28. Stearns, p. 213.
29. Seligman, pp. 5-6.
30. Stearns, pp. 167-168.
31. Stearns, 1988.
32. Al Siebert, "The Survivor Personality," *Association for Humanistic Psychology Newsletter*, August-September 1983, pp. 20-21.
33. Cited in Stearns, p. 241.
34. Stearns, p. 186.

5

EXPECT PERFECTION, BUT ACCEPT IMPERFECTION
Max and Adrianna Norton

"We love those who know the worst of us and don't turn their faces away."
Walker Percy[1]

"The greatest disease of mankind is the absence of love."
Mother Teresa[2]

"Avoid confrontation, hardness meeting with hardness. The soft voice is heard long after the shout. Gentleness is stronger than anger.
"Winning is a kind of losing and losing is a kind of winning. If there must be winning and losing, treat them as the same."
Ray Grigg[3]

Adrianna Norton and her 4–year–old son, Robyn, both had doctor's appointments in Salida, a small California town. When Robyn was finished with his appointment, he asked his mother for money to buy some candy. Adrianna complied and then visited the doctor herself. When Robyn didn't return, Adrianna went looking for him. She did not know that her little boy had been killed by a car as he attempted to cross the street.

MAX NORTON

Max Norton was born in Idaho in a family of eight children, but his family moved to California in the mid-1920's. "We left Idaho because my father was in the farming business, and he went broke. He then became an irrigation engineer in the San Francisco Bay area."

He describes a family that was close and had strong Mormon values. "I don't remember ever being punished as a child. My parents outlined for us what the value of life was."

The family was bonded by tragedy. "My father was employed by Modesto Irrigation District building dams. The company furnished us with a house. Then the house caught fire. Four of us were locked in the basement because our cousins were playing a trick on us. They threw a lot of stuff up against the door and locked us in. My dad was working, my mother was next door, and my baby brother, Gale, was upstairs asleep. We finally pushed away the debris and we ran up to the front of the house. My older sister, June, ran into the house after my baby brother. My mother who was visiting some neighbors down the street saw the fire; she ran home and pulled my sister out. Then she ran back inside the house and carried him out. She was severely burned, and the baby burned to death. Her arms were in a distorted position until 1955 when surgery techniques were perfected, and they then managed to straighten her arms."

This event had a great impact on the Norton family. "It brought us together as a family. We couldn't live there anymore, because of the trauma of the incident. We left and went to Modesto to live. By that time the depression began, and times were very hard with people out of work."

Max became an important caretaker for his mother. "I became the one that my mother turned to even though I wasn't the oldest. We would go to the movies nearly every day and sit through the silent pictures. She was so traumatized she lost her ability to speak and read. She would ask me to try to figure out what they were saying. By the time I entered first grade, I was a reader—I taught myself to read by going to these silent movies. Her severe depression lasted for about 3 or 4 years and then she began to come out of it."

"My father was very supportive of her. He was depressed too, but not as much as she was. When I look back on it now, after knowing more about psychology and human behavior, I think they sublimated their depression. They wouldn't share it with us because they did not want to make us depressed also. They would talk optimistically and be very positive. They did not dwell on the negative. They only taught us hope."

"The only time I can remember my mother crying was when WW II started, and I had received my induction papers. I had gone home to see her for the last time before I was to report for duty. I arrived home real late and went into my parents' bedroom. She left the lights off so I would not see her crying. She said, `Is that you, Max?' I said it was and I went to her. She was crying. She said, `They're going to take all of my remaining sons, and I know you will never come back.' I promised her I would come back, but that was a real moment of despair. My brother was already in the war, and I was going."

Although the Nortons had little money, Max said, "My folks were always very generous, and they never allowed us to think we were poor. It was during the depression that we welded together as a family with a lot of love between the remaining seven brothers and sisters."

"It was us against the world, and we knew that we had to stick together. We went out and sold newspapers and watermelons, and we brought the money home to buy food for the next day. It was very tough, because there was no social security and jobs were very tight."

"We had a strong religious background. We were taught that everything is celestial. You might have problems now, but what was most important was your spiritual life."

ADRIANNA NORTON

Adrianna was born to a Dutch farm family in Medesto, California. She was the oldest child in a family of three daughters and one son. As the oldest child, she was often in charge of the others. But when she was about twelve, the situation changed. "Something was wrong with my heart. I was very weak and very small. My younger sister had to take over the hard work around the house like scrubbing floors and vacuuming. I couldn't do outdoor work, either, or help my mother care for the younger children."

"My mother worked outside in the garden much of the time. She is a very strong person. She still lives next door to me, and my brother and I care for her. She refuses for anyone to live with her, or for her to live with anyone, so we have to be around in case she needs anything."

MEETING AND MATING

After the Second World War, Max went to Hollywood and tried to make a career in acting. "But the strikes came to the movie industry and it was difficult to find employment. This was during the McCarthy era when many people in the movie industry were being persecuted. All the writers were given a bad time. I got fed up with Hollywood and went north back to school."

The move was portentous. Max went to the University of Pacific in Stockton where Adrianna was a student. He was about 27 and she was 19. He said, "There were a lot of returning veterans after the war who decided to return to school."

Adrianna recalls, "We were in a class with about 100 people. In order to get my teaching credential I had to take the class. I also had to pass a swimming test, but I couldn't pass the test, because of my heart. So every semester I had to take a swimming class and after swimming, I had to go to this class that I didn't like and I would fall asleep. I was dozing and Max got up to give a report. I heard his voice in my sleep, and it was really hypnotizing. I fell in love with his voice first. I couldn't get to him, because I was in the back of the class, sleeping."

"During the summer session we took an ornithology class. I loved bird watching. Max took the class to meet some of his requirements. There he was sitting across the table from me, and I heard his voice and he had beautiful blue eyes. He was absolutely adorable back then. It was probably lust at first sight."

"He thought I was stupid when he first met me. I was looking at him when the teacher asked what a certain bird was. Max said I had it in my hand and I didn't even realize it. I was younger than Max, and I was a typical blond who didn't act very intelligent."

Max remembered, "She was across the room and I was circulating some specimens of birds. I thought I was pretty bright, and I thought she was pretty good–looking."

"He gradually got interested in me, and we started talking and then we realized that we were from the same place. We were raised about 5 miles from each other. He found out that I was from a farm family just like he was. After about a year he decided he wanted to marry me. I had no thoughts about marriage, because I was only 20.

Max was a communication disorder major and Adrianna was in music. As an organist, she would practice in the chapel. "I would go listen to her when she was practicing. But she didn't know that I was there, listening. She finally found out and she was flattered."

Max views their relationship as one of complementarity. "I think we had a trade–off. She brought an appreciation of classical music and of the fine arts and I brought another kind of dimension to her life. We are opposites." He added, "Our personalities are different. I feel comfortable being around audiences and around people. However, I think of myself as being introspective and more of an intellectual type. She's more humble about her intellectualism."

People who marry each other nearly always have some similarities and some differences. Kierkegaard wrote, "Each one of us is an exception."[4] The Nortons' personalities and interests were different, but their common background allowed them common ground on which to base a relationship. As Erik Erikson would observe, this gave them "a web of expectations, traditions, and prejudices."[5]

One of their common traits which we will explore later in this chapter is that the two make each other happy. "She's good at making me feel good. We never run each other down. I have never deprecated her. I never hold her responsible for anything. I never evaluate her or label her."

An Eastern philosophy maintains that if "there has been naming so there has been dividing."[6] One of the reasons for the Nortons' successful marriage is that they do not engage in labeling each other. By avoiding naming, they maintain a wholeness or unity.

A bit of wisdom in one of Jackson Brown, Jr.'s books tells us, "Choose you life's mate carefully. From this one decision will come ninety percent of all your happiness or misery."[7] Clearly the choice that Adrianna and Max made is responsible for their long and happy lives together.

After Max and Adrianna graduated from college, Max got a job in the school district. He attended Stanford University and received his master's degree in speech pathology and psycholinguistics and then the couple married in 1952.

Adrianna said, "We did not get married in a church. The Mormon church would not marry us because I was not a member, and the Dutch church wouldn't marry us because he was not a member. We had a garden wedding at my parents' home. My parents were not happy. He was older, he was a Mormon, and he was a Democrat. He had a lot going against him when it came to my parents. But they have come to love him."

After their wedding, they both took jobs in education. She said, "We were very fortunate to both get teaching jobs in our hometown. He was a speech therapist, and I was an elementary teacher."

Adrianna made another major change when she left the Dutch Church in which she had been raised and became a Mormon. Adrianna said, "Max and I had already decided that our spiritual beliefs were as one. To please my parents, he came to the Dutch church for a year. But I knew I was going to join the Mormon church even before he did that. I joined two years later just before my first child was born. I did it because I wanted him to be brought up in the Mormon church. Do you know what this child has done? He went back to the Dutch church."

Adrianna added, "My spiritual beliefs about eternal life are important. I didn't agree with everything in the Dutch Reformed Church. I had visited Salt Lake City before I met Max, and I believed that Mormonism was the true religion. I found out he was a Mormon and that piqued my interest. We had like spiritual beliefs and that was important to me."

Early Marriage

One of the clouds that marred the sunny days of their early married days was Adrianna's health. Max said, "When we got married, my father–in–law told me that Adrianna wouldn't live any more than 10 years because she had a congenital heart problem. He thought I should know that and that we should avoid having children."

Adrianna wanted to have babies, however, and she had two sons within the first five years of their marriage. Max recalled, "Having the babies made her weak, but I couldn't deny her and she wanted to have them. She had to be fulfilled in this way. I tried to discourage her, but she wanted to have the children."

In addition to Adrianna's health problems, their second child was born with neurofibromatosis—a disease of the nervous system. Adrianna said, "It's a 50-50 chance that you could inherit it or it is spontaneous. He got the disease spontaneously."

Adrianna said, "The doctors did not find out what was wrong with my heart until 1956, after I had the two children. They discovered a large hole in the heart. Then I had to wait for 2 more years until the surgery for this was perfected. They were still losing one out of four patients, so it was very risky." Adrianna had one of the first open heart surgeries done at Stanford in California.

Adrianna said, "Max has been the perfect father. He has done 'everything' for these children since they were born. I was very lucky to have been married to him when I was ill. I don't think anyone else would have been so supportive."

After her surgery, Adrianna's doctors insisted that she have no more children. "But I wanted a baby girl. My father would get angry at Max with every pregnancy, telling him I was going to die." Adrianna did not die, but she had very difficult births. "Then after the third child, the doctor said he would not take me as a patient if I got pregnant again."

Although Adrianna's father was concerned about the couple's decision to have children, in other ways he was very supportive. Max said, "Her family is quite wealthy and this was an advantage. My father–in–law was determined that I would be self–fulfilled. He kept saying to me that I should go back and get my doctorate. I didn't have the money. He kept after me, until I went back to school, and he sent us money to live on every month. By that time, we had three children and I was able to finish the doctorate because of his generosity. He believed in me and I was determined not to let him down. From the moment I married her, he placed confidence in me and in the marriage."

ROBYN'S DEATH

Max got his Ph. D. at Denver University and the family moved back to Modesto, because they had started a new university and Max was hired to create a speech pathology curriculum. Not long afterwards they lost their third son.

Adrianna said, "Robyn was hit by a car and killed. Both of us had doctor's appointments and that's where I was. He had cut his chin and the doctors had taken the stitches out. After he was done, he went out to get some candy. There was a grocery store next door, and that was where I thought he had gone. Time kept going by, and he didn't come back. So after I was done, I went looking for him in all the stores. I had no intuition about the child being killed. I couldn't find him because in the meantime he had been hit and was taken to the hospital. I never saw what happened."

"Coincidentally, Max came home from the college at that moment and was at the store where I was when they told us that he had been hit by a car and taken to the hospital. Max was there. We both went to the hospital, and they told us that he had died from head concussions and brain damage. That was one of the lowest points in my life, because I felt responsible."

She continued, "At that moment I was wondering how we were going to get through the next couple of days. The next few months after that were very low, because I felt responsible. I felt that after all Max had done for us, that I had caused him this grief."

Max recalled, "She had terrible nightmares, she blamed herself, and she had terrible depression. Whenever I thought of Robyn, it brought back nightmares about the fire and the death of Gale, my younger brother, and I became depressed myself."

The couple agrees that they were so consumed by their own grief that they could not focus on their older two sons' needs. Adrianna said, "We treated them wrong. We never told the kids anything about what had happened and didn't take them to the funeral. The children were at home when Robyn was hit by the car. The only counseling they got was from uncles and aunts."

"The oldest one was only eight years old and he was the strong one of the family and he took over. The second child had a lot of emotional problems because Robyn was his playmate. He had a terrible time.

"This same summer, we all went to Mexico for a family vacation and the doctor had given the youngest tranquilizers because he was suffering a lot of grief. He had an extreme reaction to the drug and tried to run into the ocean and drown himself. Luckily his cousins were around to save him. I was out of it. His cousins saved him."

How Did the Couple Cope?

Like many other fathers who have lost children, Max used his work to escape the pain. "I went to work every day. I put myself into a time warp. I could go to the University and work, but the minute I came out I was a basket case."

"I was in denial and I would tell myself that it was only a dream and it never happened. When I got home each night I would realize again that it did happen."

Max grieved for many years. "It was about 10 years before I could even talk about him."

Adrianna added, "He couldn't see a picture or mention his name. He wouldn't go to the cemetery, but neither could I. Max went into denial for 10 years—usually it only happens for a few months."

Max said, "I began to heal and one reason was because I could draw upon my early childhood experiences."

Adrianna was so depressed that she could not function. Max said, "Adrianna wasn't leaving the house because she was so depressed. She didn't cook or clean or take care of the boys. I would come home and try to help out. I hired a housekeeper who came in and took over and nursed Adrianna. Most of the time Adrianna would sleep and stay in the house. She was dysfunctional for some time."

Adrianna agrees with Max's assessment. "During this time, I was not the stronger one. I was the one that felt all the guilt but Max never blamed me. It was self–induced and it was me feeling this way and making myself feel this way."

"The first couple of months, I slept. But finally, Max told the doctors, and they had me take a mood elevator so I could function. I still had two kids that I was neglecting."

Robyn Reappeared

Max and Adrianna both believe that Robyn returned to them. Max said, "One day, about two months after his death, my son walked in the door. He was dressed in white and he said `I will not be back, but you will be alright.' He walked out of the door."

The event helped him to heal. Adrianna said, "That was a turning point for Max so he was able to go on."

Adrianna saw Robyn at a different time. "The church teaches us, that I will see Robyn as a little boy, but I saw him as a grown young man, when he appeared to me. I was home alone and I was just looking out the window and there he was. He didn't look at me, he was talking to other people. I knew it was him, but I was just an observer. I know that was not a self–induced daydream. It is just as clear to me today."

Max said, "That kindled her interest in life–after–life research and the near death experience."

Adrianna gave some thought to their experiences and began to read about similar events that others had written about. As a consequence the two eventually joined the International Association for Near Death Studies begun by Kenneth Ring.

Adrianna believes that her reading led her to an important awareness. "I realized that this had happened to me when I was 5 years old. All my life I had been repressing it. I thought it was a nightmare. I had a hole in my heart and a very high fever. I remembered I was very sick, and then, all of a sudden, I found myself at the top of ceiling looking down on my body and then I went into a black room and it was very threatening. There was black matter clawing at me. I thought this was a nightmare. Then I went into an opalescent sea and felt wonderful. That was as far as I got."

"All of my life when that memory would occur to me, I would repress it as a nightmare. I didn't want to think about it. But it never went away. It is still real 50 years later."

"That event had colored all of my relationships. I feel love towards everyone. There are few people that I don't like. I have always been happy, even when I was sick."

"That is a universal reaction that everyone has with these near death experiences. When they come back, all they care about is love. They say that the way we treat others is the most important thing. Love and kindness are most important. That is the way I feel."

Belief in a Reunion

Adrianna looks upon Robyn as living in the spiritual world, and he is real to her. She is only separated from him in a physical way. "I finally have been able to accept the fact that Robyn is happy where he is. Everyone who comes back says that, because they don't want to come back, because they are happy."

"He is happy and leading a productive life wherever he is. He is having just as many opportunities where he is now. I know that we will see each other again."

Max said, "The religious influence was very present and was there all the time. Mormonism says that life is eternal. Even though we couldn't understand why it happened, we knew that in the end we would be reunited with Robyn.

Their religious beliefs also encourage them to presume that Robyn's death served some purpose. Max said, "I still don't understand why he was taken, the Lord has not revealed it to me. We all have to have a sense that there is a purpose for what happens in life."

Another Child

The event that probably changed their lives the most was another child. Adrianna recalled, "The doctors finally consented to let me have another baby. Jenni was born two years later. She was a girl, and everyone was glad."

The pregnancy was not without complications. "A month before she was born, I had a new heart problem. It was not related to the hole in my heart. The women of the church had given me a surprise shower, and I literally had a heart attack. When this happened, the baby did not get any oxygen."

"When the doctor checked me, he heard a heart beat, but he did not know how the baby would be affected. The doctor had told my mother that that was the worst day of his life. But she was born with no problems. When the doctor saw her, he was so happy because he could tell that she was perfect. Life was absolutely wonderful after Jenni was born."

Max smiled, "She became the pet, because now she was the youngest. She's 10 years younger than her two older brothers."

Helping Others

Adrianna's recovery has also been a result of her help to others. She said, "[A step] in recovery "is how can I use this experience to help other people. And that is what I do through the support groups I am in. Some mothers have told me that I have saved their lives.

Adrianna's attitude is similar to the 64-year-old who told author Jackson Brown, Jr., "I've learned that regardless of how little you have, you can always give comfort and encouragement."[8]

Adrianna said, "We encourage parents to come back to this support group, week after week, even though it is painful for them. We tell them they are going feel worse tonight and tomorrow, but then you are going to feel a little better and when you come back next week, you may feel terrible again, but it will get better."

"We see so many mothers who don't go to the group or think they don't need it, and they stay away for a year or two, but they still have to come and go through the pain. Putting it off does not help."

Support groups may be important for the health of the marriage. Adrianna observed that you cannot expect your spouse to help you since he or she is experiencing his or her own grief. "Couples who do not stay together do not have enough people around them to help them. Women rely on their husbands but the husbands are also patients."

Other family members may not be as helpful during this period, either. "You expect your parents to help, but if they haven't lost a child then they can't help. You expect your brothers and sisters to help, but they can't help, because they are suffering too."

"A value of the group is that these are people who can help you because they understand. There is no use in talking to someone who has never been through it; they don't understand. They want to care and listen, but everything they say will be a knife in your heart. It has to be someone who has already been through it. A hundred years ago, every woman lost a child and had to go through it, and there was always someone to turn to."

"You have to find someone. That is why the group is so good. We always have lots of hugs, of course. At the beginning of the meeting, everyone hugs each other. At the end of the meeting, everyone hugs each other."

"People who don't stay married to each other, do not know how to relate to other people. They need other people and they are expecting too much from their spouse. They will say that no one understands."

Adrianna said, "They are self–pitying people." Survivors avoid self–pity. This lesson is taught in the book, *Coming back: Rebuilding lives after crisis and loss.* The author writes:

At the Feast of Tabernacles it is the Jewish custom to build a *sukkah*, a temporary structure in the garden or yard. For eight days the structure stands as a reminder of the temporary booths in which the ancient people of Israel dwelt during forty years of wandering in the wilderness. The *sukkah* must be insubstantially built to convey the idea that human beings should never be haughty and that things of luxury are not lasting and do not bring lasting happiness. The roof must be partially open so that one can see the stars as a reminder of God's protection and blessings.

A structure that preferably has four walls but sometimes has three walls with one side open, the *sukkah* may represent the fragility of life. "Life would be preferable with four walls, but most people have to learn how to live with three walls because few of us have escaped tragedy, disappointment, or misfortune," said Rabbi Simon Glustrom of the Jewish Center in Fair Lawn, New Jersey. In a recent conversation, Rabbi Glustrom was using the three-walled *sukkah* as a symbol for describing how to cope with human brokenness. The insubstantial structure symbolizes God's protection under which frail human beings are able to stand erect and manage to survive.

From the vantage point of a three–walled structure from which one can look to one's neighbor's *sukkah*, continued Rabbi Glustrom, "we are clearly reminded that we are all united together in pain and sorrow. Because a wall of our own is missing, we see that our neighbor, too, is missing a wall. While another person's pain doesn't necessarily lessen our own," he continued, "by looking past our predicament to the other person's *sukkah*, we move from self-pity to the healing that comes when we try to bind up other people's wounds."[9]

Expressing Grief

Adrianna said, "There are typical steps that one must go through when recovering from the death of a close family member. You can't repress it, you must suffer the grief to its fullest. The old practice of wailing and moaning is very valuable. It would be valuable today, but people don't do it. It is very necessary to get rid of all this grief.

"Expressing feelings is important. We encourage mothers to write down every thing they feel. If they don't want to read it or keep it they can burn it or throw it away. They need to write down their feelings or express it to someone else. If you don't have someone to talk to, then write it down."

> ## The Secret of Surviving Couples:
> ## *Expect Perfection, but Accept Imperfection*

The secret provided by the Nortons is that they view each other as perfect beings and simultaneously accept all of the imperfections the other might hold. Couples cannot merge and maintain their merger without this contradiction. On the one hand, we must believe that our spouses are the best they can be. On the other hand, we must understand that they will behave in ways that we cannot explain.

Unconditional acceptance

Unconditional acceptance is essential to the survival of a family. Yet it stands in sharp contrast to other American values. Robert Bellah and his associates write, "Given the enormous American emphasis on independence and self–reliance. . . the survival of the family, with its strong emphasis on interdependence and acceptance, is striking. In many ways, the family represents a historically older form of life."[10]

Adrianna Norton understood the importance of acceptance within her family life. "You learn to be grateful for whatever you have. That is one step toward recovery. Just be grateful for what you have and learn to accept it." Her fate was worse than some people, but she accepted her situation and her life with gratitude and love.

Families must represent security and stability, if they are to be maintained. "The family," according to David Schneider and Raymond Smith, is a realm of "diffuse, enduring solidarity," as opposed to "the anxiety, competitiveness, and achievement–orientation of the occupational realm."[11]

The family requires both women and men to indulge their more feminine, relational sides. The Nortons were both in touch with their empathic, caring selves. In other words, they were both able to perceive the other person's view of the world as though it were their own. Adrianna said, "Max is both feminine and masculine, but I am mostly nurturing and feminine. I really don't have a drive or ambition." Max added, "The men in my family are very nurturing. When the children were growing up, I knew what they were doing. I never punished them." Max's behavior was consistent with the wisdom provided from Goethe who wrote, "Correction does much, but encouragement does more."[12]

In order for marriages to succeed, men must successfully engage in traditionally feminine behaviors. The family setting is one where feminine, rather than masculine, traits are valued. Men have to participate in what has been a "woman's sphere."[13]

Expecting perfection, but accepting imperfection, encourages our spouse to be better. Goethe wrote, "If you take people as they are, you make them worse than they are. If you take people as they could be, you make them achieve what they would be."[14] When we provide messages of admiration and respect tempered with acceptance and approval, relationships blossom.

Max Norton has shown his psychological stress at various stages in his life. The losses he has known have caused him to become clinically depressed. Adrianna talked about the most recent incident. "During the past year, Max had two siblings and a close friend pass away. His depression became so overwhelming that he had to turn to Prozac."

"He felt so bad that he couldn't get out of bed and he couldn't face his class. He was losing touch with reality. He couldn't see why I wanted to live with him, because he was in such bad shape. I tried to argue him out of this and help him back into reality. He would feel worse because he realized he was wrong. It just kept intensifying, and he dug a deeper hole." Within a few months, Max recovered fully.

Throughout this experience, Adrianna saw Max for what he could be, not for what he was. Although his illness was challenging, she stood by him. One seventy–year–old person remarked that one of the most important lessons learned in life is that "kindness is more important than perfection."[15] Adrianna practices this lesson.

Max understands the way Adrianna sees him. "She exists on a

spiritual plane and she lifts me up and makes me exist and aspire to something better than myself. She makes me become a better person."

Max chose his wife wisely. The philosopher Robert Nozicvk wrote in *Philosophical Explanations* that "there is benefit of knowing people who bring out the best in us, who inspire us to grow in new and positive directions."[16] Adrianna probably does make Max a better person than he would have been without her.

At the same time, Adrianna does not simply genuflect to any of Max's behaviors. She observed that in many ways she is the stable person in the relationship, while Max is the emotional one. She said, "It seems like every day, he has a new idea and a new challenge. We are going to go to England next summer to study stained glass!" I say `No, Max, we're not.' Then the next day there is new idea. One time he was going to move to Washington and take a position in the U.S. Department of Education. He was going to accept a Dean's position in Texas once, too." In spite of any idiosyncratic behaviors, Adrianna sees her husband as just about perfect.

Max shows the same behavior to his wife. When Robyn was killed, a less loving husband might have blamed his wife for allowing a small child to leave the doctor's office in search of candy. Max never blamed Adrianna. The two are in complete agreement on this memory.

No Blame

Max said, "We did not let the death of our son destroy our marriage. I never, in any way, held her responsible for the death of our son. I never blamed her and would tell her that over and over again. She has finally overcome the guilt. Today she can say that she was at fault, but that she can accept her fatal mistake."

Max's lack of blame may have come from the sense of humility he has. To blame a spouse suggests the other's superiority. The person placing blame holds an assumption of blamelessness. Grigg writes, "Practice humility and do not try to get ahead of each other. A winner requires a loser . . . We are born in humility and we die in humility. From beginning to end, it is a proven path."[17]

Adrianna said, "Those who get a divorce blame each other for the death of their child." Elisabeth Kubler–Ross wrote that we all need to acknowledge that "I'm not okay, you're not okay, but that's okay," so we can stop passing along our pain to subsequent generations and start loving.[18]

A similar sentiment is offered in the book, *Love is Letting go of Fear*. The author writes, "Have you noticed how often you feel that you are a victim of the world in which you live? Because most of us perceive many aspects of our surroundings as insane, we are tempted to feel helplessly caught in a trap. When we allow ourselves to think we are living in an unfriendly environment where we must fear being hurt or victimized, we can only suffer."

"To be consistent in achieving inner peace, we must perceive a world in which everyone is innocent."[19]

People who accept each other unconditionally may have happy married lives and they may also be generally more satisfied with other relationships. Rather than encourage "no fault" divorces perhaps we should try to practice "no fault" marriages and other relationships. People would be accepted for all of their oddities and differences in behavior.

A wise 51–year–old stated that a most important learning is that "relationships are more important than rules."[20] As younger people we may cling to rules in order to do the right thing. As we age, we may learn that our relationships should take precedence over them. When we value relationships, it becomes increasingly difficult to blame others for their actions.

Placing the Other Person First

Unconditional acceptance may involve putting the other person ahead of oneself. Robert Bellah and his associates write, "Love is . . . a willingness to sacrifice oneself for others. . . "Love" is "saying you come first, even ahead of me, where possible."[21]

Les Newman, an Evangelical Christian and businessman married for a few years states, "I think real love is something where there is that chemistry, but there is also that mental decision that there's going to be a conscious effort for two people to do what's best, instead of what's best for one individual."[22]

Adrianna and Max have such a relationship. She said, "I have such bias. I think that people who are true Christians have learned to be unselfish, but people who are organizational Christians may not have learned that. They may still be feeling self–righteous and `holier than thou.' I am talking about unconditional love. Christ never took anything for himself, he was totally giving. He suffered everything and was willing to do this for the good of others."

"Max will suffer anything for me and the children. He will endure anything, even for his brothers and sisters."

She concludes, "One reason I wanted to marry him was because I felt he was going to devote his life to helping other people, which is what he did—professionally and in his family. He was always the person who was giving instead of taking."

This quality of giving has important health benefits, as well. Bernie Siegel reports that a survey was done to "determine whether there was a statistical correlation between selfless service to others and survival." The answer, he reports "was a resounding yes!"[23] People who give to others not only know the joy of giving, they also have longer lives.

Eleanor Roosevelt observed that "The giving of love is an education in itself." While everyone does not learn this lesson, some are wise in this schooling. In *Live and Learn and Pass It On*, a fifty–eight year old writes, "I've learned that, ultimately, takers lose and givers win."[24] The Eastern philosopher, Lao Tzu, wrote, "Kindness in words creates confidence, kindness in thinking creates profoundness, kindness in giving creates love." Max and Adrianna's love story is about their kindness in giving.

Accepting Differences

Unconditional acceptance is sometimes difficult because each of us remains a mystery to others. Although people married for a lifetime bond and "become one" on many levels, they may still not know each other fully. Willa Cather wrote, "The heart of another is a dark forest, always, no matter how close it has been to one's own."[25]

Individuals not only have different experiences, but they also perceive the same event differently. Because of these differences in perception, communication is rendered difficult. Sometimes we use the same language to express different perceptions or thoughts. As a consequence, we can never be sure our messages are understood in the way we intended them to be sent. Alexandra Penney observed that "There is never total honesty in any situation, because there is never total truth."[26]

Emphasizing Similarities

Although we are different from each other and sometimes sound as though we are speaking a foreign language, we want to accepted. One way we can show approval of others is to emphasize our similarities rather than our differences. In the movie *Harold and Maude* Bud Cort asks Ruth Gordon, "How come you are so good with people?" and she says, "They're my species, you know."[27] She clearly understands that as humans we are fundamentally more alike than we are different.

Indeed, it is when we realize that we have shared experiences, thoughts, and ideas that we bond with others. C. S. Lewis wrote, "Friendship is born at that moment when one person says to another, `What! You, too? I thought I was the only one.'"[28]

The similarities that are shared may be negative ones. Shared pain bonds people. Siegel writes, "Once you share your pain, it makes it easier for others to share theirs."[29] The parents of a nine–year–old boy who helped their son fight off his tumors in an unsuccessful battle with death grieved for their son. Through their experience, they also became closer. "We are still after six months grieving very hard." Author Bernie Siegel noted, "It was in their pain that they discovered `the tie that binds' all human hearts to each and one another."[30]

When people are in pain, we may incorrectly believe that they need information rather than time to share their grief. One wise middle–aged person said it is important to know that "people are more influenced by how much I care than by how much I know."[31]

The word "care" comes from the Gothic *kara* which means "to grieve, experience sorrow, cry out with."[32] When we really care about another person, we join him or her in pain. Hugh Prather writes, "I can be of no real help to another unless I see that the two of us are in this together, that all of our differences are superficial and meaningless, and that only the countless ways we are alike have any importance at all."[33]

Extending Forgiveness

Unconditional acceptance does not mean that people become blind to the errors or mistakes that are made. Sometimes it is tied to the awareness of problems and our forgiveness of them.

Forgiveness, like acceptance, is powerful in human relationships.

> Forgiveness is the vehicle for changing our perceptions and letting go of our fears, condemning judgments and grievances.

> We need to remind ourselves constantly that Love is the only reality there is. Anything we perceive that does not mirror Love is a misperception. Forgiveness, then, becomes the means for correcting our misperceptions; it allows us to see only the Love in others and ourselves, and nothing else.

> Through selective forgetting, through taking off the tinted glasses that superimpose the fearful past upon the present, we can begin to know that the truth of Love is forever present and that by perceiving only Love we can experience happiness. Forgiveness then becomes a process of letting go and overlooking whatever we thought other people may have done to us, or whatever we may think we have done to them.[34]

Forgiveness of ourselves and others does not come easy for any of us. In *Live and Learn and Pass It On*, a fifteen–year–old wisely states, "I've learned that learning to forgive takes practice.[35] For many people, it is a lesson that is not learned until later in life. Judy Collins observed "How life catches up with us and teaches us to love and forgive each other." Nonetheless, we should never under–estimate the power and value of forgiveness.

Expecting Perfection

In many of these ways the Nortons accept each other unconditionally. They accept all imperfections. Do they believe, like the 56–year–old interviewed by Jackson Brown, Jr., that "attractiveness is a positive, caring attitude and has nothing to do with face lifts or nose jobs."[36] Or, do they honestly not see the imperfections brought by age?

The Nortons maintain that they expect (and see) perfection. Max said, "I like Adrianna physically. I think she is the most beautiful women I have ever met and she still is to me."

Adrianna added, "We see each other the way we originally saw each other when we met."

"I see her the way I saw her on the lawn at the university. I still have the same passion for her as I did then."

William Shakespeare wrote over 300 years ago:

> To me, fair friend, you never can be old
> For as you were when first your eye I eyed,
> Such seems your beauty still.

This chapter suggests that we should never underestimate the power of love.

REFERENCES

1. Walker Percy, *Love in the Ruins*, reprinted in *Reader's Digest*, May, 1988, p. 137.
2. Cited in Bernie S. Siegel, *Peace, Love, and Healing: Bodymind Communication and the Path to Self-Healing* (New York: HarperPerennial, 1990), p. 199.
3. Ray Grigg, *The Tao of Relationships* (New York: Bantam Books, 1988), p. 101.
4. Cited by Ellen Goodman, *Turning Points* (New York: Fawcett Crest, 1979), p. 6.
5. Cited in Goodman, p. 5.
6. Grigg, 1988, p. 39.
7. H. Jackson Brown, Jr., *Life's Little Instruction Book* (Nashville, TN: Rutledge Hill Press, 1991), # 93.
8. H. Jackson Brown, Jr., *Live and Learn and Pass It On* (Nashville, TN: Rutledge Hill Press, 1992), p. 110.
9. Ann Kaiser Stearns, *Coming Back: Rebuilding Lives after Crisis and Loss* (New York: Ballantine Books, 1988), pp. 280-281.
10. Robert N. Bellah, Richard Madsen, William M. Sullivan, Ann Swidler and Steven M. Tipton, *Habits of the Heart: Individualism and Commitment in American Life* (New York: Harper & Row, 1985), p. 87.
11. David M. Schneider and Raymond T. Smith, *Class Differences and Sex Roles in American Kinship and Family Structure* (Englewood Cliffs, NJ: Prentice Hall, 1973), pp. 14, 103.
12. Goethe, cited in *Reader's Digest*, December, 1986, p. 207.
13. Bellah, et al, 1985, p. 89.
14. Paraphrased in Pesach Krauss and Morrie Goldfischer, *Why Me? Coping with Grief, Loss, and Change* (New York: Bantam Books, 1988), p. 21.
15. Brown, Jr., p. 31.
16. Robert Nozicvk, *Philosophical Explanations* (Cambridge, MA: The Belknap Press of Harvard University Press, 1981) cited in James W. Pennebaker, *Opening Up: The Healing Power of Confiding in Others* (New York: Avon Books, 1990), p. 143.
17. Grigg, p. 23.
18. Siegel, p. 182.
19. Gerald G. Jampolsky, *Love is letting go of fear* (Berkeley, CA: Celestial Arts, 1979), p. 91.
20. Brown, Jr., 1992, p. 147.
21. Bellah, et al., p. 95.
22. Cited in Bellah, et al., p. 95.
23. Siegel, p. 219.
24. Brown, Jr., 1992, p. 65
25. Willa Cather, *Love: an Illustrated Treasury* (1992), p. 11.
26. Quoted in Quotable Quotes, *Readers Digest*, 138 (April 1991), p. 33.
27. Reported in Siegel, pp. 41-42.
28. Sol Gordon, *When living hurts* (New York: Dell Publishing, 1988), p. 159.
29. Siegel, p. 204.
30. Siegel, p. 252.
31. Brown, Jr., 1992, p. 131.
32. Siegel, p. 228.
33. Cited in Jampolsky, p. 6.
34. Jampolsky, p. 65.

35. Brown, Jr., 1992, p. 117.
36. Brown, Jr., 1992, p. 44.

BE OPTIMISTIC, BUT ACCEPT REALITY
Mike and Chris Downard

"The first and necessary step of grief is discovering what you have lost. The next step is discovering what is left, what is possible."[1]
John Schneider

In an interview on Westwood One radio, Eric Clapton was quoted about his son's death. "Loss and emotional trauma are almost like everyday feelings. You become ... not happy with that, but happy despite that."[2]
Charles Leerhsen

Personal control means the ability to change things by one's voluntary actions; it is the opposite of helplessness.[3]
Martin E.P. Seligman

When Erin Downard was less than two years old, her parents learned that she had the incurable disease, Metachromatic Leukodystrophy, and that their little girl's life expectancy was only projected as four years of age. Later that same year, they added Jamie to their family. Within six weeks of her birth, test results revealed, that against all odds, Jamie had the same disorder as her sister. After five years of nursing the two little girls, the Downards lost them only 3 months apart.

Michael Downard

Michael Downard grew up in a family with a mother who stayed at home and a father who owned and operated a laundry and dry cleaning business. He is a middle child with a sister who is three years older and a brother who is nine years younger. His childhood in a small college town was idyllic and unblemished with problems. Mike began working for his dad when he was only 12 or 13, and took a more active role in the business as an adult. When his dad died at the age of 72, in the early 1980's, of arterial disease, Mike was well equipped to run the business.

Mike married a woman, named Lynda, when he was about 28 years old. She was an education major at Ohio University in Athens. After she graduated, the couple married. Differences in temperament, however, caused the two to drift apart. When the marriage fell apart, Mike met Chris.

Chris Downard

Chris Downard's early life was not as tranquil as Mike's. Her parents fought constantly, and when she was 12 years old, the two divorced. On the one hand, the parents' divorce was a relief; on the other hand, it was upsetting because the children had had no forewarning.

Chris and her four–year–older sister and her four–year–younger brother all stayed with their mother. While their dad would visit with them, they often had to initiate visits on holidays such as Christmas, Father's Day and his birthday. He developed lung cancer and died at the age of 52 when Chris was 25. She did not completely deal with his death until at least a decade later.

Like Mike, Chris had been married and divorced. She married when she was only 18, became pregnant, and had a son whom she named Bill. She explains the divorce by saying, "We wanted different things. I wanted picnics, and he wanted parties." After 7 years of marriage and with a 6–year–old in her custody, Chris was single again.

MEETING AND MATING

Chris had been divorced for 3 years when she met Mike. Although she had dated, none of the relationships were serious. Mike recalls that they met because of his divorce. He recalls, "She helped finance my divorce. Linda wanted to get out of town and she didn't want anything but cash, so we re–financed the house. Christy did the re–financing at the bank."

Chris recalls that a bank manager played cupid. "Dave was worried about me and felt I needed a man. He came running into my office one day to tell me that Mike Downard had separated."

The two did not date for some time. On Friday evenings, many young working people would gather at a local bar, the Greenery, for drinks and snacks. One night they met at the bar and Mike asked Chris to dinner. He recalls, "She didn't even like me at first. We were both seeing other people at the time we went out. We started seeing more of each other, and I realized that something was going on between us. I told her that I loved her. She said, `You dumb ass.' I thought this wasn't the way it should be."

Chris explains, "I said that because he wasn't supposed to fall in love with me. It was to be just casual dating."

Mike admits, "I was more serious at first then Christy was, but eventually we got married. She has mentioned several times that she had second thoughts on the day of the marriage."

Chris said, "I was just scared of marriage. I kept wondering if this could work. I have told him a thousand times that I am glad that he hung in there."

EARLY MARRIAGE

The couple married in 1981. Chris brought her son Bill who had been born in August 1970 with her and Mike brought with him a laundry business which provided financial stability. Mike moved into the house that Chris and Bill had shared for a number of years.

Not long after they were married, the couple learned that they were to have a baby of their own. Chris worked through her pregnancy and in May of 1982, she gave birth to her second child,

Erin. Three months later she went back to her job, and a cousin cared for the little girl.

THE DAUGHTERS' DEATHS

The Downards' family life was uneventful for the next year and a half. Erin grew and responded normally. Then the couple had a Super Bowl party when Erin was about 20 months old. Chris noticed that she was not progressing like other children her age. She recalls, "We had a child here who was about the same age as Erin, and he was climbing and running. Erin walked, talked, and said her ABC's, but she didn't run or climb."

"I had known that Erin hadn't felt well, and she had been constipated. I took her to our doctor on the 10th of February." Although he could not find anything that was seriously wrong, the couple was referred to another physician in Columbus who was also puzzled. This doctor put Erin through a series of tests in Children's Hospital. During the following week at home, the couple saw a dramatic decline in Erin's abilities: She could no longer walk from one chair to another. Additional tests were ordered. By the time they received all of the test results, Erin could no longer even sit up. In a six week period, she went from being perfectly normal and healthy to being able to do nothing.

Erin was diagnosed with a rare genetic disorder known as Metachromatic Leukodystrophy. In order for a child to be born with this disorder, both parents must possess a recessive gene. The odds of two people ever meeting that have this recessive gene are one in 400,000. Even when two people marry and have children who possess the recessive gene, the chances of a child ever being born with this disorder are only one in four, or 25%. The Downards learned that a child with this disease atrophies and finally dies. The life expectancy of such a person varies, but most children do not reach their teenage years.

Chris knew that she was pregnant when Erin started having problems. She was seven months pregnant when Erin was diagnosed. She inquired about the possibility of having a second child with Metachromatic Leukodystrophy and was assured that the probability was very low. In June of 1984, 25 months after Erin was born, the couple added Jamie to their family. Within six weeks, the test results revealed that Jamie had the same disorder as her sister.

For nearly five years, the Downard couple nursed their little girls. Other family members tried to help, but they were intimidated by the girls and the situation. Chris recalls, "My mother wanted to do something, but she was not able to take care of the girls. No one could take care of them. No one could hold Erin but us; she would push them away and fight."

The couple was on call 24 hours every day. When the girls were hospitalized, one member of the couple always stood guard. Chris said, "I wouldn't even go down to the cafeteria to get coffee or anything unless Mike was there to relieve me."

At home, the couple closely attended to their daughters. Mike said, "The girls were always with us." Before Jamie was born, he held Erin constantly. Chris said, "When I went to the hospital to have Jamie, thank God, it was during the night. Mike was probably in the hospital with me a total of five minutes. Erin needed daddy. Mike would walk outside with Erin on his shoulders." Mike added, "I slept with her on my chest."

When Jamie became ill, he gave her the same close attention. He said, "I'd be watching T.V. and she would be on my lap. Instead of setting her down, when I had to go to the bathroom, I would just take her with me. She always laughed at the noise from the tinkling. One day I realized that she didn't laugh anymore."

The entire house was set up for the girls. The living room and kitchen were set up with an oxygen machine, a breathing treatment machine, and a suction machine. The couple learned to read the various machines, and they became better acquainted with the meaningfulness of the girls' vital signs than did the physicians. Mike said, "It was refreshing after awhile, because the doctors became comfortable with their lack of knowledge, and they would come to us and ask us what was going on." Chris added, "They would even ask us what kind of medication we wanted for the girls." Mike concluded, "The doctors relied on us to tell them what was wrong with the girls and what was normal for them."

The couple took the girls everywhere with them as long as the girls were able. The only time they would take an evening out for themselves was to go out for dinner alone. Chris said, "Once every three months, Mike and I would go out to dinner by ourselves. My cousin would come over and watch the girls 'cause after Erin got sick, she was the only person who could hold her besides ourselves." Even then, they did not relax. Mike said, "We would generally go to the Sportsman (a favorite restaurant), and when we got there, Christy would call home to see how everything was going."

Although the couple provided almost exclusive care for the children, they also had the knowledge that the children knew they were loved and cared for by them. Mike said, "They knew up until they died that we were their parents and that we took care of them."

Neither member of the couple realized the strength or perseverance that they possessed. A wise 69–year–old told H. Jackson Brown, Jr. that, "I've learned that you can keep going long after you think you can't."[4] Surely this was the Downard's experience as well. Mike said, "I know I could do anything for Erin and Jamie, but I couldn't do it for just anyone." He added, "I remember when the girls had to have feeding tubes and we didn't think we would be able to do that for them, but it became so natural. Chris agreed, "I never thought I would be able to insert those tubes; it was something that skilled nurses did."

As the girls' bodies failed, their personalities changed. Mike said, "Both of the children could be real tyrants. They acted like month–old–babies, because they were totally dependent on us. Erin would throw fits that would last for about an hour. Her body would get rigid and she would raise Cain." He added, "It is real odd, Erin was passive and laid back before she was sick. If we would tell her no, that was it. She would listen without talking back at all. When she got sick, she turned into a fighter. Jamie, on the other hand, was about as rotten as they come, but when she got sick, she became more calm."

As the Downards moved through the 1980s, they continued to add more work and worry to their load. They shared the care for the girls and the work that needed to be done around the home. Mike also continued to work at the laundry and dry cleaning business, although he cut his hours back. He sometimes relied on his brother, Jim, to take up the slack. During the last year of the girls' lives, the couple hired nursing to help them.

Other events transpired in the family during the girls' illnesses. Chris's son, Bill, was a high school student during most of the time that the little girls were sick. He played basketball and soccer and the family attended most games. Mike said, "We took both of the girls and loaded up all the stuff to care for them." Bill later graduated from high school and began college.

In 1987 Chris learned that she was pregnant with her fourth child, and tests run in the first trimester provided the family with hope and optimism. The fetus had no physical or genetic problems. A third daughter, Allison, was born later that year.

By this time, Erin and Jamie had no control of any muscular movement at all and communicated to their parents only with their breathing, the only action they had any control over. During their illnesses, the girls became very sick many times but the Downards never gave up hope. They may have known in their head that their daughters' deaths were imminent, but in their hearts, they did not view their deaths as a possibility.

Ironically, the girls died only 3 months apart. Jamie died at 4–and–a–half years in January, 1990, and Erin died 20 days before her 7th birthday in April of the same year. Mike said, "Erin got pneumonia a couple of times and the last time she just couldn't fight it off."

Jamie's death was without warning and the couple never did learn the specific cause of her death. Just before Jamie's death, Erin was diagnosed with respiratory failure. Because they were so attuned to Erin's critical problems, they were taken by surprise when Jamie succumbed.

Chris discovered the death of her daughter, Jamie. She recalls, "My routine in the morning was to give one girl her breathing treatment and drainage and then to get the other one up and to do the same for her. After this, I would feed them. Well, I got up that morning and walked into their rooms and Erin was lying in bed with her eyes open. Jamie was still in the same position as when I had put her to bed. When Jamie would wake up, she would arch back. I looked at Jamie and thought she was still asleep. I went out to put my tea kettle on, came back in their room, and decided to check Jamie again. I put on the light and I discovered that she wasn't breathing. I grabbed her out of the bed and screamed. Mike told me later that one of the fears that he had had was of waking up and hearing me screaming."

Erin's respiratory failure lasted for a long time. Her fragile condition made it impossible to allow friends or family members who were ill with ordinary colds or flu to be allowed to be near her. The nurse the Downards hired, Dee, contacted the flu and took a week off from caring for Erin. Mike caught the flu, as well. Chris was run ragged caring for both the girls and Mike. The day that Dee returned to work, Erin was particularly sick. Mike had planned to go to work that day, but Dee advised him not to. Erin became even worse as the day progressed. The family physician paid two visits to their home and told them that they could put Erin in the hospital, but it would not produce any change in her condition. Chris recalls, "We had another oxygen tank brought in for her." The couple could do no more, and later that day, Erin died.

With each girl's death came love and concern from friends and family. People in the community grieved with the couple for their losses.

How Did the Couple Cope?

The Downards coped with their situation by accepting each other as different people; they never blamed each other; and they relied on each other, rather than religion or other forces.

Accepted Each Other's Differences

When their daughters died, the couple experienced different emotions. Mike said, "I think I felt I had some relief. I remember the night that Erin died, I thought, `There is nothing to fear anymore, the worst has already happened.' It was like you had fallen off a cliff and you were no longer afraid of doing it, because it had already happened. There was nothing worse that could happen to the girls, because it had already happened. We had experienced constant anxiety and fear that we were going to lose them, and then we did. The anxiety and fear were gone. The girls were beyond any more hurt."

Chris experienced the deaths differently. She said, "My feelings were more selfish. I kept thinking about my loss. Michael and I knew that the inevitable had finally come upon us. For five years we had been trying to prepare ourselves for that very event, but there was no way that we could be fully prepared for the pain we would feel or the loss we would suffer. I still have a hard time with the feelings I have."

The couple had to deal with the loss of their children and also the loss of a way of managing their lives. Chris said, "Michael and I had become accustomed to a way of life, a way that became routine and typical to us, but totally nuts and chaotic to ordinary families. The only life we knew was a day packed with a million things that had to be done. After Erin's death, we tried to keep busy with Allison and the laundry business, but we had too much time on our hands."

They also lived in a house that held many traumatic and terrible memories. Their living space had been reconfigured to serve as a care center for two terminally ill people. When they lost their daughters, the home held memories of the many years of care and the girls' eventual deaths. Although they considered selling their house, they concluded that the house was not only where the girls and died, but also where they lived. It was the site of much suffering, but it also had been the haven of a great deal of happiness. Ultimately, the couple decided to remain in the house that had served as the family home throughout their married life.

Never Blamed Each Other

Although some couples who lose children through inherited disease fall into the trap of blaming each other, Mike and Chris never did. Chris said, "We never blamed each other for what was going on. There was no blame on anyone." Mike added, "I never blamed Chris or myself. The only person that had any control over this was God. This was something that we were totally aware of. I don't think that anything could have been done differently. I also never felt any guilt.

Relied on Each Other, rather than Religion or Others

People sometimes focus on their own needs rather than on the needs of others. Martin Seligman writes about the contemporary tendency to emphasize one's self above the common cause. He describes this as the "waxing of the self" and the "waning of the commons." Seligman observes that the "society we live in exalts the self. It takes the pleasures and pains, the successes and failures of the individual with unprecedented seriousness."[5] At the same time, he believes that we diminish the importance of the role of country, God, family, or any purpose that transcends our lives. Seligman states, "In the past quarter-century, events occurred that so weakened our commitment to larger entities as to leave us almost naked before the ordinary assaults of life."[6]

The Downards do not emphasize themselves over their family. The couple is clear that their strength comes from each other. Mike said, "I get my strength from Christy. She is always there for me. Some people draw their strength from religion which is fine for them. What Christy did was tangible, obvious, every day, and constant. You could see it. It wasn't a theory or asking God to give her strength. She was doing something all the time. It was not something theoretical. It was how we lived. That was how I got through it."

Chris found no comfort in religion, either. She said, "People would tell us that this is God's will and it was happening for a reason. But your children are suffering, and you don't want to hear this."

Mike said, "I remember walking out into the yard with Erin in the earlier stages of her illness when she would have crying fits. She was an outdoor girl and I would take her outside to try and calm her down. I can remember the anger in me and I just wanted to scream at heaven and say, `Why are you doing this. Is this your plan?'"

Both Mike and Chris disagree with those who use religion or "God's will" as an explanation for life events. Mike said: "I cannot believe it is God's will that the innocent should suffer, but I also believe that God does not intervene in our daily lives. People can draw great strength from their belief in God, but it irritates me when they claim God's blessing on their particular endeavor, no matter how trivial."

Chris added, "I learned about a boy in another high school who was in a wheel chair and needed therapy but had a mother who was so narrow–minded that she refused medical help. She felt that God would take care of him. That really upsets me."

Mike concluded, "Just the other day on the news there was commentary on teenagers' rights. Some parents were featured who refused to have cosmetic surgery for their daughter. She had been born with facial deformities and it was her parents determination that it was God who wanted her to look like that, because she was born like that. I thought to myself that this child should be taken away from these people. How could you let your child have other children ridicule her and laugh at her? They should put their faith in God to guide the hands of a surgeon to mend their daughter's face."

The Downards' strength comes from each other rather than from outside forces. They view each other as the source of their strength. Those who are able to survive harrowing experiences often believe in something bigger than themselves. In one person's words, "You have to have an anchor point or points, a beacon, a candle in the window—something that won't ever change, that you can visualize or hold on to."[7] For Mike and Chris, the other person served as a beacon.

The Downards also dismiss metaphysical forces in favor of the concreteness of each other's every day actions. This tendency is related to their secret of survival: they are optimistic, but they accept reality.

The Secret of Surviving Couples:
Be Optimistic, but Accept Reality

Many paths lead to the same house. Couples cannot simply follow the road taken by others. Mike said, "There is never one same formula for a great lasting relationship. You do not choose to be put in the situation you are in, but you and your counterpart have to take the route and choose the best way each knows how to deal with problems." Mike and Christy Downard took a path which emphasized optimism, but acknowledged their reality.

Be Optimistic

If, as one observer noted, a hero is a person who can change his or her fear into positive energy, the Downards qualify as heroes.[8] Throughout their daughters' illnesses, they continued to turn their fear into positive energy and hopeful action. They demonstrated the wisdom of the notions that "everything looks impossible for the people who never try anything"[9] and "what isn't tried won't work."[10]

The Downards remained optimistic throughout the entire course of their daughters' illnesses. They never gave up hope that a cure could be found. Chris said, "We did a lot of research because we wanted to do everything we could to help find a cure. We never gave up hope." Mike added, "It wasn't false hope. What we were doing at the time, we thought would work and it will. Unfortunately, time ran out for Erin and Jamie. We worked with Tom Wagner (a world–renowned genetics researcher at Ohio University) who advised us and gave us leads of who to contact about genetics and research."

The couple learned that John O'Brien had been doing genetics research on MLD at the University of California that held some hope for them. The California group had lost their funding, but the Downards were able to fund their work for another year. Because the research was restarted, O'Brien and his group were able to gain additional external funding to carry on their project.

Karl Menninger, a world–renowned physician, suggests that it is the duty of physicians to "estimate probabilities and to discipline expectations." More importantly, he adds, "leading away from probabilities there are paths of possibility, towards which it is also our duty to hold aloft the light, and the name of that light is hope."[11] The Downards were given hope by physicians and researchers across the country.

They also sought help at the University of Minnesota where work on bone marrow transplants was being conducted. After they went to Minnesota, they tried to find a donor for the bone marrow. No family member provided a match so the couple sought unrelated people to serve as a donor. They contacted the Anthony Nolan foundation in England which was able to find a donor, but no one who was completely a match. By this time, Jamie was in very bad shape. They were told that the probabilities of the operation succeeding were very low; Jamie was given only a 10% chance of living with bone marrow from an unrelated donor. The couple finally decided that they would not risk the surgery.

Nonetheless, the couple remembers the hopefulness of the trip and the care that was provided by family members. Chris said, "We were so optimistic that this was going to work when we went there. My uncle had a house in Minnesota; he went to Phoenix in the winter. My cousin picked us up at the airport and took us out to the house. We thought everything was going right. They left us a car to use, and we had a home to use. It was really nice."

Chris Downard's positive memories of a very painful time is similar to the attitudes held by those who survived captivity during the Second World War. In describing the survivors, one author explained, "Optimists always believed there would be a tomorrow with better opportunities, whereas a pessimist was fully convinced we would never make it and, if you took him seriously, could assure you there was no use in trying."[12] The Downards, like the captivity survivors, maintained their optimism in the face of horrible circumstances.

Another activity which marked this time was a letter writing campaign. The Downards encouraged others to write letters that would support research in related areas. Hundreds of letters were written supporting experimentation that might help their girls. Chris said that the letter writing campaign bore some fruit, "Mike had a friend that he went to college with who taught biology classes in Kentucky, and he turned his class loose on this as research because of the letter writing campaign."

Chris concludes, "I think what got us through this was hope." Two authors explain Chris Downard's wisdom:

> There are no hopeless situations in life; there are only people who have lost hope. Mark Twain wrote about the man who wasted many years in prison because he didn't realize that his jail door was unlocked. Many doors that we consider closed will open if we just summon the vision and the will to try them. When you unlatch the right door, your own special song will emerge loud and clear—and you'll be on your way to finding your life's meaning.[13]

Throughout the illnesses of their daughters, Chris and Mike Downard exhibited their hopefulness.

Many people would have become pessimistic or depressed given the situation that the Downards were given. Martin Seligman notes that, "The defining characteristic of pessimists is that they tend to believe bad events will last a long time, will undermine everything they do, and are their own fault." He contrasts them with optimists who "think about misfortune in the opposite way. They tend to believe defeat is just a temporary setback, that its causes are confined to this one case. The optimists believe defeat is not their fault: Circumstances, bad luck, or other people brought it about. . . Confronted by a bad situation, they perceive it as a challenge and try harder."[14]

Pessimism and depression may be related phenomena: "Pessimists give up more easily and get depressed more often. . . A pessimistic attitude may seem so deeply rooted as to be permanent."[15] Sigmund Freud maintained that depression was anger turned against the self. Tim Beck, at the University of Pennsylvania, holds that "Depression is nothing more than its symptoms. It is caused by conscious negative thoughts."[16]

Depression is not uniformly distributed between women and men. Women are twice as likely to suffer depression as men are. Seligman explains that women are more likely to "think about problems in ways that amplify depression. Men tend to act rather than reflect, but women tend to contemplate their depression, mulling it over and over, trying to analyze it and determine its source. Psychologists call this process of obsessive analysis *rumination*, a word whose first meaning is `chewing the cud.'" He goes on, "Rumination combined with pessimistic explanatory style is the recipe for severe depression."[17]

When we explain events pessimistically, we are likely to feel helpless and hopeless. When we are optimistic about life events, we tend to be more energized. What can we do to ward off feelings of passivity, helplessness, and depression? Two possibilities exist. We can distract ourselves—try to think of something else. Or, we can dispute our pessimistic thoughts. By arguing about the causes of events, we may be more likely to be able to challenge negative thoughts when similar contrary events occur again.

Optimism is a choice. The philosopher Viktor E. Frankl writes, "Everything can be taken from a man but one thing: the last of the human freedoms—to choose one's attitude in any given set of circumstances, to choose one's own way." We all are free to choose optimism or pessimism. We can ruminate and be depressed or remain positive in our outlook. Carl Jung maintained that "It all depends on how we look at things, and not on how they are in themselves."

Physician Bernie Siegel tells a humorous story which illustrates this point. He explains:

> Whenever I have somebody who's ninety or ninety–five in my office. . . I walk in and say, for the student's benefit, "I guess you've had a tough life." And the answer is always, "No, I haven't had a tough life. That's why I'm ninety–five." "But," I say, "didn't your house burn down?" Yes. "Child run away from home?" Yes. "Youngest son die?" Yes. "Husband die?" Yes. "Second husband die?" Yes. And then she'll say, "Gee, I guess I have had a tough life."[18]

Siegel's point is well–taken. No one who lives over 90 years escapes pain, but many older people do not view their circumstances negatively. They view their lives with optimism.

The humorous story is similarly told of the person who falls out of a window at the top of a thirty–story building. As he falls past each floor, people lean out and say, "How are you," and he says, "I'm alright so far." When we take each event that we are given in–crementally, rather than as an overwhelming series of insurmountable problems, we can move through a great deal of tragedy.

People who are optimistic live longer, and have better lives. The lives of pessimists often are sour and short. Each determines his or her own reality. Both ultimately see the truth of their own lives. In fact, they create that truth.

Some couples do not believe they can resolve the conflicts they will encounter, while others have an optimistic viewpoint. A couple's belief in their ability to deal with problems and to resolve conflicts is more predictive of marital satisfaction than many other predictors.[19] Couples who positively construct their abilities to handle conflict are more satisfied than are couples who hold a negative perspective. This is similar to the observation in another chapter concerning self–disclosure that positive distortion may be a healthy and useful part of a satisfying marriage.

Accept Reality

While the Downards demonstrated optimism, hopefulness, and a lack of depression throughout their ordeal, they did not lose touch with reality. The couple remained realistic. While they were caring for Erin and Jamie, they also tried to have other children. Chris said, "We elected to have Allison. We got pregnant in the first month we tried. A lot of people thought we were crazy, but we decided we needed something positive in our lives." After Allison was born, the couple tried to have another child. This last pregnancy resulted in a miscarriage. Chris concluded, "I think now we are finished trying to have children."

The couple also demonstrated their realism as they memorialized their daughter's life through two bronze statues that mark their graves. Mike said, "We wanted something tangible for them, more than just a stone. Their lives were very important. The outfits were patterned after outfits that they really did have and wore a lot. Chris said, "It was really difficult. The sculptor wanted a profile picture of them, but we didn't have one. You just don't take profile pictures. So he molded and molded and we would go out and look at them and make changes. He worked for a year and a half. There is a good likeness to the statues. They are not perfect, but they are a work of art. Mike said, "Fred (the sculptor) is a tremendous person. He did the sculptures, he was very patient, and he never got upset with us." Chris said, "I am glad the statues are there. It was Mike's suggestion."

The statues were a last gift to Erin and Jamie. Many couples find that the funeral service and other related events serve a comforting purpose. As the couple worked on the statues with the sculptor, they had a concrete project in which to pour their energy. Perhaps without realizing it, they were helping themselves to heal. The creation of the statues gave them an opportunity to ritualize their loss.[20] Many people in their community find comfort in the bronze statues that stand as a memory of the Downard daughters.

The couple exhibited their hope and optimism through their daughter's illnesses and death. They remain hopeful for themselves as well as for the future for Bill and Allison today. They also recognize that the tragedies that they have endured have yielded some positive outcomes. Mike said honestly, "I do believe that there are some positive things that came out of this—but I don't think it is worth the trade. The suffering that Erin and Jamie went through was terrible. The suffering that we went through is selfish. It is our loss. We are sorry for ourselves. Their suffering is different. They had a year and a half of normalcy in their lives. The rest of their lives was hell."

At the same time, the Downard's marriage was strengthened by their loss. Mike said, "I think that our tragedies with our girls certainly strengthened our relationship." One of the characteristics of those who are able to survive adversity is the ability to convert misfortune into something that produces growth or somehow benefits others.[21] The Downards exhibit this quality.

The Downards are survivors. "A survivor is a person who, when knocked down, somehow knows to stay down until the count of nine and then to get up differently," said Dr. Joy Joffe, a psychiatrist who was on the faculty at Johns Hopkins Hospital in Baltimore. "The nonsurvivor," she added, "gets up right away and gets hit again."[22]

What does the term to "stay down until the count of nine" mean? Ann Kaiser Stearns suggests that it means "to plan ahead how to handle the next blows before they come." She goes on, "When even the best–laid plans are undermined or sabotaged, those who triumph plan for the triumph and more on that course of action."[23]

The Downards may also be called "roundtrippers." Bernie Seigel provides the origin of this term. When he was caring for a terminally ill woman, her husband said he wasn't worried about her because she was a "roundtripper." The man explained, "When I was in the service, and we were caught in a foxhole without supplies or ammunition, we would only send out the men we knew would come back. You could always trust them to do what was necessary, so we called them roundtrippers."[24] The Downards have also gone roundtrip.

The Downards do not have a perfect relationship. At the same time, they have a marriage which serves as a model. Their situation is similar to one depicted in a play about author Lillian Hellman. In one scene, Hellman is speaking to Dashiell Hammett in the final few months of his life, summarizing their thirty–year love affair. While the couple had a number of good years, they also had experienced a great deal of pain. Too, cancer and a coma would soon take him away from her.

"It's been *fine!*" Hellman exclaims.

"Fine's too big a word," replies Hammett, a person she always admired for his precise truthfulness. "Let's just say, 'We've done better than most.'"[25]

The Downards who combine optimism and hope with a realistic perspective of their life together might similarly conclude that if their marriage has not been fine, they certainly have done better than most.

Gerald Jampolsky observes that "We are never presented with lessons until we are ready to learn them."[26] Just like the Downards, we can perceive our own life experiences not as problems, but rather as opportunities for learning. We can experience a sense of lasting love and marital happiness when the lessons are learned.

REFERENCES

1. Psychologist John Schneider, Michigan State University, cited by Ann Kaiser Stearns, *Coming Back: Rebuilding Lives after Crisis and Loss* (New York: Ballantine Books, 1988), p. 10.
2. Charles Leerhsen, "His saddest song," *Newsweek, 119* March 23, 1992, p. 52.
3. Martin E. P. Seligman, *Learned Optimism: How to Change Your Mind and Your Life* (New York: Pocket Books, 1990), p. 6.
4. H. Jackson Brown, Jr., *Live and Learn and Pass It On* (Nashville, TN: Rutledge Hill Press, 1992), p. 69.
5. Seligman, p. 282.
6. Seligman, p. 284.
7. Robbie Risner quoted by Stearns, p. 177.
8. Paraphrased from A. S. Neill, as quoted in M. R. Rosenburg, *Quotations for the New Age* (Secaucus, NJ: The Citadel Press, 1978).
9. Jean-Louis Étienne, reprinted in *Reader's Digest*, December, 1990, p. 17.
10. Claude McDonald, *The Christian World*, reprinted in *Reader's Digest*, July, 1990, p. 147.
11. Karl Menninger, *The Vital Balance* as cited in Bernie S. Siegel, *Peace, Love, & Healing: Bodymind Communication and the Path to Self-Healing* (New York: HarperPerennial, 1990), p. 117.
12. Manny Lawton, *Some Survived: An Epic Account of Japanese Captivity During World War II* (Chapel Hill, N.C.: Algonquin Books, 1984), p. 76, as cited in Stearns, p. 188.
13. Pesach Krauss and Morrie Goldfischer, *Why Me? Coping with Grief, Loss, and Change* (New York: Bantam Books, 1988), p. 153.
14. Seligman, pp. 4-5.
15. Seligman, p. 5.
16. Seligman, p. 74.
17. Seligman, p. 75.
18. *Man's Search for Meaning* quoted in Bernie S. Siegel, *Peace, Love, & Healing: Bodymind Communication and the Path to Self–Healing* (New York: HarperPerennial, 1989)
19. Siegel, p. 46.
20. The importance of grieving is discussed by Daniel Goleman, "Mourning: New Studies Affirm Its Benefits," *New York Times*, February 5, 1985.
21. Stearns, p. 193.
22. Stearns, p. 157.
23. Stearns, p. 157.
24. Siegel, p. 219.
25. *Zoe Caldwell as Lillian*, a play by William Luce, directed by Robert Whitehead, performed at Johns Hopkins University, Baltimore, Maryland, December 4, 1986, and cited by Stearns, p. 293.
26. Gerald G. Jampolsky, *Love is Letting Go of Fear* (Berkeley, CA: Celestial Arts, 1979), p. 124.

Maintain Control, but Relinquish It

George and Janet Voinovich

"I sometimes use the analogy of life being equivalent to a game of cards in which we have no say over the hand dealt us. We do, however, have control over how we play the hand. There's no point in blaming the dealer for a bad hand. The trick is to play it out with all the skill and determination at our command."[1]

Pesach Krauss and Morrie Goldfischer

"God does not play dice with the cosmos."[2]
Harold Kushner

"Stress is life, that's all. It's God's way of showing us we're alive and kicking. We just got to kick a little harder sometimes."[3]

Dolores Curran

George V. Voinovich became the 65th Governor of Ohio on January 14, 1991. His name is frequently mentioned as a potential candidate for the United States Presidency. Some pollsters have suggested that he is one of the few people who might challenge the incumbent President in 1996. Whatever contests lay ahead, George, and his wife, Janet (Allan) Voinovich have already faced a more difficult test. On October 8, 1979, their youngest child, 9–year–old Molly, was hit by a van and died instantly.

Janet Kay Allan and George Voinovich met in the autumn of 1959 at a Republican campaign event for Cleveland mayoral candidate Tom Ireland. George had already graduated from Ohio University and was a law student at Ohio State. Janet was working in the office of a Cleveland–based company. They did not date until the next summer, while working on Richard Nixon's campaign.

Janet Allan Voinovich

Janet grew up as the youngest of three daughters in a traditional middle–class Republican family in Lakewood, on Cleveland's West Side. Her father worked his way up during a 50–year career at a Cleveland electrical parts company. Her mother stayed at home to raise the girls. Although they were not wealthy, the family life provided by the Allans was snug and secure.

Janet was bright, but shy. As one of the top four students in her graduating class, she avoided making a speech at graduation by taking an elective. Rather than take a required public speaking class, she enrolled in an additional English course. She had no idea that years later she would have to place her introversion behind her.

George Voinovich

George was born on July 15, 1936, and grew up on the east side of Cleveland. His grandparents had emigrated to the United States from Yugoslavia. Unlike his wife–to–be, George demonstrated early his public speaking skills and his leadership ability. He served as the President of the Student Council in his high school, and he held other important positions in a number of clubs.

Janet was captivated with George from the start: "He had a kind of directness about him that was almost unsettling. He zeroed in on people. There was none of this light fluff I was used to."[4]

Years later she added, "I think he was probably the least superficial person I had ever met in my life. He was so interested in whatever went on about him in the country and in national affairs. It was the depth of the person that really just turned me on. He just burned a hole in your eyes because he really cared about what you were saying. And it was just like, 'Whoa! This is a real person here.'"

Although the couple enjoyed a long courtship, Janet admits, "We really knew early on."

Religion was important to both Janet and George, but they were of different religions. Nonetheless, they were not deterred from marrying. Their religious differences were always apparent to them, but Janet explains how they felt. "Some things took a back seat to the relationship. We looked at what we had in common, not what set us apart."

The couple was engaged Easter Sunday, 1962, and married on September 8, the same year, at her Presbyterian Church. Six weeks later they married again in his Catholic Church in an effort to bridge their religious differences. Janet never converted to Catholicism, but she has worshipped in Catholic churches since her marriage.

The couple's babies arrived early and close together. George's political career developed swiftly, too. Janet already had two toddlers, George and Betsy, when her husband was elected to the Ohio House in 1966. By 1970, when he left the House and his weekly commute between Cleveland and Columbus, the family had four children—Peter and Molly had been added—under the age of seven.

George and Janet's marriage mirrored their own parents' traditional lives. George was deeply committed to his career, and Janet was content at home. She did not return to work or to college after they were married. "George was so involved in politics, and my life was so intertwined with his there was no time left over," she said.

Janet acknowledged that their choices traded monetary gain for family closeness. "I share George's values," she said. "We are very family–oriented. Faith and family are at the pinnacle."

While Janet was managing her children and home, George was making political strides. After serving as a member of the Ohio House of Representatives, he served as the Cuyahoga County Auditor from 1971 to 1976 and as a Cuyahoga County Commissioner from 1977 to 1978. George Voinovich served as Lieutenant Governor of the state for a short time in 1979 and then was elected Mayor of the City of Cleveland for the decade spanning 1979 to 1989. When he was elected Governor of Ohio in November, 1990, he and his running mate Lieutenant Governor Mike DeWine garnered more than 55 percent of the vote.

The tranquil home life and triumphant career were upended on

October 8, 1979. The couple's 9–year–old daughter, Molly, was a fourth grader at Oliver Hazard Perry Elementary School in Cleveland. Until the year before, Molly had been bused to Longfellow Elementary. The program for gifted children in which she was enrolled was eliminated at Longfellow and Molly was transferred to Oliver Hazard Perry, which was about a half–mile from her home.

A number of unusual events transpired on this rainy day in October, just six days after her father had finished first in Cleveland's mayoral primary. First, Molly had decided to have lunch at a former babysitter's house, instead of going home. Second, she returned to school about 10 minutes later than usual because of the rain and her prediction that her friends would not be out on the playground. Thus, the crossing guard normally on duty at the intersection where the accident occurred was on her break because the lunch period was over.

Finally, George Horacek, a 19–year–old repairman for Audio Craft Company, went on a call only to discover that a number had been left off the address of his service call. As a result, he said, he ended up near Lake Shore Boulevard instead of where he should have been. When Horacek discovered the error, he was proceeding to a nearby interstate. Witnesses told police Horacek was driving 40 to 45 miles per hour in a 20 m.p.h. zone and that he ran through a red light.

Molly Voinovich waited until the light turned green and then crossed Lake Shore Boulevard at Schenely Avenue in the crosswalk. Horacek, in his service van, was westbound on Lake Shore. As the car in front of him slowed for a red light, he pulled to the right and into the curb lane. He struck Molly as she stepped off the curb into the crosswalk. Horacek never saw the red light nor the little girl.

Molly was killed instantly. The impact threw her body 146 feet through the air. An Emergency Medical Service rescue squad took her body to Euclid General Hospital where she was pronounced dead at 12:55 p.m. Police said she suffered severe head injuries.[5]

At the time, her father was meeting with Sebastian J. Lupica, secretary-treasurer of the Cleveland AFL-CIO Federation of Labor. He received a telephone call saying that Molly had been in an accident and had been taken to the hospital. He and Janet left immediately. Later, they sought solace and seclusion in their home.

George Voinovich demonstrated extraordinary dignity the day after Molly's death. While he anguished over Molly's passing, he also offered compassion for the driver of the van that struck her.

"I feel bad for the driver, he's got a family, too" Will Largent, a longtime friend of Voinovich, quoted the lieutenant governor as saying.[6]

Molly Voinovich was not forgotten. Two days after her death, the children enrolled at her elementary school held a memorial service for her. Molly's teacher, Nathaniel Austin Jr. described her as a child "who got along well with everyone." He added, "She was a real little lady for someone only nine years old."[7]

Three days later, her funeral was held at Holy Cross Church in Cleveland. Father Martin J. Scully, pastor of Holy Cross Catholic Church, celebrated a funeral mass at which Auxiliary Bishop Anthony Pilla and 18 priests participated. Molly's brother, George, 15, and sister, Betsy, 14, both read excerpts from the Scriptures at the service.

When it was time for her other brother, Peter, 11, to read, he was overcome with emotion. Betsy took his place while Peter embraced George and wept. Betsy, an accomplished flute player, played a song for her sister.

The Reverend John Murphy told the Voinovich family, "I can only say to you that you received a gift for nine years. It was yours for only nine years and had to be returned."[8]

The Cleveland newspaper, *The Plain Dealer*, eulogized Molly the day after her funeral mass: "Molly A. Voinovich was a girl who loved her family, her friends and classmates and life itself—and in return was loved by everyone."[9]

Janet Voinovich remembered her daughter more than a decade after her death, "She was a very happy child. She was the youngest of four, so she had everybody giving her love. Wherever she turned, it was there. She had kind of an enchanted existence."

People from around the country sent messages and memorials to Molly and her family. Former Governor James A. Rhodes called the Voinoviches at the hospital shortly after the accident to offer condolences. He called the child's death "a numbing shock to all of us who have become so close to the Voinovich family the past two years."[10]

George Voinovich told a reporter two weeks after Molly died that he and his family had received several thousand cards and messages and said they would try to answer them.

"The people have been so good," he said. "There are a lot of good people out there."[11]

In retrospect, the last few days of Molly's life were important ones. The week before she died, Molly was helping her father campaign for Mayor of Cleveland and she was spotted wearing a tee shirt that stated, "Together we can do it."

Because her father was campaigning for mayor, Molly had been regularly observed by the news media. This allowed Joseph Wagner to be able to paint a word picture of her. He captured her spirit in Cleveland's newspaper, *The Plain Dealer*, the day after she died:

> To Molly Voinovich, the campaign trail was a yellow brick road. Molly skipped along, carefree, forever smiling, completely unawed by the world of politics that swirled around her. She was a Brownie, enjoyed Barry Manilow, loved gymnastics and learned to play the piano.
>
> Though her father, Lt. Gov. George V. Voinovich, held the second highest office in the state, and had been a VIP in local politics her entire life, she never pulled rank on anyone.
>
> Too many families of politicians suffer or are destroyed, but, to the Voinoviches, politics became the tie that binds.[12]

Wagner added some other observations in his October 9th article:

> The family was together last Tuesday evening in a Collinwood restaurant eating their election day dinner, one of their many traditions. Molly ordered a hamburger, french fries and a Coke.
>
> They were late for dinner, slowed up because Molly had spilled shoe polish on her knees.
>
> While a television blared early results showing Voinovich with the lead, Molly, her sister Betsy, and brothers George Jr. and Peter engaged their father in a game of pinball bowling.
>
> Molly kept rolling splits and when she finally threw a strike, the family cheered.[13]

Wagner concluded his observations, revealing a little more of Molly's personality:

Sure of victory, Voinovich led his family out of the suite to a celebration, but they were delayed because Molly had forgotten her shoulder strap purse. She just couldn't go anywhere without that purse," a friend said.

"The fact that her father was winning didn't awe her at all," said Ed Richards, a friend of the family.[14]

Some people thought that George Voinovich would drop out of the mayoral race. Although he had won the primary just six days before Molly died, he still had a tough battle on his hands. Cleveland voters were to choose between him and the incumbent Mayor Democrat Dennis J. Kucinich in the November 6 general election.

Five days after Molly's death, Voinovich was asked about his intentions. The then–Lieutenant Governor was subdued and stated that he did not know when his campaign would resume. He asked the voters for their understanding.

"I never gave any consideration to dropping out of the mayor's race," he said in a statement to *The Plain Dealer*.[15]

"I'm certainly going to continue, but because of my family situation, I don't exactly know when I will resume my campaign."

"My family wouldn't want me to quit. And, they never thought of me being a quitter. I want to be of service as mayor. And, I want to serve my fellow man."

"My family feels that the best way I could serve is to just keep going on and I hope people understand this situation."[16]

People who knew George Voinovich did not entertain the idea that he would quit. His campaign staff was not surprised.

"They always expected he would stay in the race," said Wil Largent, a Voinovich campaign aide and longtime friend. "He's not a quitter."[17]

Although Voinovich did not drop out of the mayoral race, his campaign did take a far different turn. Less than two weeks after Molly's death, the candidate made an announcement. He told reporters that he would conduct a "positive campaign." He said he would prohibit television commercials that attacked Mayor Dennis J. Kucinich's administration.

The family's role in the campaign changed, too. Voinovich explained that his wife and their three surviving children would not be involved.

The Voinovich campaign that resumed two weeks after Molly's death allowed the candidate to spend maximum time at home with Janet and the three surviving children—George, Betsy, and Peter. Attacks on the opponent were noticeably absent in the new campaign. They were succeeded by a series of endorsements by Clevelanders. Voinovich did not appear on these commercials.

Two weeks later Clevelanders selected him as their Mayor.

"THY WILL BE DONE"

Hugh Prather offers the forward in Gerald Jampolsky's book, *Love is Letting go of Fear*. He concludes his remarks:

> A man who had finished his life went before God. And God reviewed his life and showed him the many lessons he had learned. When He had finished, God said, "My child, is there anything you wish to ask?" And the man said, "While You were showing me my life, I noticed that when the times were pleasant there were two sets of footprints, and I knew You walked beside me. But when times were difficult there was only one set of footprints. Why, Father, did you desert me during the difficult times? And God said, "you misinterpret, my son. It is true that when the times were pleasant I walked beside you and pointed out the way. But when the times were difficult, I carried you."[18]

George and Janet Voinovich may never have heard Prather's story, but they have lived it. When George's campaign for mayor was over, he and his family and friends were still grieving for "Molly Dolly," as they had called Molly. How did George and Janet cope with the loss of their child? Their religious beliefs were cardinal.

Perhaps the couple had read and understood the second verse of the Twenty–sixth Psalm: "Examine me, O Lord, and try me." If they had not done so before Molly died, they surely came to understand the essence of the Old Testament verse in the days that followed her passing.

The Greek word *therapeia* means "doing God's work." Bernie Siegel, writes, "Anything that offers hope has the potential to heal."

At the same time, Siegel gives grievers the permission to be angry with their God. He writes, "But it's okay to be angry—even with God. As one of our group members said, "I fired God a long time ago."[19]

George and Janet Voinovich did not fire their God. Indeed, their religious faith carried them through the first days of acute grief and into the never–ending chronic grief experienced by parents of children who have died. For them, God represented an anchor in the storm–tossed waters.

People who knew the family hoped that their strong beliefs would help them. Former Governor James A. Rhodes had offered condolences while the Voinoviches were still at the hospital immediately after Molly's death. He later told reporters, "The unexplainable and untimely loss of their child will be a crushing blow to George and Janet and I pray that their strong religious faith will sustain them in the dark hours they are now experiencing."[20]

Rhodes' prayers and those of others were apparently heard. Janet Voinovich cites faith as most important in their survival:

> What brought us through the event was that we are very strong in our faith: "Thy will be done." We live with that in a daily way. We feel that we are each here for a given period of time. In Molly's case, the Lord, in His infinite wisdom, chose for her to be with us for nine years before she went on. We had that joy. To some people it might just sound like we're justifying it or explaining it away. If that's the case, so be it, but it is what our faith teaches us. When it happens, you grab on to anything you can. In our case we really happen to believe it. In fact, "Thy will be done" is inscribed on Molly's gravestone with her name.

Janet Voinovich interrupted her explanation with tears. She continued:

> Tears are for so many reasons. We know she is in a glorious place now, and our grief is because we miss her, but she's already home. We're homesick. We do truly believe we will see her again. That is probably the single most motivating thing that keeps both George and me going. That's the underlying strength that supports us. If we lead halfway decent lives, we will be reunited with her.

The experts agree that the Voinoviches' faith was instrumental in their survival. Bernie S. Siegel, in *Peace, Love, & Healing* writes, "I think spirituality is part of healing, and because I think death is not just an end but perhaps a beginning as well."[21]

Ann Kaiser Stearns, in her book, *Coming back: Rebuilding Lives after Crisis and Loss*, explains the importance of prayer during times of crisis:

> Prayer during the most difficult period of a crisis or on a routine basis is helpful to many. Prayer can provide an outlet for haunting feelings of fear, yearning, anger, guilt, or loneliness. Meditation and prayer can provide a sense of hope, courage, calm, or simply the feeling that one is doing *something* and is not completely powerless.[22]

Janet Voinovich's faith helps her forgive the driver of the van who killed Molly, as well:

> In the case of an accident, I guess, somebody caused Molly to die. Well, I just tend not to think about it. Sometimes I think of that poor soul (Horacek). He wasn't drinking so I don't have that to cope with. He was just in a hurry. It almost breaks my heart for him because he has to live with this. What an awful thing to live with! But at the same time, I don't want to know who he is; I've forgotten his name.
>
> If you say "thy will be done" then who's to say the method? I mean Molly could have died from a lingering illness which we would have had to watch everyday.
>
> There are those who say "what is worse, seeing your child die slowly or just getting a phone call?" They're all awful. There's no way to prepare for it.
>
> But I can't use my qualities and the like that God gave me in doing blame. I'm very sad, and very sorry for that kid. Maybe he's married now with a family. Maybe he realizes now more than ever. He's got to live with that. And I don't want him to ... if he can make a contribution to society by raising a good family or by helping someone. Maybe he does, maybe he's a really good guy. But I really don't want to know.

Our days are numbered for some reason. Molly's babysitter, Mona, lived to be ninety–seven. She was a wonderful lady. And she went through Molly's death. Molly had lunch at their house before she returned to school.

Tom, Mona's husband, who used to walk Molly up to the corner, didn't do it for some reason on that day. There are all these what if's. I had my moments with the crossing guard, "You knew Molly was ... why weren't you there?" You can go on but you can't get Molly back—ever. Why bring down upon those people the kind of thoughts, they probably have them, themselves. They all have had their what if's. "I should've walked up with her." "I should've been there." "I should've said `you've gotta be home for lunch.'" If she had come home for lunch I would've driven her back to school because it was cold. So, you just can't live your life ever with what if's. And the sooner you can erase those what if's by the knowledge that "what is to be, is to be" and was for whatever reason. I find solace in the fact that Molly died instantly.

Janet Voinovich found peace by believing in a force that was larger than life. Her religion and her God sustain her. Ann Kaiser Stearns writes, "A belief in something bigger than self seems to typify the triumphant survivor."[23] This "larger than life" belief provides a beacon of hope. Such an unchanging force provides the survivor with a sense that some things are stable. The dramatic crisis filled with life and attitudinal changes is subsumed by a larger context in which the event is diminished.

Few people in Ohio are aware of the religious differences in the first family of the state. George is Roman Catholic, and Janet is Presbyterian. "It's interesting that I have never become Catholic because I'm at Mass every Sunday or Saturday night of my life and I enjoy it thoroughly," Janet said. "There are just one or two fundamental beliefs that I just choose to cling to of my own," she explained.

The Voinovich children were raised as Catholic but Janet thinks that they would answer a question regarding their religion as "Christian." She added:

> They thoroughly believe in God and they pray. They're not
> each in church every Sunday; some are, some aren't. I have
> no problem with that because they are good people with
> strong beliefs. They believe that Jesus Christ was the son
> of God. Although we believe in one God, Jesus is his son.
> I've been reading a lot about Islam, because we're going to
> be in a lot of countries where that is the prominent religion,
> and it is interesting how much religion is actually the same.

If Janet Voinovich had disagreements with some of the tenets of
the Catholic Church, why didn't she continue to attend services in
her own Presbyterian tradition? Part of her answer is contained in
her explanation that religions tend to be fundamentally similar. She
offered another reason. "I tried to keep going to the Presbyterian
church at the beginning, but it's too hard to do both. I'm not much
of a loner in that respect, and I wanted to go where my husband
went. So we attended Mass as a family." This response foreshadows
the second aphorism that helped the Voinovich marriage survive the
death of their child.

"TOGETHER WE CAN DO IT"

At the same time that the Voinoviches relinquish control over life
events to a power greater than they are, they also believe that they
can work toward certain goals together. Indeed, George Voinovich
used the "together we can do it" slogan from his early political days.
And Molly wore the shirt with this inscription the week before her
death. This assertion incorporates two beliefs: people need each
other, and they can accomplish their goals.

Janet talks about this trademark. "Do you know we use that
today? He's [George has] kind of taken that on as his personal motto.
There are very few speeches where he doesn't use it."

The maxim marks Janet's attitudes and behaviors, too. As a child
and even in her early marriage, Janet Voinovich was shy. She
avoided public speeches. After Molly's death, Janet overcame her
fear. When her husband was elected Governor in 1991, she told
Mary Bridgman, a *Columbus Dispatch* Accent Reporter, "If you
believe in something strong enough, you can do it—sweaty palms
and all."

She added, "I will be at my husband's side to greet and welcome people and fill whatever roles I need to fill."[24]

Janet was asked during the gubernatorial campaign how the couple would fare if her husband lost the election. They would adapt, she said. "He can go back to being a lawyer, and we can make money!" More seriously, she added, "We are blessed with a great relationship. No matter what happens, we will be OK."[25]

As Ohio's First Lady, Janet Voinovich has been more than "OK." Alan Johnson explained in an article in *The Columbus Dispatch* on April 28, 1992:

> Janet Kay Allan Voinovich, a wallflower during much of her husband's 10 years as mayor of Cleveland, has blossomed as Ohio's first lady over the past 15 months.
>
> The woman who once had to force herself to accompany her husband, George, on campaign appearances and who agonized over speaking in front of an audience, now delivers speeches, reads to schoolchildren, gives interviews and does public service TV ads with the poise of a veteran.
>
> Mrs. Voinovich regrets the loss of privacy that goes with being the governor's wife, and she feels the sting, perhaps more than her husband, when critics harpoon him.
>
> Still, for Mrs. Voinovich, these are the best of times.
>
> "I think this is a real high point in my life," she said. "I'm almost surprised to hear myself saying that. There's a real feeling of fulfillment."
>
> "As every day goes by, I feel more comfortable. It's like any new job. You begin to feel your way around."
>
> "You're afraid of making mistakes, but you make mistakes. That's how we all learn.
>
> "As far as giving speeches, I would never say,`Yeah, I'll go do that.' It was very difficult during the campaign, but it goes with the territory. The more I do it, the easier it becomes."
>
> "When I was first lady of Cleveland, it was a tremendously different role," she said. "I had speeches and dedications and dinners, but not as much on my own as I am here."

"Now, when I go out to do my thing, it's what I would normally have done with George in the old days."[26]

Ann Stearns observes that "How well we live with a significant loss can be greatly influenced by caring people who share with us our time of crisis and its aftermath."[27] People in crisis typically recall the situation surrounding a major crisis with crystal clarity. Stearns writes:

> If our memories are of unkind and insensitive interactions with friends, family members, and the people representing various institutions, our torn emotions can be difficult to mend. Essential to the strength of the fabric of our lives is the knowledge that other human beings can be trusted in our times of greatest vulnerability.[28]

Stearns' advice has scientific backing. In general, people who have social support systems fare better than do those with few friends or family members. People who have supportive friends are less likely to become either mentally or physically ill than are those who do not.

Stearns feels that being able to socialize with friends and family members during the mourning period is important. She provides an example of a couple who had lost their son:

> As month after anguishing month passed, Jan and Ed were comforted in their longing for their lost son by the poems, cards, phone calls, letters, and other tributes they received. Friends and family continued to "keep" and honor Mark by donating money in his name to children in need, by freely talking or writing about him, and by remembering him on social occasions such as on his birthday or holidays.[29]

Janet Voinovich similarly talked about the comfort she found when friends recalled stories about Molly:

> Barbara [one of her friends] and I were having lunch and she said something about Molly and then she said "Oh, I'm sorry." And I said, "Barbara, what do you mean you're sorry?" I said, "I love to talk about Molly. I love for people to remember this, that, or the other about Molly."

Then we were at a reception at a friend's house. We had been at their home prior to a parade in Chagrin Falls with all the kids years before. And she reminded me that night, she said, "Oh yes, do you remember, Molly left her ring. It was just a dime store ring, but I had to package it up and mail it to you." I said "Oh, Jane what a wonderful story." I had forgotten that. I told her, "It may be the little ring that I have hanging in my kitchen window on a little elephant that we got at Mohican State Park for a dollar or two.

I told George that night that I had a new story. You think there's never anything new to learn as far as Molly's concerned and here's this retelling of this whole story that I completely forgot.

The "together we can do it" attitude also is apparent in the empathy Janet shows when she learns of others who have lost children. "When we lost Molly, we got letters from people we did not know from Adam, just because it was prominent and in the papers, from people who had lost children. They were so beneficial, because they had been there."

People who have lost children have experienced the worst pain a parent can know. They have learned that all of us are vulnerable to mishaps and diseases resulting in death. They also seem to know almost intuitively that they must share their grief with others. Dinah Shore aptly observed, "Trouble is a part of your life, and if you don't share it, you don't give the person who loves you enough chance to love you enough."[30] By sharing their pain with others, they allowed them to provide not only support, but love as well.

Janet Voinovich did not let her experiences pass her by. Having been the recipient of so much kindness and generosity, she began to return the gift of understanding to others. She seemed to understand that opportunities to care for others sometimes knock very softly. She recalled:

After a year or two, I took my pen in hand. When I was aware of someone who had lost a child, I would sit down and write a letter. I got involved with Ronald McDonald House up in Cleveland. I wrote letters on behalf of the house. We lost a lot of kids there.

I keep a file of nice things I've read which have particularly helped me and I'll enclose them when I write to someone.

> You never know when you're going to read that one thing
> that will click, maybe even a few months later, that will
> help you go through.

Janet Voinovich has done so much for so many. People who have
been the recipients of her notes, poetry, and books have surely
benefitted. But Janet's actions probably have helped her own
grieving process. She has not allowed self–pity to develop because
she continues to focus on people who have situations that are as
devastating, or even more difficult, than her own.

Many people have found comfort in caring for others. Indeed,
when we focus on other's problems, we begin to experience less pain
ourselves. Janet Voinovich, and others like her, have learned that to
give is to receive.

Bertha von Suttner wrote that "After the verb 'To Love,' 'To Help'
is the most beautiful verb in the world."[31] The Voinoviches' service
to others both publicly and privately demonstrate their
understanding of the role of helping others in one's relationships.
George Eliot observed, "What do we live for, if it is not to make life
less difficult for each other?"[32]

Two popular musicians have lost their children in recent times.
Eric Clapton and Eddie Rabbitt both lost young sons. Both men
found that writing and singing songs about their loss was
therapeutic. In a *Newsweek* article, Charles Leerhsen with Marc
Peyser, write about Clapton's award–winning song:

> Clapton's new music has all the warmth and sensual
> appeal of just–baked bread. If it has all the permanence,
> too, so be it; at a time when his songwriting is, as he says,
> "a process of self–healing," that may not matter. "I
> wouldn't want to insult [my audience], he said on MTV's
> "Unplugged" program last week, "by not including them
> in my grief." He is consistently moved, he says, "by the
> sympathy I get from people who come up to me."[33]

Eddie Rabbitt's life was changed when his young son, Timmy
succumbed to biliary atresia, a debilitating disease that often affects
the liver. Eddie observes, "I weave the pain and suffering [of
Timmy's death] through my songs." He adds, "It's a piece of
wisdom, but you pay for wisdom."

The songwriter and his wife experienced a great deal of love from others after their son's death. Eddie said, "It makes a lot more love come out. . . Even though it comes out of a sad seed, it blossoms into a beautiful flower."[34]

Both of these men understand that sharing one's pain is necessary to healing. Their unique talents allow them to do it with a large number of others. They, too, seem to understand that "together we can do it."

This adage is not only about the support we can provide to each other. It also suggests that people in happy, surviving marriages have a sense of the "little engine that could." They have a belief that they can make a difference.

George Voinovich clearly talks like a man who believes he can accomplish anything. When he learned that he was to become Ohio's 65th Governor, he told a jubilant crowd, "I grew up on the east side of Cleveland, and now I'm governor of Ohio. It just has something to say about setting your goals. . .and working toward those goals. I think it sends a good message to the young people that, if you work hard, you can accomplish anything."[35]

Another way that the Voinoviches express their "can do" attitude is in the fund they established in Molly's name. The family contributes to it annually on the anniversary of her death. Proceeds go to the school she attended and to one other school, a different one each year. While the second recipient changes each year, it is always a Cleveland public elementary school that has a gifted and talented program.

On the first anniversary of Molly's death, George, with Janet next to him explained, "When God took Molly and lots of people wanted to do something, we suggested contributions to the school's major works program. Molly was a student in the program, and we were very proud of that program. It seems to be a good way to remember her."[36]

In *The Ultimate loss: Coping with the death of a child*, Joan Bordow writes:

> Accepting things as they are and opting for life is a matter of choice. We can accept life the way it is or we can attempt to have it the way it isn't, to live in the past or to try to make it different. We can be the author of our lives or can be controlled by our circumstances.[37]

Bordow is speaking specifically to parents who have lost a child, but her advice is well taken for couples who have not, but who do wish to have a loving, lasting relationship.

Having an internal locus of control—believing that you, not others, control your destiny—can make a difference in many aspects of life. For example, medical and social scientific research shows that one's attitude can even affect disease. A study published in *Social Science Medicine* in 1992 showed that chronic diseases were not only determined by genetic factors, but also by individuals' attitudes about their illnesses. People view illness in a variety of ways including illness as a challenge, as an enemy, as a punishment, as a weakness, as a relief, as a strategy, as irreparable loss or damage, and as a value. The way one views illness affects one's emotional reaction and coping strategy. Patients who view their disease as a challenge or as a value have internal control and are more likely to have mental well-being and adaptive coping.

The Secret of Surviving Couples: *Maintaining Control and Relinquishing it*

Neither of these two conflicting philosophies is sufficient in itself. Happily married couples know that they must exert control and they also must relinquish it. People who believe too strongly that they can accomplish anything will be disappointed.

Gerald Jampolsky, in *Love is Letting go of Fear*, explains:

> Although we want to experience peace, most of us are still seeking something else that we never find. We are still trying to control and predict, and therefore we feel isolated, disconnected, separate, alone, fragmented, unloved and unlovable. We never seem to get enough of what we think we want, and our satisfactions are highly transitory. Even with those people who are close to us, we often have love/ hate relationships. These are relationships in which we feel a need to get something from someone else; when the need is fulfilled, we love them and when it is not fulfilled, we hate them. Many of us are finding that, even after

obtaining all the things we thought we wanted in terms of job, home, family, money, there is still an emptiness inside. Mother Teresa of Calcutta, India, calls this phenomenon *spiritual deprivation.*[38]

Florence Littauer, a speaker and author, grew up in the depression, learned about marital problems firsthand, and then lost two sons. In her book, *Make the Tough Times Count: How to Rise above Adversity,* she explains:

> Early in life I developed a talent for straightening out other people. Innately I believed I could spot faults in others and improve them if they would only listen to me. My mother called this my Cinderella complex—always ready to transform any damsel in distress.
>
> I had grown up as the oldest child in a family of three and felt I was a born leader. When my father died, I simply took control of my family. My grieving mother, who was weak and exhausted, allowed my strong will to reign, and no one questioned my authority. It was the same when I taught school. My pupils doted on my every word. Not until my marriage had anyone ever suggested I needed help.[39]

Later in her book she writes about the deaths of her sons.

> Those two tragedies showed me for the first time that there are things in life money and willpower can't do anything about.
>
> Never would I say losing my sons was a positive experience or I'm glad it happened, but I do have a heart for people with hurts that I did not have before. By the grace of God, I have learned to make beauty out of ashes. I have learned to make the tough times count.[40]

Littauer did not learn until mid–life that she could not simply maintain control over herself and over others. She also had to relinquish control. Some of us learn this lesson even later, or not at all.

The issue of trying to exert too much control and not relinquishing it is relevant to all marriages, but it may be particularly apt when couples have lost children. Ronald Knapp, in *Beyond Endurance: When a Child Dies*, clarifies:

> You know, there is a myth circulating today, and that is that childrearing is easier than in earlier times because of modern medicine, child psychology, modern appliances, etc. Actually the opposite is true. These modern "conveniences" make the matter worse. For example, the improvements in medicine in recent decades have increased the undercurrent of anxiety surrounding childrearing practices within most families. In the past, children often got sick. In the past, they often died. This was to be expected. There was nothing to be done about it; it was a part of the reality of life.
>
> Today, however, we as parents have entered into a paradoxical situation. Even though we may be more aware of all the terrible things that can happen to children, we really don't consciously expect them. We don't expect life–threatening illness; we certainly don't expect death. Instead, today we believe we are sophisticated and knowledgeable enough to recognize possible symptoms and conditions early and to take proper preventive action. As parents living in today's world we pride ourselves on our rationality and on our *control* of the events around us.
>
> In the past, children died. It was part of the nature of things. No one held parents responsible. Today. . .the onslaught is devastating. Many parents have come to believe that they must accept full responsibility for the safety and welfare of their children far beyond reasonable limits.[41]

The dialectic of relinquishing control and believing one has control is demonstrated by the Voinoviches. These seemingly contradictory beliefs reside in their belief systems side by side. Janet observed:

> I use "together we can do it" along with the state motto which is "with God, all things are possible." So, those two things are interwoven. [George's] "together we can do it" motto was folded into the family. No matter what befalls us, together as a family we can do it, we can cope. With God, all things are possible. I believe that with God, all things are possible *and* together we *can* do it.

In H. Jackson Brown, Jr.'s popular book, *Live and Learn and Pass It On*, two people offer apparently contradictory "learnings." The first, a 60–year–old, states, "I've learned that if you depend on others to make you happy, you'll be endlessly disappointed."[42] The second, a person who is 82–years–old, notes, "I've learned that it is impossible to accomplish anything worthwhile without the help of other people."[43]

Their comments, taken together, comprise the truth of the dialectic of maintaining control and relinquishing it. We must work with others to accomplish our goals. However, we can not depend on either ourselves or others. A greater force may intrude.

Others have provided credence to this need to believe both in ourselves and in others. "Support from others is important to all people," wrote George Vaillant in *Adaptation to Life*, "but there is much that humans must do for themselves."[44]

Bernie Siegel writes, "Leave your troubles to God when there is nothing you can do to change them. This combination of a fighting spirit and a spiritual faith is the best survival mechanism I know. . . the Serenity Prayer, which was written by Reinhold Niebuhr, the twentieth–century theologian, and has been adopted, in the shorter version that I quote here, by Alcoholics Anonymous: `God grant me the courage to change the things I can, the serenity to accept the things I cannot, and the wisdom to know the difference.'"[45]

The prayer is not quite right. Usually our own power and the powers of others, including greater forces, are not separate. They are synthesized in the dialectic of maintaining control and relinquishing it. Few events are totally under our control or totally left to chance.

The lesson of the Voinovich couple is quite clear. People who desire long, strong marriages understand when they should seek and maintain control and when it should be relinquished. Kenny Rogers would tell us that they "know when to hold 'em and when to fold 'em, they know when to walk away, they know when to run." Happily married people are those who manage the dialectic of maintaining and relinquishing control.

REFERENCES

1. Pesach Krauss and Morrie Goldfischer, *Why Me? Coping with Grief, Loss, and Change* (New York: Bantam Books, 1988), pp. 47-48.
2. Harold S. Kushner, *When Bad Things Happen to Good People* (New York: Avon Books, 1981), p. 54.
3. Dolores Curran, *Stress and the Healthy Family: How Healthy Families Control the Ten Most Common Stresses*. (San Francisco: Harper & Row, 1985), p. 216.
4. All of the quotations from Janet Voinovich are from an interview with her conducted in 1992, unless stated otherwise.
5. Horacek was charged with aggravated vehicular homicide which generally occurs when a person recklessly causes the death of another. Horacek was placed in the City Jail and then released on a $2,000 bond. He was sentenced after pleading guilty to the charge. Common Pleas Judge Ralph McAllister sentenced Horacek to six months in prison and a $1,000 fine, but he suspended the jail sentence and $500 of the fine, pending Horacek's completion of two years of probation. Horacek could have received as much as five years in jail, plus a fine of up to $2,500.
6. "Hundreds gather to mourn with Voinovich family," *The Plain Dealer*, October 11, 1979, p. 8A.
7. John P. Coyne and Joseph D. Rice, "Voinovich Child is Killed by Van," *The Plain Dealer*, October 9, 1979, p. 1A.
8. "Molly Voinovich eulogized as girl who loved life itself," *The Plain Dealer*, October 12, 1979, p. 5A.
9. "Molly Voinovich eulogized as girl who loved life itself," *The Plain Dealer*, October 12, 1979, p. 5A.
10. Coyne and Rice, October 9, 1979, p. 1A.
11. Joseph D. Rice, "Voinovich makes return to campaign," *The Plain Dealer*, October 20, 1979, p. 18A.
12. Joseph L. Wagner, "Carefree Molly, beloved child in a political family," *The Plain Dealer* October 9, 1979, p. 14A.
13. Wagner, October 9, 1979, p. 14A.
14. Wagner, October 9, 1979, p. 14A.
15. Joseph L. Wagner, "Voinovich will stay in the mayoral race." *The Plain Dealer*, October 13, 1979, p. 1A.
16. Wagner, October 13, 1979, p. 1A.
17. Wagner, October 13, 1979, p. 1A.
18. Hugh Prather, "Forward," in Gerald G. Jampolsky, *Love is Letting Go of Fear* (Berkeley, CA: Celestial Arts, 1979), p. 9.
19. Bernie S. Siegel, *Peace, Love, & Healing: Bodymind Communication and the Path to Self-Healing* (New York: HarperPerennial, 1990), p. 164.
20. Coyne and Rice, October 9, 1979, p. 1A.
21. Siegel, p. 254.
22. Ann Kaiser Stearns, *Coming Back: Rebuilding Lives after Crisis and Loss* (New York: Ballantine Books, 1988), p. 23.
23. Stearns, p. 177.
24. Mary Bridgman, "One will be First Lady," *The Columbus Dispatch*, October 21, 1990, p. 1C.
25. Bridgman, October 21, 1990, p. 1C.

26. Alan Johnson, "Janet Voinovich becoming more at ease in the limelight," *The Columbus Dispatch*, April 28, 1992, p. 7B.
27. Stearns, p. 15.
28. Stearns, p. 15.
29. Stearns, p. 16.
30. Quoted in *Great Quotes of Great Women*.
31. Quoted in *Great Quotes from Great Women*.
32. Quoted in *Great Quotes from Great Women*.
33. Charles Leerhsen with Marc Peyser, "His Saddest Song," *Newsweek*, March 23, 1992, p. 53.
34. Tim Allis and Bonnie Bell, "Still grieving after the death of his young son, Eddie Rabbitt finds solace in country music," *People Weekly*, 31 (April 17, 1989), p. 83.
35. Jim Massle, "Voinovich is greeted by crowd here as he lays claim to victory," *The Columbus Dispatch*, p. 6D.
36. "Voinoviches designate fund for schools in memory of daughter," *The Plain Dealer*, October 9, 1980, p. 8A
37. Joan Bordow, *The Ultimate Loss: Coping with the Death of a Child* (New York: Beaufort Books, Inc., 1982), p. 66.
38. Jampolsky, p. 12.
39. Florence Littauer, *Make the Tough Times Count: How to Rise above Adversity* (San Bernardino, CA: Here's Life Publishers, Inc., 1990), p. 159.
40. Littauer, p. 143.
41. Ronald J. Knapp, *Beyond Endurance: When a Child Dies* (New York: Schocken Books, 1986), p. 123.
42. H. Jackson Brown, Jr. (1992). *Live and Learn and Pass It On*. Nashville, TN: Rutledge Hill Press), p. 96.
43. Brown, p. 112.
44. Cited by Stearns, p. 179.
45. Siegel, p. 174.

LISTEN IN ORDER TO BE HEARD

Roy and Eleanor Souders

"True listening, total concentration on the other, is always a manifestation of love. An essential part of true listening is the discipline of bracketing, the temporary giving up or setting aside of one's own prejudices, things of reference and desires so as to experience as far as possible the speaker's world from the inside, stepping inside his or her shoes."[1]

M. Scott Peck, *The Road Less Traveled*

"True listening has its spiritual component as well. When you allow another person to express himself without threat, you give him dignity, a feeling of control, and a sense of freedom even if all external circumstances deny his freedom.

To my mind, just as the so-distant sun with its hidden physical energy streaming through the universe nourishes the flower that turns toward it and opens its petals, so the sunlight of God's hidden spiritual energy and presence, the stream of loving-kindness, nourishes and strengthens one's soul, opening it up like a flower in all its beauty.

So that when you give that kind of dignity to . . . your mate, and he or she listens to you in turn, both of you dip into that spiritual energy stream and nourish each other."[2]

Pesach Krauss and Morrie Goldfischer,
Why Me? Coping with Grief, Loss, and Change

ELEANOR SOUDERS

Eleanor Souders is today a warm and affable middle–aged woman of medium height and weight with short, graying hair and glasses. She was born in Oklahoma City, Oklahoma, nearly 60 years ago. Eleanor was the youngest of three children in her original family. As she was growing up, her family moved frequently for job opportunities and for health reasons. "We moved to California from Oklahoma when I was a child because of my sinus condition. The doctor told my father I should go to a dry climate, and we chose an area that wasn't right, but he didn't know that and so that was how we got to California."[3] Today she lists her self as a Methodist, a former school teacher, and a housewife. She makes her home in a small picturesque town in Northwestern Ohio.

ROY SOUDERS

Roy Souders was also born in Oklahoma, but he was the second oldest child in a family of four children. Roy is four years older than his wife, has a full head of gray hair and a tall, slender body. He has been very successful in the insurance business, is a sought–after public speaker, and is civic– and community–minded. Roy's understated wisdom is apparent from the first moments of interaction.

COURTSHIP AND MARRIAGE

Eleanor and Roy view themselves as conservative in many matters, but when they met, they threw caution to the wind. The couple knew each other for a couple of months, dated for only two weeks, and immediately became engaged. Their engagement in February of 1955 was followed shortly by a wedding ceremony late in May. Although they have been happily married for nearly forty years, they are still reticent about their swift courtship and their whirlwind wedding. After offering some caveats, Roy admitted, "I was ready to get married." Eleanor added, "I didn't want to let him go."

Although the couple courted in haste, they were not children when they met and married. Roy was a returning veteran from the Korean War and Eleanor had already finished two years of college and was beginning her junior year. Roy began his first year of college at Central State University in Oklahoma as a twenty–four–year–old because he had spent a year working after high school, then two years in a business college, and finally, four years in the Navy.

After their wedding, they returned to college. Eleanor had one year to finish and Roy had two years to go. The couple managed financially because Roy had the GI Bill, and he was working at full–time job that was not too demanding. They also postponed having children.

The couple made their initial home in a suburb of Oklahoma City. After graduation, they lived in Oklahoma for another three years before moving to Missouri where they lived in three different places in seven years. They moved from Kansas City, their final residence in Missouri, to San Francisco. After living in California for nearly four years, they were transferred to Boston. Two–and–a–half years later, they were relocated to Ohio. Did they mind all of the moving around the country? Roy said, "I think, from a family standpoint, that all that moving around forced us to be more self–reliant. It made our family stronger."

Eleanor agreed, "We got into these new situations and we needed to count on each other."

While Roy was building his reputation in the insurance business, Eleanor taught school. When they began to have children, Eleanor quit working. She returned as a substitute after their daughter was in the first grade. Then she served as a substitute teacher. She said, "I started substituting and that set very well with our moving and being with the children. I kept very busy."

The couple did not begin having children as quickly as they had developed their relationship. Their first child, Neal, was born on February 4, 1958. Fifteen months later, on May 24, 1959, their daughter, Rebecca, completed their family. Eleanor said, "Neither one was planned. It worked out that way, you have two children and you love them and take care of them."

The relationship between the children mirrored the relationship between the parents. Eleanor said, "In fact our daughter said she always got things for Neal. She was kind of like the wife that always gets the drink and takes care of the other person." At the same time, Neal looked after Becky. Eleanor recalled, "When we moved here she was a freshman in high school and Neal was a sophomore and that was very hard for Becky. Girls of that age are not as receptive to meeting people as boys are. Becky had a really hard time, and so she relied more and more on Neal.

NEAL SOUDERS' DEATH

On June 19, 1979, the Souders waited at home for their son, Neal, to come home from college. The University of Toledo was officially out for the academic year. Neal had just moved from the dormitory to an apartment and was going to bring some of his things home. He told his parents that he was just going to stay for a night or two before going back to Toledo.

Eleanor recalled, "It was a Tuesday night. When he didn't get here for supper, I didn't worry about him getting here because he didn't say what time he was going to be here. He just said he was going to be here sometime. I had fixed his favorite casserole. I had made him a small one and was going to send it back with him. I was sitting on the patio reading the paper."

Roy interrupted, "You had twice commented that you were concerned because he was late."

"I always worried about anyone on the road." Eleanor explained.

Roy added, "She felt she should have a premonition."

"I should have known that he died. How could someone you gave birth to die and you not know it? I should have been tuned in," Eleanor said.

"She made a comment about him being late and I said, `Oh don't worry, let's go ahead and eat because we don't know when he's coming.' So we ate supper and then we were out on the patio and she made another comment. It was 15 or 20 minutes or so and the doorbell rang."

Eleanor knew when she answered the doorbell and found a highway patrolman and one of her neighbors at the door that Neal was dead. Eleanor said, "There was no question."

Roy started into the house from the patio. "I came trailing in and she met me right here in the dining room and she said, `Neal's been killed in an accident.' And the highway patrol man hadn't said anything yet so we walked in."

The highway patrolman and the neighbor waited at the door. The officer asked if they could come in. Eleanor invited them to do so and then went back to her husband's side. The officer said, "There has been an accident, and it's a fatal accident." Roy said, "I'll never forget those words. That's exactly what he said."

Eleanor remembered, "He was very kind, very considerate. It was hurting him to do it, and of course it was hurting our neighbor."

After a few minutes, the neighbor asked who they would like her to call. The Souders named friends who had lost a child seven years earlier. Roy explained, "I knew they would help us. It seemed like they were here in five minutes." The couple's closest friends came immediately as well. They also called their friends from out of town.

Roy recalled, "That evening we went to bed, but we did not sleep a wink. We just laid there and we'd get up and we'd watch television and we talked and we'd go back to bed. I am not a night person, and I need my eight hours. and I'd say `I've got to get some sleep.' And I'd lay there. It was just a horrible night."

"The next morning, Becky flew in from Massachusetts. She had been visiting friends in Boston. Our best friends in Boston had a daughter, Jaymie, who was in between Neal and Becky in age, and Becky was visiting them. Jaymie flew in with Becky."

"Our friend David took off from work and drove us to the airport. Before we left for the airport, David went down to the drugstore and said, `They need something, they can't sleep.'"

Roy added, "I told him to only get enough for one night. I just felt like I had to have some sleep, but only the one night I needed the medication. I am a little afraid of sleeping pills anyway."

What exactly happened to Neal? Apparently he was driving home in his Volkswagen. Eleanor explained, "We had given it to him on his birthday in February, just that year when he was 21. He wanted that car because it was so economical, and he learned to drive in a Volkswagen. I had always driven a Volkswagen. And so we felt badly that we had given him that car that wasn't safe."

Roy clarified, "But the patrolman said it wouldn't have made any difference if he had been driving a Cadillac because of the way he got hit. He would have been killed."

The size of the car may not have made a difference, but the couple do feel that Neal might have been at fault. Roy said, "I guess he was the cause of the accident. The road took a long slow curve to the right, and there was a witness that was somewhere behind Neal, and he said that he slowly went across the center line. And the highway patrolman said he suspected that maybe he was fiddling with the radio, and the road just kind of moved under him. He looked up and saw this pickup coming straight at him. A Volkswagen has very quick steering, you know. He whipped it back so quick, and by that time the guy in the pickup had made his evasive move. He came over and Neal's car had turned sideways, and he just came right into the door.

Eleanor is less sure of the details. "I don't know. Maybe there wasn't room for the pickup to go to the ditch . . . That's what I couldn't understand. And he had just purchased the pickup and maybe wasn't used to driving it. He was a deputy sheriff in Toledo."

The man in the pickup was not hurt at all, but he had a ten–year-old boy in the vehicle whose arm was broken. Although the Souders initially wanted to talk to the driver of the pickup, their insurance company advised them not to. Eleanor was sure that the driver would have felt remorse, but when she learned that he attempted to gain money out of the accident, she decided her initial impression was wrong. She admitted, "I didn't worry about it after that." Roy, too, had strong feelings about the driver for some time.

The couple felt anger where Neal was concerned, too. Eleanor said, "I was angry with Neal. He'd always been a good driver. He had never had an accident. He'd been driving for five years. He was a careful driver, and I never worried about him having the keys."

Roy added, "I can remember being angry with him for making the mistake; however, I have driven—I don't know how many times— and caught myself going left of center, and it just wasn't at the right minute. Neal just got caught."

He explained, "But you reach a point after a time when it doesn't matter why it happened because you're not going to change it."

HOW DID THE MARRIAGE SUCCEED?

Eleanor and Roy Souders have a strong marriage. How did they survive the death of their college–age son? They frequently mention the support they received from others, the role of their religion, their opportunities to talk about their son, and, most important, the role of communication.

Support from Others

Roy talked about the people who helped his family when Neal died. "We had tremendous support in this town." The Souders knew a number of couples who had lost children. These people, too, were instrumental in helping the Souders cope with their loss. One couple, in particular, had lost their daughter seven–and–a–half years earlier, and were always available to the Souders. Eleanor said, "Neal died in June. All that summer we knew we could just call and say `Are you at home? We need to come over.' They would just sit and talk to us and help us through it. Not everyone can sit and talk to you because they don't understand."

Importance of Religion

Also important to the Souders is their relationship to the Church. Eleanor said, "I grew up in the church." She explained that since her original family had moved so frequently, they needed to make friends fairly quickly. The obvious place for meeting people was at church. "The church people were our friends and then we branched out with other things. The first place we always went was to the church. And the church, the congregation, has never let me down. I have always found fellowship there, and support, and friends that I could count on."

Roy did not have a strong religious base as a child, but he became active in church after he met Eleanor. She recalled, "Roy was baptized just before we were married. He'd never been baptized, but he was going to the Wesleyan Foundation, the Methodist campus program. He thought he wanted to be baptized, and so he was."

Roy smiled, "Which didn't upset Eleanor, at all."

Talk About the Person Who is Gone

When a family member dies, others are often not sure what they should say, or if they should talk at all about the departed person. Eleanor and Roy were clear in recommending communication about the person who is gone. Eleanor said, "You feel like, at low times, that people have just forgotten that he ever lived." She added, "But we were fortunate that I had two friends at church who asked about Neal often and would say his name, and that is so important. I don't care who it is that you have lost—your father or your mother or anyone—you don't want that person forgotten."

She recalled how pleased she was when people would send photos and other mementos relating to Neal. "My sister–in–law sent us a picture, we were there for Christmas, the Christmas before Neal died. Roy's parents had celebrated their fiftieth wedding anniversary, so we all went home and Luanne (her sister–in–law) had taken pictures. A couple of years later, she found a picture that they had taken in the living room. One was especially good of Neal, and she wanted us to have it."

This sister–in–law was also particularly good about talking about Neal. "He liked to sing and she would talk about the things he had sung. She would say, `Could you believe that he would stand right up there in front of everyone and sing?' It was almost instinctive that she seemed to know that that was important to say."

The Souders mentioned a number of couples—some of whom had experienced a similar loss—who regularly spoke to them about Neal.

The Secret of Surviving Couples:
Listen in Order to be Understood

The most important lesson the Souders provide to couples seeking strong marriages is the importance of communication. They explain, and their behaviors illustrate, how essential effective interaction between spouses is to a good relationship. They also identify some of the barriers to successful communication including gender differences, stress, and conflict. The Souders believe that while expressing oneself and being honest are important ingredients to a good marriage, it is more important to use silence, listening, and understanding.

Communication is Essential

If you ask a layperson what the most important ingredient in a good marriage is, he or she would probably reply, "communication." Indeed, many humorous stories about marital problems are told that illustrate problems in communication. Authors Krauss and Goldfischer provide an example about a married woman who wished to obtain a divorce. She came to her attorney seeking help.

> "Do you have grounds?" the attorney asked.
> "Oh, yes, we have half an acre."
> The lawyer paused, then continued. "Do you have a grudge?"
> The woman responded, "Oh, no, we have a carport."
> In desperation, the lawyer plunged ahead, asking, "Does he beat you up?"
> She enthusiastically responded, "Oh, no, I get up earlier than he does."
> Unable to contain himself any longer, the exasperated attorney shouted, "Madam, exactly why do you want a divorce?"
> Innocently she replied, "Because it's impossible to communicate with him."[4]

This story based on the misunderstanding of terms is a good example of what some might label "a failure to communicate." However, communication between marital couples is far more complex than understanding that words that sound the same may be mistaken for each other.

As a communication professional, I am oftentimes wary about prescribing "communication" as a solution to marital problems. The term has become so overused that it has virtually lost its meaning. Many people believe that "communication" simply means "talk." Yet we know that talk, in and of itself, does not solve problems. Communication is a tool, or a means to an end, it is not the end, itself.

The original definition of communication is to "understand and share meaning."[5] When individuals successfully communicate with others, they establish "common understanding, a common tradition, common ideas, and common ideals."[6] The establishment of such commonalities is sometimes overwhelmed because of gender differences between the interactants, because of difficulties in the situation—such as the loss of a child, because couples do not know how to express themselves, or because couples do not know how to deal with conflict. Such problems can be overcome by learning how to express feelings, learning when to fall silent, learning how to more adequately listen, and learning how to show understanding.

The most important element of a successful marriage that the Souders discussed was communication between the spouses. Roy began, "You probably know better than I do, but my feeling is that the critical factor in a strong marriage is communication." Communication, in its original sense, is most critical.

PROBLEMS IN COMMUNICATION BETWEEN SPOUSES

Gender Differences in Communication

Most couples do not automatically have a common understanding. Communication is especially rendered difficult in heterosexual relationships because women and men speak and listen differently. For example, women often use talking to build rapport with others while men use talking to provide reports to others. Women may see communication serving a relational need while men may use communication to handle tasks that need to be performed. Women often create equality and similarity through their talk while men frequently communicate in order to establish their status and power. Women are generally more responsive and tentative in their talk while men are typically more likely to be assertive and certain.[7]

Misunderstanding, then, can easily occur in heterosexual relationships. She needs to emote, and he believes she is out of control. He falls silent, and she believes he doesn't care. Her interest in talking is met by his desire to watch television or to read the paper. Her questions, which are based on a desire to draw him into conversation, are matched with brief, deliberate answers designed to solve the problem.

Effect of Grieving on Communication

These differences in communication can create problems every day, but they may be especially problematic for grieving couples. For example, she may want to cry about the loss of the child long after he or she is gone. He may want to try to forget his pain by engaging in an alternative activity or by talking about something else. Her need to express grief and to share the experience are met by his need to assert himself and to establish his control in the situation.

The Souders discussed the gender difference that couples experience when they lose a child. Roy began, "I think it's important that there be a strong marriage before the death of a child. If the couple is not communicating and they lose a child, it is compounded because men and women grieve so differently. Men have a difficult problem of expressing themselves and women don't. People believe that men handle grief very well and women do not. I'm convinced that the exact opposite is true, women handle grief much better than men because women talk about their feelings. They have close friends, and they talk about their feelings to them. Men have friends, but we never talk about our feelings. We talk about our jobs, and we talk about the weather, and we talk about sports, and we talk about fishing, and cars and everything else, but we never talk about our feelings—or rarely we do."

"Men are more future–oriented and women are more now–oriented and I'll give you some examples. When the new son is born, when he's still in the hospital, the father is liable to buy a little baseball cap and a little glove. He's thinking about when he's going to be playing Little League and how he's going to get involved in all of that."

Roy suggested that men express their grief less obviously than do women and also that men grieve over future events that will not occur while women grieve over current events that will not occur. He provided a personal example, "I think after Neal died—you know your mind plays crazy tricks on you—I thought about the daughter–in–law that would never be, and the grandchildren that would never be. He had just finished his third year in college and I thought about the college graduation, the wedding, and other things that would never be. People laugh about women crying at weddings—I cry at weddings, because every one I go to I think about the fact that he'll never have one."

Eleanor shed many tears after Neal died, as well. Roy recalled, "This must've been a month or six weeks or two months, something like that after Neal's death. Eleanor came out of his bedroom sobbing, and I said 'What on earth is wrong?' She had found one of his dirty socks under his bed. I thought, `That's the dumbest thing I ever heard of, why would you cry about that?'"

Women are very now–oriented and they have difficulty with different things than men do. They go to a supermarket and they see groceries that are his favorite food, and they stand in the grocery store and start to cry. I can remember Eleanor going into the kitchen at suppertime and opening up the cabinet and standing there and just sobbing."

The Souder's conclusions are validated by the study discussed in Chapter 2 in which the investigator talked with 20 couples who were aged 27 to 60 years of age and who had lost a child between one month and forty–eight months earlier. Five themes were discovered: First, father's expressed concern and frustration about their wives' grief; second, wives' expressed anger over their husbands' not sharing their grief; third, a temporary halt in communication occurred; fourth, a loss of sexual intimacy occurred; and, fifth, general irritability existed between the spouses. The couples felt that "the death of the child was the most devastating thing" that they had experienced. They reported withdrawing from each other at various points in their bereavement either because of their own intense anguish or out of a desire to avoid increasing their spouses' pain. Not surprisingly, the marital relationship suffered.[8]

This study suggests that communication may be particularly difficult for grieving couples. Couples in bereavement are tossed through a variety of emotions. Elisabeth Kubler–Ross, in her landmark book, *On Death and Dying*, identified five distinct coping stages: denial, anger, bargaining, depression, and acceptance.[9] Many people experience all, or most, of these stages as they cope with the death of a family member.

When one's marital partner is similarly going through these stages, sometimes in the same order, sometimes in a different path, understanding becomes difficult. For instance, if one partner is denying the death and the other is angry, little understanding may occur. Nonetheless, it is important to allow each partner to experience the variety of coping stages.

The Development of Conflict

Conflict is inevitable among spouses. Nikki Giovanni observed, "Mistakes are a fact of life. It is the response to error that counts."

Conflict occurs because couples do not always share the same meanings for the things or events in their lives. They may interpret such events differently because of differing values, perceptions, needs, beliefs, feelings, opinions, or attitudes.

Interpersonal conflict has been defined by communication researchers Joyce Frost and Bill Wilmot as "an expressed struggle between at least two interdependent parties who perceive incompatible goals, scarce rewards, and interference from the other parties in achieving their goals."[10] Why does conflict arise? Sometimes it is a simple matter of the two people having different viewpoints or ideas.

Conflict may be more complex. All communication includes both a content and a relational dimension. When one spouse tells another to do something for him or her, the content of the message is the act that is being requested. The relational dimension of the message suggests that the first person has the right to make the request. Couples may disagree about either the content or the relational message.

For example, when a couple is grieving over the loss of a child, the husband may believe that he has the right to tell his wife to stop crying or talking about the child. The wife may disagree with the content of his message, e.g., that she shouldn't emote *and* with the relational message, e.g., that he has the right to tell her how to behave or grieve.

Problems may also occur when people believe that others should not express anger or other feelings. The inability to express feelings and to engage in conflict may doom a relationship. Family author Sven Wahlroos explains that when people state they do not like to argue, they are intimating a communication problem. He asserts the phrase "I don't like to argue" is used for one of three reasons:

> 1) The basic purpose is common but almost always unconscious and involves a middle form of the defense mechanism called denial of feeling. It appears to be an almost universal human tendency to wish to deny the existence of an alter ego. Rare is the person who admits that there is a "devil" within him (and those who do admit it usually do it for the purpose of excusing their destructive actions). . .

2) Another purpose, very common and often conscious, is to convince yourself and the world not only that you are innocent and lily white, but that it is the *other* person who *forces* you to be destructive when the discussion turns into an argument. The processes involved are blaming (conscious) and projection (unconscious). The statement "I don't want to argue" implies *"but you do"* and thus involves the pretense "I am the innocent victim of my communication partner's cruelty"...

3). A third purpose, also very common and sometimes conscious, is to avoid a discussion. The reason for such avoidance is usually some fear, perhaps of embarrassment, of being found out, of losing, etc. The avoidance may be conscious or it may involve various degrees of the unconscious defense mechanism avoidance.[11]

Couples who are grieving for a lost child may be particularly inclined to disengage from argument. They may fear the negative emotions they are experiencing. They may blame their partner consciously or unconsciously for the death of the child or for exacerbating the pain they feel. Finally, they might feel guilt—whether justified or not—about their role in the child's death.

How we view conflict is related to marital satisfaction and marital distress. Couples who blame each other more have less marital satisfaction[12] and attributing responsibility to one person, rather than sharing the responsibility for the conflict is related to more distress in relationships.[13] Grieving couples may divorce so frequently because they blame their partners and do not share their overwhelmingly negative feelings.

SOLUTIONS TO COMMUNICATION PROBLEMS

Expressing Oneself

One of the first steps in achieving satisfactory marital relationships is by talking to each other. Roy Souders understood the importance of expressing oneself when he said, "[Most important is] that you talk to one another." Such talk cannot be superficial in nature. One marital researcher explained, "You can have a 'nice' marriage where there are no conflicts, but a good marriage is one in which problems are faced, discussed and dealt with."[14]

Marital partners need to be free to express themselves to their partner. They need time to complete their thoughts and they have to be free to express both positive and negative matters. No one should be forced to disclose information beyond their limits, but every opportunity should be provided for each person to share feelings and thoughts. The suppression, control, or limitation of thoughts and feelings is generally undesirable.

Bernie Siegel, M. D., similarly believes it is essential that people learn to express all of their feelings. He suggests that the expression of feelings is essential to the healthy individual. He writes, "I believe that a healed life need not exclude the so–called negative emotions . . .Feelings are not to be judged. Anger has its place, as long as it is freely and safely expressed rather than held inside where it can have a destructive effect and lead to resentment and hatred."[15]

He clarifies his message with a story about a snake that frightened children in a particular village when they went out to play:

> The elders of the village went to talk to the snake and ask it please to stop biting the children. The snake agreed, and for the next few weeks everything went well. The children enjoyed playing outdoors and returned home each day happy and safe. The elders then went to thank the snake, but they discovered it battered, bruised and tied in knots. When they asked it what had happened, the snake said, "Well you told me to stop biting the children." "That's right," they said, "we did tell you to stop biting, but we didn't say to stop hissing."[16]

Siegel explains that, like the snake, it is essential for us to express all of our feelings, including the unpleasant ones, because otherwise they have power over us. Like the snake, unexpressed emotions may leave us tied in knots.

In one of his movies, Woody Allen quips, "I can't express anger. I internalize it and grow a tumor instead."[17] Siegel tells us that such behavior is exactly what we do not want to do. When we pretend that we are coping or fine when we really are not, we do damage to ourselves and to our relationships. He concludes, "So don't `try' to be positive—that's just performing, and it's hard work. Our goal is peace of mind, which will give your healing system a true "live" message.[18]

In *The Right to Feel Bad*, we read that people who are fully alive "experience the full range of emotions." We need to deal with the negative emotions as we learn to appreciate the positive ones. Hazelton writes, "Life is certainly difficult and even unpredictable—full of meaning and purpose at one time and utterly meaningless and purposeless at another, sometimes so desirable that we wish to freeze it at a certain point and remain there forever, and at other times so undesirable that we may find ourselves wishing we had never been born."[19] He adds, "But. . .there is no real happiness without the experience of depression to balance it. If we are not capable of depression, we are not capable of happiness either. In a very real sense, depression keeps us alive."[20]

Indeed, inhibiting our thoughts and feelings can create problems—even medical ones—for individuals. Pennebaker's research showed that the body's defenses are gradually undermined when we inhibit disclosing our thoughts and feelings. He specifies, "Over time . . . inhibition can affect immune function, the action of the heart and vascular systems, and even the biochemical workings of the brain and nervous systems."[21]

"While inhibiting our thoughts and feelings can create physical and psychological harm, confronting them can be helpful in both the short–and long–term. When we are able to either talk to others about our feelings, or even keep a written record of our feelings, we can neutralize the problems of inhibition."[22] In a marital relationship, the bond is strengthened when we can share our thoughts with our spouse.

Honesty is also important. Secrecy, hidden agendas, and misrepresentation will result in less than effective communication and less than marital satisfaction in the long run. Accurately representing our own needs, plans, and goals rather than disguising them is important. Similarly, avoiding threats and bluffs is desirable.

The Importance of Silence

On the one hand we need to talk to share our feelings and thoughts. On the other hand, we need to be silent in order to hear the thoughts and feelings of others. Krauss and Goldfischer write,

"Sometimes you have to communicate by being silent, by sharing pain, by listening, by empathizing."[23]

Silence and quiet is also important when we are attempting to be heard by others. *The Tao of Relationships* tells us to "Avoid confrontation, hardness meeting with hardness. The soft voice is hard long after the shout. Gentleness is stronger than anger."[24] Less may be more. As an inspirational writer suggests, "There are times when silence has the loudest voice."[25] Grigg adds:

> Too loud and we are not heard. Too bright and we are not seen. Too fancy and we are hidden. Too much and we are obscured. Let speaking come from deep within, from the quiet place. Let silence speak. Listen for silence. Hear the sound between words.[26]

Silence is also an appropriate substitute for potentially hurtful messages. A Russian Proverb notes, "A spoken word is not a sparrow. Once it flies out you can't catch it." It is very easy for us to say something that is harmful and yet irretrievable.

Many words and phrases have the primary feature of hurting ourselves and others. One author suggests that we should eliminate the following list of words which serve only to harm us:

> impossible
> can't
> try
> limitation
> if only
> but
> however
> difficult
> ought to
> should
> doubt
> any words that place you or anyone else in a category
> any words that tend to measure or evaluate you or other people
> any words that tend to judge or condemn you or someone else[27]

The Importance of Listening

Communication is key to successful marriages. But as we have seen, communication is far more than talk. Communication includes careful listening to both the content and the intent of what our partners are trying to convey. As one writer suggested, "The goal of communication isn't mouth to ear (surface talk) or mind to mind (facts and ideas). It isn't even heart to heart (feelings). The real goal is soul to soul—the ability to openly share joys, successes, hurts, dreams, and fears without rejection."[28] A maxim suggests a similar sentiment, "Communication is having a clear idea about the other person's joy or pain."[29]

More important than talking in communication is listening. Following the lead of *The Tao of Relationships*, it may be that it is only when we are good listeners that we can we be heard by others. Spouses yearn to be heard by each other. Family therapist Sven Wahlroos writes, "A discussion of problems between intimates, especially, requires that the other person's self–concept, feelings, desires, and goals be viewed with compassion and understanding by each participant and that such variables be seen as important elements in the discussion."[30]

Couples in satisfying relationships demonstrate a sense of equality rather than a sense of power or control over others. They do not make quick judgments or offer evaluative comments. Long ago Washington Irving wrote, "A sharp tongue is the only edge tool that grows keener with constant use." Happy relational partners do not whet this blade.

Listening is one of the greatest gifts we can offer our partners and others. In *Say Yes to Life*, Rabbi Sidney Greenberg is inspirational:

> What extravagant gifts are ours to bestow? A word of praise many yearn to hear, encouragement to lighten the burden of living, an hour to listen to a loved one's heart, an act of forgiveness to repair a family breach, a thoughtful deed to brighten a dreary day—these gifts we too often withhold are so desperately needed and so amply at our disposal.
>
> As we bestow these gifts on others, they come back to enrich our lives.[30]

Listening is very difficult work. Sometimes we have to listen for what is not being said as well as what is being offered. Too, it may be the softest rather than the loudest message we need to be hearing. To paraphrase one wit who said, "Marriage should be a duet—when one sings, the other claps,"[31] when one person speaks, the other needs to be carefully listening."

The Importance of Understanding

Ultimately, communication is about understanding. The importance of expressing feelings and thoughts, being silent, and listening lies in the role they play in understanding another person. Roy Souders observed that couples sometimes have difficulty in understanding each other because of gender differences. He said, "Men have difficulty in expressing their feelings, and we don't understand why women feel certain ways. Women probably don't understand why we feel like we do. Eleanor and I very early on had an understanding. This was long before we got involved in Compassionate Friends or did much reading. Right after the sock incident, I said, `I don't understand that, but I do understand that you are hurting.' So we just had an agreement that when the other one was hurting we would just go give them a hug. We tell people at Compassionate Friends, `talk to one another.'"

Extending yourself to your partner is made even more difficult when couples are experiencing severe problems such as the loss of a child. Roy said, "I think that both of you are so emotionally devastated that you just don't have anything to give to one another. You cannot imagine how fatiguing it is. You are emotionally drained, all the time, for months. And as you know, when you are out of sorts or when your husband is out of sorts, you can have some real arguments even if they're no big deal. When both of you are out of sorts for months on end, there's got to be a lot of understanding and communication."

In Jackson Brown's popular book, *Live and Learn and Pass It On*, many of those interviewed alluded to the importance of understanding other people. Here's a sample:

> I've learned that attractiveness is a positive, caring attitude
> and has nothing to do with face lifts or nose jobs. Age 56.[32]

I've learned that regardless of how little you have, you can always give comfort and encouragement. Age 64.[33]
I've learned that people don't want advice, but understanding. Age 40.[34]
I've learned that people are more influenced by how much I care than by how much I know. Age 54.[35]
I've learned that relationships are more important than rules. Age 51.[36]

Such advice is timeless. All of us want comfort, encouragement, and understanding.

Some unmarried couples spend hours trying to look as attractive as they can for their potential partner. They take pains in selecting just the right clothing to impress. They spend hours having their hair cut and styled, adding make–up, even undergoing cosmetic surgery, in order to look as good as possible. They do not know that their attitudes, their expression, their ability to understand the other person is more important.

Other people attempt to build up great reservoirs of financial wealth in order to be attractive or in order to feel secure. Erich Fromm observes, "Not he who has much is rich, but he who gives much. The hoarder, who is anxiously worried about losing something, is, psychologically speaking, the poor impoverished man, regardless of how much he has. Whoever is capable of giving of himself is rich."[37]

Marriage is not the only arena in which understanding is important. In general, we appear to be having difficulty with this ability throughout society. Physicians have been identified as one group who seem to express less human understanding today than in the past. One of the profession's own, Bernie Siegel, feels that communication is essential to medicine and suggests that it should be taught in medical school. He writes, "It was common knowledge among doctors from Hippocrates on that we need to tend to the patient as well as the disease . . . I can't help noticing that our power to heal people and their lives seems to have diminished as dramatically as our power to cure diseases has increased. . . Science has become God, and separated itself from the patient."[38] Franz Kafka offered an answer for why this situation accrues, "To write a prescription is easy, but to come to an understanding with people is hard."[39] Whatever the cause, it is clear that people, even in the helping professions, may be showing less understanding and less humanness today than they have in the past. Is it any wonder that one out of two marriages end in divorce when understanding is less and less valued?

Understanding in marriage may be as simple as listening, as offering a hug, or of providing a few words of encouragement. A Japanese proverb suggests that "One kind word can warm three winter months."[40] A small investment may pay large dividends if we only know what to invest.

Grigg offers the benediction. "Great mountains do not cover the entire earth; waterfalls are not the whole river. Most of the extraordinary is ordinary. Man and woman grow together in the rhythms of the everyday; daily chores, comfortable silence, desires rising and fulfilled. From easiness with the ordinary, togetherness comes quietly in the shared and simple commonplace."[41]

People seeking happiness in marriage may want easy steps to success. They may desire scientific formulas. They might prefer specific actions to recommendations about listening, understanding, recognizing gender differences, and communicating with their partners. And yet, "Happiness in this world, if it comes at all, comes incidentally. Make it the object of pursuit, and it leads us on a wild–goose chase, and it is never attained."[42] Marital happiness cannot be found by seeking it. It is in the realm of the mysterious rather than the scientific.

REFERENCES

1. M. Scott Peck, *The Road Less Traveled*, cited in Pesach Krauss and Morrie Goldfischer, *Why Me? Coping with Grief, Loss, and Change* (New York: Bantam Books, 1988), p. 85.
2. Krauss and Goldfischer, p. 85.
3. All direct quotations are from a personal interview with the Souders in 1992.
4. Krauss and Goldfischer, p. 81.
5. See, for example, Judy C. Pearson and Paul E. Nelson, Understanding and Sharing: An Introduction to Speech*Communication* 6th Ed. (Dubuque, IA: Brown & Benchmark, 1994).
6. R. Hutchins, in D. Bolander (Ed.), *The New Webster Quotation Dictionary* (United States of America: Lexicon Publications, Inc.), p. 50.
7. See, for example, Judy C. Pearson, Richard L. West, and Lynn H. Turner, *Gender and Communication*, 3rd Ed. (Dubuque, IA: Brown & Benchmark, 1995); Deborah Tannen, *You Just Don't Understand: Women and Men in Conversation* (New York: William Morrow & Co., 1990).
8. Reiko Schwab, "Effects of a child's death on the marital relationship: A preliminary study," *Death Studies, 16 (2)* (March-April, 1992): 141-154.
9. Published in 1969.
10. Joyce L. Hocker and William W. Wilmot, *Interpersonal Conflict* (Dubuque, IA: Wm. C. Brown, 1985), p. 9.
11. Sven Wahlroos, *Family Communication* (New York: Macmillan, 1983), pp. 73-74.
12. Alan L. Sillars, "Interpersonal perception in relationships," in W. J. Ickes (Ed.), *Compatible and Incompatible Relationships* (New York: Springer, 1985), pp. 227-305.
13. G. Bernal and J. Baker, "Toward a metacommunicational framework of couples interactions," *Family Process, 18* (1979), pp. 293-302.
14. Alexandra Penney, "How to Make Love to Your Husband," October, 1988, p. 37. (Condensed from *How to Make Love to Each Other*.)
15. Bernie S. Siegel, *Peace, Love, & Healing: Bodymind Communication and the Path to Self-Healing* (New York: HarperPerennial, 1990), p. 27.
16. Siegel, p. 29.
17. Cited in Siegel, p. 33.
18. Siegel, p. 33.
19. In Lesley Hazelton, *The Right to Feel Bad—Coming to Terms with Normal Depression* (New York: Dial Press, 1984), cited in Sol Gordon, *When Living Hurts* (New York: Dell Publishing, 1988), pp. 22-23.
20. Hazelton, cited in Gordon, pp. 22-23.
21. James W. Pennebaker, *Opening Up: The Healing Power of Confiding in Others* (New York: Avon Books, 1990), p. 13.
22. Paraphrased from Pennebaker, p. 14.
23. Krauss and Goldfischer, p. 87.
24. Ray Grigg, *The Tao of Relationships* (New York: Bantam Books, 1988), p. 101.
25. Leroy Brownlow, *Today is Mine*, cited in *Reader's Digest*, April, 1991, p. 33.
26. Grigg, p. 15.
27. Gerald G. Jampolsky, *Love is Letting go of Fear* (Berkeley, CA: Celestial Arts, 1979), p. 41.
28. J. Johnson, "Happily married...what's the secret?" *Today's Christian Woman*, January-February, 1993, pp. 29-34.

29. Mort Katz, as quoted in M. R. Rosenburg, *Quotations for the New Age* (Secaucus, NJ: The Citadel Press, 1978).
30. Cited in Krauss and Goldfischer, p. 167.
31. Joe Murray, cited in *Reader's Digest*, December, 1990, p. 17.
32. H. Jackson Brown, Jr., *Live and Learn and Pass It On* (Nashville, TN: Rutledge Hill Press, 1992), p. 44.
33. Brown, Jr., p. 110.
34. Brown, Jr., p. 116.
35. Brown, Jr., p. 131.
36. Brown, Jr., p. 147.
37. Erich Fromm as cited in Krauss and Goldfischer, p. 89.
38. In Siegel, p. 121.
39. Franz Kafka as cited in Siegel, p. 130.
40. Japanese proberb printed in *Reader's Digest*, December, 1986, p. 207.
41. Grigg, p. 67.
42. Nathaniel Hawthorne as cited in *Reader's Digest*, March, 1990, p. 13.

STAY AS YOU ARE, BUT CHANGE
Marilyn and Glen Heavilin

"We hide to protect ourselves from change, because change is so frightening."[1]
Philip and Vicki Emmert

"Change your thoughts and you change your world."[2]
Norman Vincent Peale

"The ancient sages taught, `Yield and be whole. Bend and overcome. Empty and be full.'"

"The hard and unbending are broken by change; the supple and yielding give way and prevail."[3]
Ray Grigg

In 1964, Marilyn and Glen Heavilin lost their son Jimmy when he was seven–weeks–old, the victim of crib death. In 1965, Christmas day, they had twin boys, Nathan and Ethan, but Ethan died of pneumonia when he was ten–days–old. Seventeen years later, they lost their second twin, Nathan, to a drunk driver.

Most marriages die after the loss of a child. How can a couple manage to remain together and have a good relationship after three such tragedies? Marilyn and Glen Heavilin illustrate the principle that we must change and yet remain the same.

MARILYN WILLETT HEAVILIN

Marilyn Willett was born and raised in Flint, Michigan. She was the daughter of a shopworker in a Chevrolet plant. She was raised in a religious family and became a Christian as a very young child. Her relationship to God has changed over time, but her religion has remained central to her life.

Marilyn describes herself as "basically the only child." She explains, "My parents adopted my cousin when I was 12, and he was two–years–old. So I have an adopted brother who's ten years younger than I am."[4] Marilyn exhibits many of the characteristics of the only, or oldest child. She is strong–willed and responsible.

Although the Willett family was small, their home became a center of activity. Marilyn's parents were warm, friendly, and they prized conversation. College students, visitors, members of their Sunday School classes and others often came to the Willett home for home cooked meals and fellowship.

At the same time, Marilyn was surrounded by death since she was a child. One of her earliest recollections which she shares in the first chapter of her inspirational book, *Roses in December*, is that her four–month–old cousin died when Marilyn was five years old. Since Marilyn was the only child in her original family and since there were no other grandchildren nearby, she always regarded the cousin as her baby.

The cousin suffocated in the night, perhaps from crib death. The baby's death was traumatic, but her parents instinctively knew how to help her deal with the death. They allowed her to see and touch the baby after death. They encouraged Marilyn to talk about her which helped the little girl cope with the loss. Before she was 12 years old, Marilyn also lost several grandparents.

GLEN HEAVILIN

Glen Heavilin was born in 1938 in Indianapolis, Indiana, and he was to be the oldest of seven children. As the oldest, he was given a great deal of responsibility. "I was the resident babysitter,"[5] he recalled. With nine people in their family, the Heavilins had little money for entertainment and social occasions. He remembered, "If it was a social activity that involved expense, it rarely happened, because taking nine people to an event was a major expense. Most often we'd go to picnics in the park."

The size of the family also affected the communication patterns. While Marilyn's smaller, original family reached out to others for companionate time, the Heavilins learned to curb communication. Glen said, "Conversation was real different at our house than it was at hers. With seven kids, you were pretty much taught to be quiet unless you were spoken to. Around our dinner table we had a lot of brain teasers and verbal discussion of that kind. It was always pretty well directed. You didn't just say what was on your mind. Mom and dad pretty well controlled the conversation."

The Heavilins believed in basic values and tended to be conservative. "You didn't venture out into questionable areas. Adventure was not really part of our vocabulary. Honesty and hard work were rewarded, and virtue was its own reward. I think my mom would be the kind of person who would take a leap, but she was just really burdened down with this humongous family, and I think fear and uncertainty removed all the daring adventure." Apparently their family philosophy paid off: Glen graduated second in his high school class.

Glen's father was a lab technician in a factory and his mother was a homemaker. The timing of his birth, just before the start of World War II, was significant. He said, "One of the impressions I had from my childhood was that I had to finish college. My dad wasn't able to finish college, due to the war, the family, and other responsibilities."

Glen's family was not as strongly religious as Marilyn's was. His family did not attend a formal church, and his personal commitment to Christianity did not occur until he met Marilyn's family at the age of 19. Nonetheless, Glen was raised with a Judeao–Christian ethic. Although their original families had somewhat different backgrounds, they had similar moral standards and ethics.

Glen Heavilin, unlike his wife, had little experience with death as a child and young man. Marilyn observed, "The only funeral he had ever attended before his own son died was his grandfather's. And that was the year we got married."

MARRIAGE AT FIRST SIGHT

Although Marilyn had grown up in Flint, Michigan, she went to college in Indiana at Taylor University. Glen, at the same time, was traveling from Indiana to attend the General Motors Institute in Marilyn's hometown of Flint.

Marilyn's father was the Sunday School teacher of the college age group in a large, very active Baptist church in the area. Although Glen had not really been in the practice of going to Church, he had attended Sunday School during his high school years.

While he was in the registration line at General Motors Institute, a young man stood behind him whose father was a Baptist minister. This fellow had been ingrained in church attendance. He invited Glen to go with him the following Sunday. Glen was uncertain at first, but the friend added, "They've got really cute girls there." Glen decided, with that bit of persuasion, that it was God's will.

He went to the church and attended a Sunday School class, as well. The Sunday School teacher turned out to be Marilyn's father. Mr. Willett visited Glen in his boarding house, and Glen became a Christian during this time.

When Marilyn came back from Taylor University, her father introduced her to Glen. He had had Glen over to the house along with many other young men for Sunday dinner several times and when Marilyn came home, Glen visited again.

Marilyn said, "Then I took over; I've been doing it ever since."

Marilyn knew from the beginning that they would marry. She said, "The first time I dated him it was love at first sight. I knew on the first date that he certainly was the marrying type as far as I was concerned. This goes back to my temperament. I am very organized and make charts and lists. Since I was 15, I'd had a chart that I revamped every year as to what I wanted in a husband. I had worked on this many times. I had been engaged before I met Glen and had broken that engagement. I was pretty aware of what I wanted by that time, and Glen had all the qualities on the list."

Was it marriage at first sight for Glen? He was honest, "No I don't think so, not necessarily the first time. I was just a sophomore in college, and I wasn't really looking at girls in the marrying mode."

Marilyn's inclinations were to become reality. Her strong will and her charm soon persuaded Glen to her way of thinking.

The General Motors Institute has an interesting schedule. People who attend, go to school for eight weeks in Flint and then they rotate to a GM plant in their own area to work for eight weeks. This schedule continues for a four year period. When Glen and Marilyn met, he was halfway through one of his eight week rotations in Flint.

The couple met on the first of October, and Glen left for Indiana at the end of the month. During the next six weeks, Glen visited Marilyn. When he came to see her at Thanksgiving time, he proposed marriage. At Christmas, he gave her a diamond, and the following October they were married. For the 1950's, their courtship was a whirlwind.

The couple was married on October 25, 1958. Marilyn's parents were not opposed to their marriage, but Marilyn remembers, "Glen's parents wondered what in the world he saw in me." Their reservations were based on their perception that Marilyn was "headstrong."

Indeed, Glen's mother argued against her son's choice. Glen recalled his mother saying, "Don't you realize this girl is so radically different than you are? You're not going to be able to live with her, and it's going to be terrible. So don't do it."

Glen's father, a man of few words, said little about the intended marriage. Glen said, "He's the kind of person who thinks things will work out."

Glen's mother was a strong and critical voice in her husband's dealings as well. Glen said, "I can think back where my mom had decided my dad was supposed to do something, and if he didn't, she would verbally berate him for failing to take the action that he should have taken. When we were in high school, we built a house on this piece of property we had out in the country. We had an old house there and needed to build a new one. I can remember the whole time, my mom telling my dad that that was not the way her father would have done it because her father was a contractor and had built lots of houses. When he poured the cement, she said he hadn't built the forms right. She told him it wasn't going to work. 'That's not the way my dad would have done it.'"

While Glen's mother was opposed to Marilyn because she was so strong-willed, it is ironic that she was perhaps even more forceful. Perhaps her opposition was based on the unconscious fear of relinquishing her son to another powerful woman.

Marilyn admits that she was, and is, a very determined woman.

She believes that Glen's parents might have had the feeling that their son would be overpowered by her. Was that concern well–founded? Marilyn answers, "He's not [overpowered], but there have been times that he was." She added that the relationship between her and her in–laws is excellent today, "Glen's mother and I get along quite well now. They are accustomed to me."

The couple's religious differences may have figured into the equation, as well. Marilyn feels that Glen's parents may have been afraid that she was going to indoctrinate him into something that would pull him away from them. She recalls, "I think at that point my religious beliefs just had a greater influence on him. My life centered on the church, and theirs did not. Glen came from a Quaker background, so they don't believe in sacraments as far as communion and baptism and things like that. After he went to our church, he was baptized which had nothing to do with me. I think that worried them, that things were different."

Marilyn and Glen had been raised differently and they exhibited different personalities and preferences from the beginning. Glen said, "Marilyn was a much more social person. They were always always having visitors into their home. In our home we had seven kids already, so we didn't invite people in."

After Marilyn and Glen were married, they moved to Indianapolis, Glen's hometown. They lived outside of the city for seven years and then moved to California, where they were members of Campus Crusade for Christ International. They later left this organization to work in the field of education.

THE DEATHS OF THE HEAVILIN CHILDREN

By the time the Heavilins moved to California, they had had all five of their children. In 1964, when their oldest son, Matt, was five years old, and his sister, Mellyn, was three, the couple had a little boy named Jimmy. Marilyn writes, "When Jimmy was seven weeks old, Glen walked into his room early one morning and discovered he had died of crib death during the night. As we waited for the coroner that day, I scooped Matt and Mellyn up in my arms and took them to my next door neighbor's home, trying to explain to them that Jimmy was now in heaven."[6] With Jimmy's death came the death of one of Marilyn's dreams, "...that we would live happily ever after in a lovely home with healthy, wonderful children. I hadn't left any room in that dream for problems—at least not problems such as the death of a child. I believed bad things wouldn't happen to good people. Jimmy's death didn't fit into my dream of a perfect, trouble-free life."[7]

A year and a half later, the couple believed that their prayers were answered with a very special Christmas present. On Christmas morning, Marilyn gave birth to twin sons, Ethan and Nathan. Their joy was shortlived.

Marilyn recalls the twins' birth:

> My parents brought Matt and Mellyn to the hospital on Christmas afternoon. Although they were not allowed to visit me, my room was on the ground floor, and we arranged to have the twins in my room so that Matt and Mellyn could view them through the window.
>
> I can still see their hopeful little faces pressed against the window. Surely our pain from Jimmy's death would go away now that they had two brothers.
>
> We brought Nathan home on New Year's Eve, but Ethan needed to gain more weight before he could be released.
>
> I visited Ethan each day, and I saw that he was not gaining weight; in fact, he was losing. Soon my greatest fears were confirmed: Ethan had pneumonia. The doctors worked hard to save him, but he died when he was ten days old.
>
> I had to tell my children that another brother had left them and was now in heaven. My dear Matt who had proudly taken pictures of his twin brothers to school for his classmates to see now had to tell them that one of his little brothers had died.
>
> I remember thinking then, *little children shouldn't have to deal with the fact that babies can die.* I wish no one, not even adults, had to deal with such terrible heartbreaks.[8]

Marilyn recalled her feelings the night she learned that she had lost Ethan:

> I remember struggling with my pain and thinking, *God, this isn't fair. How can you do this? I thought you called me to be a*

mother, and I was doing a good job at it. Now you are taking another child away.

Ethan's death destroyed my dream that people who experience a major trauma will be exempt from any further cataclysmic events. I was vulnerable. It could happen again—even if I was a good person. And I watched the dream of raising identical twins die right before my eyes.[9]

The Heavilin's stress was overwhelming. Marilyn recounted her burdens, "In the 22 months prior to the time we came to California, I had three babies, two funerals, and four major surgeries. The fourth surgery resulted in a total hysterectomy. I had a hysterectomy at the age of 27. I came to California recovering from that and also the deaths of two children and I had a seven–year–old, a five–year–old, and a five–month–old."

The next seventeen years lulled Marilyn into believing that while she had dealt with the most difficult pain a parent can experience, no further tragedies would visit their family again. She writes, "Our family slowly regained its equilibrium, and the children grew up. Matt and Mellyn graduated from high school and went on to college. Mellyn married, and Nate became a junior in high school."[10]

Most of us believe that bad things do not happen to good people. We also believe that if we have known pain and suffering, that surely we will be spared in the future. Finally, we believe that as our children grow older, they are safer from harm.

Marilyn and Glen Heavilin probably believed all of these things, too. Their belief that bad things do not happen to good people was dashed when their son, Jimmy, died. Their belief that they had experienced pain already and would not again was destroyed when their son, Ethan, passed away. Their last belief, that older children are safe from harm, was similarly ravaged. On February 10, 1983, their son Nathan, the remaining twin, was killed by a drunk driver.

Marilyn writes, "Nathan was on the way home from a high school basketball game when a drunk driver crossed the center line and hit Nathan's car head on at sixty–five miles per hour. Nathan lived long enough to arrive at the hospital and for us to get there, but after three hours we were once again hearing the words, `I'm sorry but your child is dead.'"[11]

With Nathan, another of Marilyn's dreams died. She explains, "I allowed myself to feel safe and secure. I dreamed dreams of

Nathan's high school and college graduations, our children's weddings, and our children's and grandchildren's presence in our family for the rest of my life. I dreamed that my three remaining children would live successful lives, have happy families, serve God and, most of all, outlive me. I still could not let go of my dream of everything going my way. . . Many of my dreams for my family died with Jimmy and Ethan. But the death of Nathan affected me in ways that reached beyond my family."[12]

The Heavilins have lost three children in separate incidents. Their older two children have survived. Marilyn said, "Number one and number two are still with us, and technically, I have lost my third child three times. It was the third child in the family each time that died. It was number three."

Few couples lose one of their children; the number who have lost three children in separate events is very small. The Heavilins' experiences allow them to compare the experiences of losing an older child with younger children. The couple was very careful to observe that no matter what the age of the child or the number of deaths experienced, it is the worst grief an individual ever knows.

After prefacing her remarks with this caveat, Marilyn added that the worst pain occurred when Nathan died. " . . .the death of Nathan was the hardest, I think partially because it was someone else's fault. It was so sudden. It was also because I had had him for 17 years. I look at the doorjamb and there are his handprints up there. He kept jumping to see if he was tall enough to hit it yet. Of course, I used to yell at him for all those dumb dirty fingerprints up there, and later I wouldn't have washed them off for anything in the world . . . There are so many more reminders of what you've lost . . . It was such a surprise to me, and I just was not prepared for that at all. And then of course it was the third time."

MARITAL STRESS

The deaths of their children took a toll on the Heavilin marriage. The couple never thought about divorce because of their religious beliefs, but the marital road was rocky for some time. Marilyn admits, ". . . there were days when we each wished the other wouldn't come home. Everything seemed quite peaceful as long as we didn't have to talk to each other and didn't have to agree on anything." [13]

She added, "I've met people who actually got to the point that they prayed that the person would die because that seemed to be an escape since they didn't believe in divorce. I never went that far, but there were moments that I wouldn't have felt too bad. I would rather have been a widow than a divorcee. After losing three children, nothing seemed beyond being able to handle as far as death goes. There certainly were moments that my life would have been not too difficult if I hadn't had to deal with Glen Heavilin. He was my nemesis."

The problems between Glen and Marilyn were exacerbated by the nature of Nathan's death. In some ways, the two earlier deaths were no one's fault. Marilyn said, "It was quote, unquote 'an act of God.'"

But Nathan died at the hands of a drunk driver. Marilyn recalled, "We had a manslaughter trial for a drunk driver, and of course, that never goes the way you wanted it to, and ours didn't."

"We had an insurance situation that was very difficult, also. Nathan had three teenagers in his car who were personal friends of ours. I was the academic counselor at the high school that they all attended. It became really messy. The drunk driver had no insurance. We had uninsured motorist insurance, and it was a large amount."

"One of these families became selfish. They saw how much money they could get and decided to see if they couldn't get the Heavilin's money too, the portion that should have come to us because of Nathan's death. Instead of this ending within 90 days or so, which it should have, it took 15 months."

"The manslaughter situation lasted longer, too. That trial was postponed 11 times, and it was a real frustration to me."

The problem was aggravated by the difference in personalities between the spouses. Marilyn wanted to manage and control the situation and Glen wanted to keep the peace. She states, "I want perfect control. I want justice and fairness. I want things to be logical and organized."

She adds, "I felt completely out of control. I was unable to prevent my son's death; I could not control the insurance company; I couldn't control the district attorney. I couldn't even control my own calendar. My schedule was subject to sudden change because of attorneys and judges whom I didn't even know!"[14]

Marilyn was angry at her husband because he would not confront legal officials about their son's case. Marilyn said, "I had always thought that the man should handle any confrontation in the family. He should protect me. He should take care of me. I would get so upset by all of this legal hassle. I would say, 'Go down to the district attorney and tell him what we need to have done.' My husband would just look at me and say that wouldn't do any good. `Why should I do that?' Well, he was right. It wouldn't do any good, but why you should do it was because it would make me feel better."

Glen's reluctance to interrogate the District Attorney was based on his personality, his style of doing business, and his interests. While he cared greatly for Nathan and grieved for him, he was not particularly interested in the issues surrounding his death. His attitude was that others should be allowed to do their jobs, and they should not receive interference.

In general, Glen Heavilin is a quiet man. He said, "I am certainly much more comfortable in a quiet situation than I am in a chaotic situation. I don't consider myself, even yet today, skilled in conversation. In a group setting where three or four people are talking, I don't talk because I can't figure out how to get into the conversation. . . I am just mystified at this art of how you know when it's your turn to talk and how you can enter that conversation without cutting somebody else off. It's just a real mystery to me."

Glen's original family contributed to his communication style. He admits, "At home, we were taught that you didn't interrupt other people, and you waited until the adult saw you waiting, and asked you what is it that you want. You never initiated a conversation with anybody. You always took your place in line and you waited patiently until the responsible person saw you, called on you and said, `What is it that you want to say.' And so I find the mechanics of how I want to carry on a conversation are very much like that. I wait for the other person to recognize that I'm standing there wanting to say something, and of course, in group settings, that doesn't seem to happen, and so that is part of what mystifies me."

As time went on, Marilyn did not view her husband as a quiet, logical, peacemaker, but as "Mr. Milktoast." In addition, she began to think that he felt that she was wrong in how she thought they should proceed.

Another source of contention was that the two, like most husbands and wives, grieved differently. Marilyn admits, "I am very vocal. I say how I feel. If you don't like it, I'm sorry, but I still have to get it out. My husband does not vocalize his feelings. He's learned to do a whole lot better in the last few years, but at that time he just would hold it all in."

Marilyn's assumption, just like most wives, was to believe that Glen was not really grieving. Glen, like most husbands, began to think that Marilyn was out of control.

All of these conflicts led Marilyn to believe that her life would be better without Glen. "It seemed to me that life would be so much more peaceful . . . If he weren't around, I could do what I wanted to do. I could go to that district attorney."

In retrospect, Marilyn believes she could have done some things which would have helped her situation. She explains, "It would have been better if I had gone down to that district attorney, and even if I had yelled and screamed at the other families. It seemed like the worst thing I could do was yell and scream at all of them, so I did it to him [Glen] instead."

The other error that Marilyn believes the couple made was not to admit that they needed help. She admits, "[We also let our problems] go pretty long before we finally admitted we were really in trouble. Both of us should have spoken up sooner, and probably me more than him. I'm the more explosive type, while Glen can sort of hang in there. But by the time I really exploded, it was a gigantic explosion. It would have been better if I had let it out."

HOW DID THE COUPLE COPE?

How did Glen and Marilyn Heavilin get from the point of hoping the other would not come home or would die to the point of having a wonderful loving relationship? A predominant theme that runs through their original families and their own current family is that of religion. Their notions of religion changed dramatically as they dealt with their losses and the consequent stress.

Importance of Religion

Marilyn said, "Your faith is going to be challenged as you go through this. I think it was Sasha Wagner, one of the people from

Compassionate Friends, who said, `If you have a faith, yell at it, kick at it, scream at it, but don't give it up.'"

Today the Heavilin's faith is unwavering, but that was not always true. She said, "I'm sure that some Christians might get a little nervous about my relationship with God. I'm not worried about what I say, and I'm not afraid of admitting that I was really ticked off at Him. People who have not tested their faith get a little nervous about saying something like that. But those of us who have spent their time shaking their fist and saying, `This isn't fair,' understand what I'm talking about. My faith has gone through all of those rigors, and all of those tests, and I still find that I have nothing but the Lord. If I don't have Him, what do I have?"

"I do say that when I get to heaven, I'm going to have lots of questions. My daughter who is very pragmatic says, `No momma, when you get to heaven, you'll see Jesus, and the questions won't matter. And I say, `Honey, you don't know your mother very well.'"

Marilyn is thoughtful. "It's not so much `why me.' That really isn't my question because I realize that no one is exempt. I want to know what did God see in this, and what did He see would be accomplished with this, and did we do it? Were we obedient? Did we accomplish His plan?"

The Heavilins do not believe that the deaths of their sons were random events. Marilyn said, "I guess that would be a real theological question, but for me `no.' I don't think there are any chances with God. I don't think that when Nathan went home to see the Lord that night that God was surprised to see him. He knew he was coming. Now, I do draw the line on the idea that God told that drunk driver to go out and get drunk that night, and I don't think God is the instigator of sin, but He certainly uses all of the events that He sees are going to happen. . . As one of our pastors said, `God wasn't on vacation the night Nathan died.'"

Importance of Forgiveness

Marilyn and Glen recognize the importance of forgiveness in dealing with the death of a child or the life of a marriage. Marilyn writes, "I began to realize that as long as I harbored anger and unforgiveness toward God or anyone else, I short–circuited the availability of God's power. As I learned to be honest with God, I learned I could be honest also with the people around me."[15]

Marilyn defines forgiveness "as giving up our claim to avenge a wrongdoing."[16] She adds, "The key in forgiving is the act of *voluntarily* giving up resentment or revenge."[17] Marilyn believes that many people think that forgiveness means that you must forget what occurred and this is not necessary. "Forgiving is *not* necessarily forgetting. . . but it is possible to remember and still forgive."[18]

Dr. Lewis B. Smedes writes, "We should not make forgetting a test of our forgiving. The test of forgiving lies with healing the lingering pain of the past, not with forgetting that the past ever happened."[19]

Actress Mary Pickford adds to the conversation on forgiveness. She said, "If you have made mistakes. . .there is always another chance for you. . . you may have a fresh start any moment you choose, for this thing we call failure is not the falling down, but the staying down." People who are unable to forgive are also more likely to stay down once they have fallen. Forgiving ourselves and others allows us to stand erect again.

Forgiveness may include many people. If the death occurred at the hands of another person, the perpetrator eventually must be forgiven. Marilyn writes, "Please understand that forgiveness does not mean we are releasing a person from his responsibility in a crime or that we won't press charges or expect restitution. Forgiveness removes feelings of vengeance, resolves anger that may consume us, allows us to leave the problem in the district attorney's hands, and permits us to proceed in our healing process."[20]

Sometimes the person who inadvertently caused the child's death is the parent himself or herself. Accidents within the home, on farm yards, in playgrounds, near highways, or in urban centers occur each day. In these instances self–forgiveness becomes prominent.

Even when the parent had no connection to the child's death, guilt may be overwhelming. They may intellectually know that they could have done nothing to prevent the death, but they continue to feel responsible. Marilyn writes, "We are supposed to be able to take care of those we love. Three times in my life I have not been able to protect a child of mine from death—that makes me feel helpless."[21]

Most surprising is that parents also have to forgive the child. If the child died because he or she was being reckless, it is understandable that the parents might feel angry toward him or her. But this anger often occurs when the child died through no fault of his or her own.

There may also be times when we feel angry at our loved ones for dying and that can cause us extreme guilt. Marilyn Heavilin feels that this is a natural response. She recalls her own difficulty in forgiving Nathan for dying even though she knew he had no part in his own death. While working with a group called Phillippian Ministries, the prayer director asked Marilyn if she could forgive Nathan. Marilyn writes, "I just about jumped out of my chair. I said, `It wasn't his fault!'

> She said, 'I know that, but can you forgive him for dying?'
> 'Well, of course, because it wasn't his fault!'
> She said, 'Fine. Why don't you say that to God?'

I tried to say it, but I couldn't get it out. It took me a long time. I sat there and cried and prayed. Finally, the first words that came out were, 'Nate, why'd you leave me so soon?' I realized I was mad at him."[22]

In retrospect, Marilyn realizes that she harbored anger at Nathan for some time. She writes, "Many times as I went down the freeway I would look at the exit Nate took the night of the accident, and I would think, *Nate, why didn't you take Waterman instead of Del Rosa? Couldn't you have done better? Couldn't you see that car coming? Why didn't you get there a little sooner or a little later?* All of those things may seem silly now, yet I needed to release my feelings and admit there was something that made me mad at Nate even though I loved him and would have given my life for him."[23]

Importance of Positive Action

Just like the Voinoviches who were highlighted in Chapter 7, the Heavilins trust God with their lives, but they also are proactive in their own behavior. She analyzes their behavior. "[We] took some active steps to resolve the stress in our marriage.

First, we made a verbal commitment to each other and to God that we wanted our marriage to survive.

Second, we set aside some time where we could give our undivided attention to each other.

Then we asked each other, "What is the best thing I can do for you that would help you work through your own grief process?"[24]

Importance of Other People

The Heavilins also had support from a variety of other sources. First, they had the support of people in their church. Marilyn said, "We had this accountability to people around us that when they saw that we were in trouble, they were right there saying you need help. They didn't walk away from us and we weren't alone."

They also had the support of their original families. Marilyn notes, "We had the example of both families; there had been no divorces in either family. I didn't want to be the first one striking out. I wanted to be close to my family, I wanted them to approve of me."

They also had their two living children. Marilyn adds, "I think the closeness with our children really helped us, too, that we were able to just talk with them about our struggles rather than keeping it quiet. And so they were involved with us too."

Most important, this couple had each other. She said, "Glen and I always talked." She smiled, "I'm sure I always talked more than he, but we were open with each other. We have learned to give each other room."

She added, "Underneath all of this, I've always known that there was a total commitment there. I didn't feel that he'd run off with some other woman. Certainly that is always a possibility—I'm learning more and more—but that would not be a first option with either one of us."

Marilyn summarized all of their sources of support. "I think we had built up communication with each other, and we had a strong faith, and we had an accountability with the circle around us."

> ## The Secret of Surviving Couples:
> ## *Stay as You are, but Change*

Marilyn and Glen Heavilin may simply feel that they are ordinary people who have experienced extraordinary pain. They are, however, a truly remarkable couple who have gained wisdom from their experiences and they can provide some of the secrets of lasting, loving relationships. They illustrate the importance of a belief in a divine being, the role of communication in a successful marriage, and the influence of forgiveness. Their most important lesson, however, is that they show through their words and behaviors how important it is for couples to stay the same, but to be constantly changing.

Stay the Same

As the oldest children in their original families, Marilyn and Glen were both responsible and persistent. They would not give up on their marriage. Marilyn said, "Both of us were determined that by gum and by golly we're not going to let this go down the tube." Their determination which remains as a constant feature in their lives is essential to their success.

Researchers have found that determination is one of the cornerstones of succeeding after a crisis. Ann Kaiser Stearns interviewed survivors of tragedy and observed:

> Major losses hold back many people from life. Almost everyone has known the survivor of a tragedy who, as the years go by, seems to lack the desire to triumph over it. Such a person appears to grieve forever and never goes forward to build a new life. The triumphant survivors I interviewed had the character trait of determination. These people *wanted* to triumph over the pain or loss in their lives. And they have gone forward.[25]

Change

The terms "crisis proof family" and "energized family" have been coined to describe those families that are unlikely to become unstable when faced with major changes. Such families are characterized in a number of ways, but all of them have flexible relationships and a shared sense of power. Adaptability is a major consideration in successful models of marital satisfaction.

Change is both a God–term and a devil–word. As Ellen Goodman wisely wrote, ". . . we all yearn to be the agents rather than the victims of change. [We] . . . hope that we will be able to hold on to what is best about the past while moving into a future that in some ways offers us 'more.'"[26] Considering her own feelings about change, she adds, ". . .same internal wars. . .between the part of me that finds change exhilarating and full of hope, and the part of me that fears disruption and loss."[27]

Yet our lives are filled with changes—some beyond our control and some within our grasp. Erik Erickson noted that every crisis "is not necessarily a catastrophe. It may be a turning point."[28] That our lives will be filled with change is predictable; how we deal with those changes is not.

Authors Krauss and Goldfischer, tell us that "Windows of hope are always there to open and look out even when we feel boxed in. Our challenge is to become flexible enough and patient enough to let this happen.[29] While some events—like the loss of a child— appear to be utterly without hope, we have seen in this book miraculous stories of recovery from the acute pain experienced by the parents.

Author Ann Kaiser Stearns suggests that we not expect too much in times of real tragedy and trial:

> Certain circumstances are so overwhelmingly difficult that the best we can do to promote our eventual healing is simply to mark time, stay alive, and bear up under the worst of our suffering. Recovery begins with doing whatever is necessary for survival.[30]

Stearns tells the story of a woman she knows who lost her husband when he committed suicide. The woman was only 41 when her husband died, and she had three young children to raise by herself. Stearns met her about a year after her husband's death and the middle–aged woman told her that she runs five miles each day and swims another mile. She was concerned that her behavior was aberrant or, even, harmful.

Stearns writes:

> What a relief it was to this troubled, grieving woman to hear that my new research has shown that she is behaving like a "triumphant survivor." Particularly in the early months of a crisis event or when a traumatic loss has occurred, we sometimes survive dramatic circumstances by taking drastic action.[31]

In *The Dragon Doesn't Live Here Anymore,* Alan Cohen writes, "If you always do what you've always done, You'll always get what you've always gotten."[32] Frequently people do not understand their own repetitive nonproductive behavior. The individual who is fired from job after job for identical reasons or the woman who marries one drug dependent individual after another in unsuccessful marriages appear not to recognize that they have choices and that they can change their behavior.

Professor Al Siebert of Portland State University, explains that the personality characteristic of "being flexible and adaptable, more than anything else, is central to being a survivor." He explains, "People who are best at surviving life's difficulties and who gain strength from adversity. . . have a variety of responses available" for handling life's unexpected circumstances, uncertainty, and chaos."[33]

Just as we have observed throughout this book, couples in happy marriages hold paradoxical beliefs and contradictory behaviors. Similarly, Siebert believes that the human flexibility he has observed "is derived from the survivors' paradoxical personality traits. Instead of trying to live their lives being '*either* one way *or* another,' [survivors] are comfortable being '*both* this way *and* that. They are bold and shy, tough and sensitive, analytic and metaphoric, etc."[34] People who are able to cope with the loss of a child and who are able to have long and happy marriages do not always respond to a situation in the same way.

One of the stressors in the Heavilin's early marriage was the couple's reliance on sex role stereotypes. Marilyn allowed her behavior to be limited by traditional sex role expectations. While she wanted to contact the district attorney and other officers of the court—as a woman—she did not think it was her place to do it. She believed that her husband—the man of the family—should conduct legal matters.

Marilyn is a different woman today. She would have no problem contacting legal officers of the court or anyone from whom she needed service. She said, "In fact, now, I would just say I have to talk to him. Then I'd go."

Glen Heavilin, too, was limited by his learned sex roles. He may have been bothered if Marilyn had marched off to the district attorney several years ago. Today, he understands that the two have different needs and cannot be constrained by more traditional roles.

Glen and Marilyn Heavilin have not only discarded antiquated and limiting sex roles; they have also learned to accept each other's personality and behavioral differences. When their first children died, Marilyn responded emotionally which threatened her husband. He simply did not know how to manage or help his wife. Writer Virginia Woolf recommended that people "Arrange whatever pieces come your way." Glen learned how to do this over time.

Marilyn says that Glen is very different today. "He is very nurturing now. At times he'll just say, you need to get this out. He recognizes when it's starting to build up, and he gives me room to grieve in a way that he didn't before."

Marilyn and Glen Heavilin have learned about the importance of change. The loss of their children brought out aspects of themselves that they had not seen in each other before. At first they did not know how to respond to the other. Or, they responded in ways that were dysfunctional or hurtful. Over time they were able to apply the wisdom provided by Max De Pree, in his book, *Leadership is an Art*: "We cannot become what we need to be by remaining what we are."[35]

A third change in the Heavilin marriage lies in their ability to not dwell on the past or worry about the future. In the next chapter we will focus on the importance of living in the precious present, but the Heavilins have learned this secret, too, and their experience is important to share here. When I interviewed the couple, they were on a trip to Coronado Island in San Diego. While they were there, Marilyn said they splurged on large meals and lavish evenings out. At first they were reluctant to spend the money since they had just built an addition on their home and their money was somewhat tight.

Glen observed, "We've learned along the way, when we were young we skimped and saved and we did not do some of the things that really have built the memories." He told Marilyn, "We're here now. Let's go out and build the memories, and we'll pay for it later."

Marilyn provides another example of their appreciation of the moment:

> Last Sunday our oldest son and his wife were singing at their church. This son, to my knowledge, has never sung in a situation like that before. He's sung in groups, but he's never sung a solo.

They invited us to come, and we were almost late getting there, but this was the most important thing in the world. We had to get there. It was very interesting to us how important it was for us to hear our son sing. And it turned out we did get there, and it was one of those magic moments.

I wouldn't have missed it for anything in the world. It used to be you'd let some of those things go by and say, "Oh well, I'll catch them next time." If there's an opportunity like that, we're there. Absolutely.

They do not worry about the future nor do they assume that there will always be another day to do the things that they want to do now. In the same way, they do not dwell on the tragedies that they have endured. H. Jackson Brown, Jr. collected the wisdom of many people and published it in his popular paperback entitled, *Live and Learn and Pass It On.* Two of those interviewed understand the wisdom of not dwelling on the problems of the past. A 63–year–old said, "I've learned that I can't change the past, but I can let it go."[36] An octogenarian observed, "I've learned that when bad things happen to me, I should keep the lesson but throw away the experience.[37]

The Heavilins express the same sentiment. Marilyn writes, "Forgetting the past and looking forward to what lies ahead. . . is what Philippians 3:13 (TLB) says. Does that mean we are to forget about our children or other loved ones who have died? I don't think so, but I do feel we must release the negative aspects of their deaths so that we are free to remember them as they were before. We must release anything in the past that would inhibit our living positively in the present."[38]

All of us need a purpose in our lives. Sometimes tragedies— whether they are serious illnesses, accidents, or death—serve to alert us to the tenuousness of life. Such events may serve as positive turning points that allow us to live our lives differently and, perhaps, in better ways.

Similarly, people sometimes use goals to fend off depression, illness, or even death. College students, for example, often are able to stay healthy throughout the academic term and through final examinations. When their academic term is completed, they often let down their resistance and become ill with colds and flues.

Elisabeth Kubler–Ross tells a story which illustrates this

phenomenon. She explains that a critically ill woman was in the hospital and that she begged the doctors to help her survive long enough to attend her son's wedding. The woman told the doctors that if she could just attend the wedding, she would no longer resist death. So the doctors prescribed infusions and transfusions to make her stronger. On the day of the wedding all of her intravenous lines and tubes were removed. She was dressed beautifully and her make up made her look as though she was not ill at all. Her energy level was high as she went to the wedding. When she returned to the hospital, everyone thought she would stagger onto the ward, lie down and die. Instead, she came back and said, "Don't forget, I have another son."[39]

The Heavilins have a purpose in life, too. They live in the present by viewing their lives as tributes or memorials to their children who have died. Marilyn explains, "One of the philosophies that Glen and I have had is that what we make of our lives now since they died is a memorial to them. Whatever you do—if you become a bitter person—that's a memorial, too. You have to ask if that is what you want it to be. Is that the kind of memorial you want to give? This has caused us to work at our lives and our marriage. I believe I'm going to see my boys again someday, and I can't imagine saying to them, `When you died, Dad and I broke up.'"

Marilyn wrote that when she sees her deceased children someday, she wants to be able to say, "This has been the toughest thing I've ever gone through, but I made it count."[40] We cannot change the bad fortune that occurs in our lives, but we can control our response to it. Hugh Miller, in *Snow on the Wind*, wrote, "Problems are only opportunities with thorns on them."[41] Marilyn and Glen have redefined their problems into opportunities to help others.

The Heavilins have dedicated literally thousands of hours to helping others who have lost children. They have worked with organizations including Mothers Against Drunk Drivers (M.A.D.D.)[42] Students Against Drunk Driving (S.A.D.D.), Christian Leaders, Artists and Speakers Services (C.L.A.S.S.), and The Compassionate Friends. Marilyn has also written inspirational books such as *Mother to Daughter: Becoming a Woman of Honor*, *Roses in December*, *When your Dreams Die*, *December's Song*, and *I'm Listening, Lord*.

The response of the Heavilins to their children's death is similar to Lonise Bias's behavior six months after her basketball star son, Len

Bias, died tragically of cocaine over dose. Lonise Bias went on the lecture circuit. She called her new vocation "a mission" as she went from town to town telling young people, "You don't need drugs." Her trips were generally alone and frequently she only received airfare and no honorarium. According to *Baltimore Sun* correspondent Amy Goldstein, "although [Mrs. Bias] has no prior experience as a public speaker, her style is gripping and her message powerfully spoken."[43]

In one of her books, Marilyn Heavilin writes, ". . .you must face the pain, the fear, the despair, the anger, the stigma, the confusion and the loneliness, and you must make an active decision to turn those negatives into the positives of strength, peace, freedom, power and hope." She adds, "You can take the old song that was sung in a minor key, and you can transpose it into a harmonious melody."[44]

Marilyn considers her life's course. She reflected, "The mother side of me would still like to simply be the mom of five healthy, normal children. But the child of God side of me stands in awe at God's plan and His creativity in using me and helping me discover talents and abilities I didn't know I had."[45]

Marilyn Heavilin was asked by a bereaved parent if she would want to bring her children back to this world. Her answer was immediate, "Of course I would love to have them back; that's an easy decision." Later she thought about the question. ". . .as I reflected on all I have learned and how I have changed since their deaths, I thought to myself, *I would love to have them back of course, but I would never want to be the Marilyn Heavilin I was before they died*. I didn't know what life was all about. Through my children's deaths, I have learned that life is not just about living; it is about caring, loving, hurting and dying."[46]

Joan McIntosh wrote, "Accept the pain, cherish the joys, resolve the regrets; then can come the best of benedictions—"If I had my life to live over, I'd do it all the same." Few people have had a life as difficult as the one experienced by Marilyn Heavilin. Yet she stands tall today able to manage what she has been given. She has accepted her pain, cherished her joys, and resolved her regrets.

The Heavilins are a model couple for people who desire warm and rich relationships. Marilyn has been a full–time mother during parts of her adult life, but she has other accomplishments, as well. She earned a bachelor's degree in education, and is halfway through a master's degree. She served as a high school teacher and was the academic counselor in her son's high school. Today she spends most of her time writing and speaking.

Glen has a master's degree in business. His undergraduate work was completed at the General Motors Institute in Flint, Michigan, and his master's degree and Marilyn's Bachelor of Arts degree are from California State University in San Bernadino, near their home.

In 1966, Glen set up the computer department for Campus Crusade for Christ. He then left the organization, but he continued to work on computers. Today he is the director of data processing for the San Bernadino city schools.

The couple has two children in their thirties. Their daughter, Mellyn, has a little boy and their son, Matt, has two boys and a girl. Two of the grandchildren—Katherine Nate' and Nathanael Jacob— were named for Nathan. Matt's second son is named Caleb Ethan. Through these children, Nathan's and Ethan's names go on; through their family members and friends, their spirits live.

REFERENCES

1. Philip Emmert and Vicki Emmert, *Interpersonal Communication* (Dubuque, IA: Wm. C. Brown Publishers, 1984).
2. Norman Vincent Peale, *Reader's Digest*, September, 1986, p. 139.
3. Ray Grigg, *The Tao of Relationships* (New York: Bantam Books, 1988), p. 133.
4. All of the quotations from Marilyn Heavilin are from a personal interview conducted in 1992, unless stated otherwise.
5. All of the quotations from Glen Heavilin are from a personal interview in 1992, unless stated otherwise.
6. Marilyn Willett Heavilin, *December's Song* (San Bernardino, CA: Here's Life Publishers, Inc., 1988). All of Marilyn Heavilin's books are now published by Thomas Nelson Publishers, Nashville, TN.
7. Marilyn Willett Heavilin, *When your Dreams Die: Finding Strength and Hope Through Life's Disappointments* (San Bernardino, CA: Here's Life Publishers, Inc., 1990), p. 14.
8. Heavilin, 1988, pp. 14-15.
9. Heavilin, 1990, p. 14-15.
10. Heavilin, 1988, p. 15.
11. Heavilin, 1990, p. 16.
12. Heavilin, 1990, pp. 15-16.
13. Heavilin, 1988, p. 22.
14. Heavilin, 1988, pp. 59-60.
15. Heavilin, 1988, pp. 38-39.
16. Heavilin, 1990, p. 52.
17. Heavilin, 1990, p. 52.
18. Heavilin, 1990, p. 52.
19. Lewis B. Smedes, *Forgive and Forget* (San Francisco: Harper & Row Publishers, 1984), p. 39, cited in Heavilin, 1990, p. 52.
20. Heavilin, 1988, p. 67.
21. Heavilin, 1988, p. 53.
22. Heavilin, 1990, p. 59.
23. Heavilin, 1990, p. 59.
24. Heavilin, 1988, p. 24.
25. Ann Kaiser Stearns, *Coming Back: Rebuilding Lives after Crisis and Loss* (New York: Ballantine Books, 1988), p. 185.
26. Ellen Goodman, *Turning Points* (New York: Fawcett Crest, 1979), p. ix.
27. Goodman, p. xii.
28. Cited in Goodman, p. xii.
29. Pesach Krauss and Morrie Goldfischer, *Why Me? Coping with Grief, Loss, and Change* (New York: Bantam Books, 1988), p. 171.
30. Stearns, p. 20.
31. Stearns, p. 20.
32. Stearns, p. 70.
33. Al Siebert, "The Survivor Personality," *Association for Humanistic Psychology Newsletter*, August-September, 1983, p. 19, in Stearns, p. 191.
34. Siebert, in Stearns, pp. 191-192.
35. Reprinted in *Reader's Digest*, May, 1990, p. 152.
36. H. Jackson Brown, Jr., *Live and Learn and Pass It On* (Nashville, TN: Rutledge Hill Press, 1992), p. 64.

37. Brown, Jr., p. 93.
38. Heavilin, 1988, p. 45.
39. Retold by Bernie S. Siegel, *Peace, Love, & Healing: Bodymind Communication and the Path to Self-Healing* (New York: HarperPerennial, 1990), p. 219.
40. Heavilin, 1988, p. 50.
41. Reprinted in *Reader's Digest*, July, 1990, p. 147.
42. Candy Lightner, the founder of Mothers Against Drunk Driving, is another example of someone who has refocused her anger into positive and productive behavior. In 1980, she founded the organization when her 13-year-old daughter was killed by a drunk driver. MADD began as an organization of individuals who did not believe that the justice system prosecuted drunk drivers sufficiently.
    MADD created one of the most effective public awareness campaigns in history. Today it has over 2.8 members and supporters and chapters exist in every state in the nation. In addition, chapters exist in Canada, Great Britain, Australia, and New Zealand. The group has changed the way people think about drinking and driving.
43. Amy Goldstein, "Lonise Bias, `On Mission,' Talks to UM Drug Abuse Class," *Baltimore Sun*, December 4, 1986.
44. Heavilin, 1988, p. 131.
45. Heavilin, 1990, p. 134.
46. Heavilin, 1988, pp. 132-133.

⊗ 10

REMEMBER THE PAST, CONSIDER THE FUTURE, BUT LIVE IN THE PRESENT
George and Barbara Bush

It was the best of times, it was the worst of times, it was the age of wisdom, it was the age of foolishness, it was the epoch of belief, it was the epoch of incredulity, it was the season of Light, it was the season of Darkness, it was the spring of hope, it was the winter of despair, we had everything before us, we had nothing before us, we were all going direct to Heaven, we were all going direct the other way—in short, the period was so far like the present period, that some of its noisiest authorities insisted on its being received, for good or for evil, in the superlative degree of comparison only.
Charles Dickens, A Tale of Two Cities[1]

George Bush became the 41st President of the United States in 1989. As the leader of the free world, he held what is arguably the most coveted role for an American. His wife, Barbara Bush, was enormously popular—even rivaling her husband at various times of his presidency. We acknowledge that this couple has clearly experienced the best of times.

The Bushes have also known the depths of despair. In 1953 they lost their daughter, Pauline Robinson Bush, to leukemia.

While their life together has been a congenial one, it has not been without challenges and crises. In addition to the death of their

203

daughter, they have suffered business losses, George Bush lost two elections for the Senate (in 1964 and 1970), the 1980 Presidential nomination, and the 1992 Presidential election.

Because Barbara and George Bush have experienced "the best of times and the worst of times," their marriage serves as a model for couples who desire lasting, loving relationships. Moreover, the Bushes illustrate how we can remember the past and consider the future, but that we must live in the present. A modern proverb tells us that there is no time like the present. George and Barbara Bush personify this proverb.

BARBARA PIERCE BUSH

Barbara Pierce was born on June 8, 1925, to Pauline Robinson Pierce and Marvin Pierce. Her parents met in Oxford, Ohio. Her father was well-known on the campus at Miami University where he combined athletic skills and academic success. He was the captain of the football team and a top tennis player, but he also graduated *summa cum laude*. Marvin went on to complete graduate degrees in architectural engineering from Harvard and the Massachusetts Institute of Technology.

Pauline Robinson was a student at Oxford College in Ohio. She was a campus beauty who was three years younger than Marvin. Her father was an influential Ohio supreme court justice.

The couple married in 1918. Two children preceded Barbara. Martha was born in 1920 and James was born less than two years later. Barbara followed James by about three-and-a-half years. She was the baby of the family for five years until her brother, Scott, was added as the final offspring.

Barbara's biographer wrote, "She grew up in the shadow of a beautiful older sister who was favored by her somewhat distant mother, and the two women dominated her life until the day she married."[2] Although Barbara became more understanding of her mother over time, she continued to see her as distant and distracted.

"My mother, I'm sure, was tired and irritable and I didn't understand it at the time," she said. "But I guess I felt neglected that she didn't spend as much time on me. She had this enormous responsibility which I was never sympathetic about. Now, as a mother and grandmother, I realize what she was going through."[3]

Barbara's father, Marvin, was a successful publisher. When Barbara was born, he was working at McCall's. He became president of the company in 1946, and later became publisher. He also had a special place in Barbara's memory. She reminisces about a father who always took her side, "I think because Mother never took my side."[4]

Barbara grew up in what many have referred to as "the posh suburbs" of Rye, New York. Barbara takes exception with the description. "I'm so sick of hearing about this great wealthy background I had," she said. "I was rich only in that I had wonderful parents and a happy homelife. Perhaps compared to others we were comfortable."[5]

GEORGE HERBERT WALKER BUSH

George Herbert Walker Bush was born in Milton, Massachusetts, on June 12, 1924, to Dorothy Walker Bush and Prescott S. Bush. From his family, he inherited a proclivity for competition—both in the political and the athletic arenas. His father served as Senator from Connecticut.

His maternal grandfather and name–sake, George Herbert Walker, was a first–class athlete. He was first interested in hard contact sports and became heavyweight boxing champion of Missouri. Later he became enamored with golf and was the individual for whom the Walker Cup for golfers was named.

George Bush played tennis, golf, basketball and baseball as a child. In the summers he enjoyed swimming, boating, and fishing. At Andover, Bush managed the basketball team and became captain of the baseball and soccer teams. As one classmate recalls, "From the athletic standpoint, only time limited him. If there had been five seasons and five sports instead of three, he would have been playing all of them."[6] George completed his academically–linked sports career at Yale where he was captain of the varsity baseball team.

FIRST ENCOUNTER

Barbara Pierce left Rye, New York, in 1941, for her junior year of high school to attend Ashley Hall, a small exclusive preparatory school in Charleston, South Carolina. The Second World War began during December of that year. When Barbara went home to Rye for the holidays, she met an Andover student, also home for the holidays, who would make the war seem even closer.

She was only 16–years–old when she met George at a Christmas dance at the Round Hill Country Club in Greenwich, Connecticut. He was only 17–years–old. For both Barbara and George, it was "love at first sight."

George reflects, "I'm not much at recalling what people wear, but that particular occasion stands out in my memory. The band was playing Glenn Miller tunes when I approached a friend from Rye, New York, Jack Wozencraft, to ask if he knew a girl across the dance floor, the one wearing the green-and-red holiday dress. He said she was Barbara Pierce, that she lived in Rye and went to school in South Carolina. Would I like an introduction? I told him that was the general idea, and he introduced us, just about the time the bandleader decided to change tempos, from fox trot to waltz. Since I didn't' waltz, we sat the dance out. And several more after that, talking and getting to know each other."

"It was a storybook meeting, though most couples that got serious about each other in those days could say the same about the first time they met. Young people in the late 1930s and early '40s were living with what modern psychologists call heightened awareness, on the edge. It was a time of uncertainty, when every evening brought dramatic radio newscasts—Edward R. Murrow from London, William L. Shirer from Berlin—reporting a war we knew was headed our way."[7]

Barbara Bush did not use the events of the day to explain their initial attraction. "I could hardly breathe when he was in the room."[8] "He was the handsomest–looking man you ever laid your eyes on, bar none," she says. "I mean, my boys don't even come close to him, nor did his own brothers."[9]

Bush biographer, Pamela Kilian observes, "The Bushes have obviously repeated this story fondly for their children, each of whom adds his own spin."

"'It seems that my dad was zonked over the head by this outgoing, charming woman,' says number–four son Marvin. `And just like everything else he's done in his life, he decided that she was the one he was going to marry and so he did.'"

"'I'm told it was love at first sight,' said number–one son George. `I think Mother had heard of George Bush's reputation from a nearby city and Dad saw Mother at a party and fell in love with her.'"[10]

EARLY RENDEZVOUS

In the remaining days of the Christmas holiday, the couple managed to go out for ice cream sodas and to sports events. Although George was worried that the two would have nothing to say to each other, his fears were unfounded. They fell into easy conversation that has lasted a life time.

When the holiday was over, Barbara returned to her high school in South Carolina and George to Andover, Massachusetts. Although the couple exchanged letters almost daily in the months to follow, they saw each other only once during that spring. Then, at the end of the year, George invited her to his senior prom.

George Bush turned 18 on June 12, 1942—he was four days short of being a year older than Barbara—and promptly signed up for the Navy. Although he had been accepted at Yale, George changed his plans after the bombing of Pearl Harbor the previous December. Pre–flight training in Chapel Hill, North Carolina, followed less than two months after he turned 18.

Barbara began her senior year at Ashley Hall and visited him only once during the year. The occasion occurred when George received his wings in a ceremony at Chapel Hill. George was self–conscious about his youthful appearance and the age of his date. He asked Barbara to tell people that she was eighteen rather than the seventeen she actually was. She was relieved when no one asked her age during the weekend.

After Bush finished his training at Chapel Hill, he went to Minneapolis, Minnesota, for further training and then completed the initial flight–training course at Corpus Christi, Texas, in June. He earned his ensign's bars on June 9, 1943. Barbara graduated from high school during the same month.

George recalled, "In the eight months that passed from that first meeting until her visit to Chapel Hill, Barbara and I had progressed from simply being `serious,' to meeting and spending time with each other's families—a fairly important step for teenagers in those days. After I got my wings and went into advanced flight training, we took the next important step."[11]

TIME TO PLAN

Home in Rye, Barbara prepared to attend Smith College, but her thoughts were on George Bush. During the summer, George invited her to spend time with him and his family in Maine. Barbara spent seventeen days with the Bush family and she and George's mother, Dorothy Bush, developed a warm rapport.

George and Barbara mapped out their future. They became engaged during the visit, but they did not formally announce the engagement until December of that year. Families and friends were privy to the development, however.

"I do remember calling my family, saying that George and I were engaged," Barbara said. "The family said, `Oh, really?' It was so obvious to them we were in love that of course they didn't have to be told. It was sort of `How could you be so silly? We've known it all along.'"[12]

The official announcement of the engagement was topped off with an engagement ring. George was in Philadelphia for a commissioning ceremony for an aircraft carrier and invited Barbara and his mother. The two women traveled to the ceremony together. On the trip, Dorothy asked Barbara what kind of engagement ring she wanted. Barbara did not know that Dorothy carried with her a star sapphire ring that had belonged to one of George's aunts.

"Just before the commissioning ceremony started, George took the ring out of his pocket and gave it to me," Barbara said. "I was thrilled. I don't know to this day whether it's real and I don't care. It's my engagement ring and it hasn't been off my finger since the day George gave it to me."[13]

The couple realized that a marriage date would be far in the future because of George's military obligation. Indeed, George was assigned to a torpedo squadron readying for active duty that fall. In

May 1944 he began flying missions against the Japanese. Harrowing experiences followed.

The worst incident occurred on September 2nd when his plane was hit by antiaircraft fire. Bush bailed out and was rescued by a submarine. Nonetheless, he was out of touch with his parents and Barbara for over a month.

In the meantime, Barbara had completed a year at Smith College. She dropped out at the beginning of her sophomore year to plan her December 19th wedding. George did not come home until Christmas Eve, however, five days after their announced wedding date.

"Barbara and I were married two weeks later, January 6, 1945, at the First Presbyterian Church in her hometown, Rye, New York, with a close friend from VT–51, Milt Moore, as a member of the wedding party,"[14] George said. He was not yet twenty–one and his wife was only nineteen–and–a–half.

"I married the first man I ever kissed," Barbara said years later. "When I tell my children, they just about throw up."[15]

MARRIED LIFE

In August, Japan surrendered. Bush was discharged one month later and two months after that he was enrolled at Yale. A special program for veterans allowed him to graduate in less than three years. Before the couple left New Haven, their first child, George, arrived on July 6, 1946.

After graduation, in June 1948, the Bushes moved to Texas to learn the oil business. Their life in Texas was very different than their lives in the East and, therefore, somewhat difficult. However, they were soon transferred to California and ended up moving five times within a single year. When their second child was born in Compton, California, in December 1949, Barbara did not even meet her doctor until the day her daughter was born.

ROBIN BUSH

Pauline Robinson Bush, the couple's second child, was born in Compton, California, in December 1949. She was named for Barbara's mother, but they "called her `Robin,' as full of life and promise as the bird that comes with springtime,"[16] noted one biographer.

Barbara's mother, Pauline, died in a bizarre car accident only two months before the birth. Pauline had set a hot cup of coffee on the car seat near her one morning while riding with her husband. When the cup began to slide, Barbara's father tried to rescue it. Instead, he lost control of the car and crashed into a stone wall. Pauline died on impact.

Barbara did not attend the funeral because she was seven months pregnant. Her father, injured in the accident, discouraged her from flying across the country, afraid of more ill–fortune. Barbara agreed, but not without regrets.

"I'll never forgive myself for not going to my mother's funeral or spending time with my father in the hospital," she says now.[17]

Soon after their daughter's birth, the Bushes moved back to Texas. Their life was fairly routine with George working long hours and Barbara performing volunteer work.

In the spring of 1953, events created irrevocable change. Their oldest son, George, was six years old, Robin was three and one–half, and a new baby boy, John Ellis—known by his initials, Jeb—was an infant. Although Barbara did not observe the small bruises on her daughter's legs, she became worried when Robin began to show no interest in playing.

"I may go out and sit in the grass and watch the cars go by or maybe I'll just lie in bed,"[18] Robin told her mother one day.

Barbara brought her daughter to the family's pediatrician, Dr. Dorothy Wyvell. After Robin was examined and a blood test was taken, the pediatrician asked Barbara to return that afternoon with her husband. Barbara was understandably alarmed and quickly called George.

George Bush recalled, "I was at the Ector County courthouse, twenty miles from Midland, checking land records, when Barbara called. She said Dr. Wyvell wanted to see us, right away. Dorothy Wyvell was the children's doctor. In a town the size of Midland, more than a doctor, she was a warm, personal friend."[19]

When they returned to Dr. Wyvell's office, she greeted them at the door with tears in her eyes.

"I'll never forget it," George said. "We walked in and the first thing, she pulled a Kleenex out of the box and just kind of wiped her eye. Then she said, 'I've got some bad news for you.'"[20]

Dr. Wyvell explained that Robin had acute leukemia.

"Barbara seemed to understand the full meaning of what the doctor had said, but I didn't at first," George recalled. "When I asked what could be done, the answer stunned me. Nothing, said Dr. Wyvell. The disease was rampant. Robin's case was advanced, and she had only a short time to live. It might be a few weeks; it might be only days. Her deeply felt counsel to us was that we take Robin home, keep her as comfortable as possible, and let nature take its course."[21]

The pediatrician predicted that Robin had less than a month to live.

The Bushes were stunned.

They disregarded doctor's orders and sought help. "After we came home from the doctor's office, I called my uncle, Dr. John Walker, in New York City," George said. "He was president of Memorial Hospital there and a former cancer specialist. When I told him the news about Robin, he urged us to bring her to New York, where early research into leukemia was being conducted at Memorial Hospital by the Sloan–Kettering Foundation. Maybe nothing could be done, he told us, but we would never forgive ourselves if we didn't try. Even if the odds were a hundred million to one, said John, `You've got to give life a chance.'"[22]

The little girl was immediately admitted to the eminent New York research hospital, and was given a new cancer drug. Her condition improved.

In the next seven months, Robin and her mother flew between New York City and Midland, Texas, as she was treated again and again at Sloan–Kettering. Barbara rarely left Robin's side, whether they were in New York or Texas.

A Bush biographer wrote, "Robin was brave. She didn't know she was going to die, though she knew she was pretty sick. Barbara wouldn't allow anybody to cry in Robin's room. The worst offenders were George and his mother, Dorothy Bush."[23]

The boys, at home in Texas, needed parental love and affection, too. When their mother was home, she did what she could. When she was in New York, George became both mother and father. On the weekends, he flew to New York to be with Robin. George W. and Jeb stayed with neighbors. Eventually Dorothy Bush, George's mother, sent a nurse down to help her son with his children.

During this period, George Bush deteriorated while Barbara was more sturdy. "He was just killing himself, while I was very strong," Barbara said.[24]

Onlookers agreed with Barbara's conclusion. For instance, Lud Ashley, who knew George Bush at Yale and who was living in New York during Robin's illness, said, "I never saw Barbara cry. It was one of the wonders."[25]

"In the next six months there were periods of remission, when Robin almost seemed to be the healthy little girl we'd always known," George said. "I remember once walking with her when she was holding my hand and laughing. Because of her blood transfusions, she was especially beautiful and full of life that day. I ran into an acquaintance, we talked briefly, and as we got ready to move on, he asked, `George, how is your other kid doing—the one sick with leukemia?' He had no idea he was talking about the vivacious little girl beside me."[26]

But Robin's leukemia did not go away.

"Despite these periods of remission, the doctors kept telling us not to get our hopes up," George recalled. "Their prognosis was the same as Dorothy Wyvell's. Robin had the highest white blood cell count they'd ever seen in a patient. They'd do their best, but there was nothing known to medical science that could help."[27]

"Spring passed into summer, summer into fall," he said. "Barbara stayed at the bedside; I shuttled between Midland and New York City."[28]

The Bushes' roller–coaster life speeded up when they learned of a report that a Kansas City doctor had discovered a cure for leukemia.

"Poor George got on the phone and called and called until he got the doctor," Barbara said. "George had gotten his hopes up so."[29]

"Then one day in October, Robin started to hemorrhage. `Our uncle–doctor, whom we love more than life, thought we ought to let her go,' Barbara remembers. `The doctors at Memorial wanted to operate—I opted to go with them.' And then, talking about it 36 years later at the White House, Barbara started to cry. `She was very, very sick. She never came out of the operation.' When Robin died, both George and Barbara were with her."[30]

Their little girl passed away on October 11, 1953, about seven months—half a year more than the time she was originally given—after her disease was diagnosed. Her little body was ravaged—one leg was totally bruised and her stomach was covered with ulcers.

Robin's body was donated to research. "First of all, I know there's a God and secondly, I know Robin left," Barbara said. "We both had that feeling that she wasn't there. We combed her hair and she wasn't there."[31]

How Did the Bushes Cope?

Sequential Grieving

Sometimes couples divorce after the death of a child because they cannot talk to each other about their loss. The Bushes never let that happen. They were able to share their feelings and they also took turns in their moments of heaviest grieving. Barbara and George seemed to sense when the other needed more comfort. That is the way "a good marriage works," Barbara said. "Had I cried a lot, he wouldn't have. But things reversed after she died. George seemed to accept it better."[32]

Barbara Bush was the strong partner during Robin's illness. George Bush fell apart. He cried continuously during her last months of life, although Barbara would not allow him to do so in Robin's room. Barbara never shed a tear.[33] But when Robin died, the couple exchanged roles. Barbara crumpled. George became strong. He even returned to the hospital on the day after Robin's death to thank everyone who had helped her. Again, the Bushes took turns in their grieving. Whenever one was devastated by grief, the other showed strength.

Couples in strong marriages share their burdens as well as their joys. They allow each other time to feel sadness as well as other emotions. The death of a child truly taxes their ability to sequence their feelings.

The couple returned to Texas, where their pain became physical, "like our hearts were breaking," she said. Barbara wanted to retreat from the world. "I nearly fell apart," she said. "I couldn't put my right foot in front of my left."[34]

Barbara surrendered to her sorrow. "I just fell apart when Robin died. I hadn't cried at all when she was alive," Barbara said, "but after she died I felt I could cry forever."[35]

Meanwhile, George gained stamina. He refused to allow Barbara to escape into her anguish. "He just didn't let me misbehave. He never let me be alone,"[36]

Barbara recalled those days, when speaking to the Republican National Convention in 1988. "He held me in his arms and he made me share it and accept that his sorrow was as great as my own," she said. "He simply wouldn't allow my grief to divide us. . . push us apart, which is what happens so often where there is a loss like that. And for as long as I live, I will respect and appreciate my husband for the strength of his understanding."[37]

Barbara's husband was critical to her survival, but their children played a role as well. Understandably, Barbara became very protective of her two living children. She rarely let them out of her sight. She related, "One day I heard my son George tell a friend, `I can't play today because I have to be with my mother— she's so unhappy.' That's when I realized you either pull together or you shatter."[38] George W.'s comment was probably a turning point in Barbara's ability to cope with her loss.

Reliance on Religion

The Bushes religious background also played a role in their recovery. While Robin was ill, her father began going to church by himself early in the morning to pray.

"I can tell you that there was no one for us to turn to but God," he said. "And I really learned to pray. I would slip into our church sometimes when no one was there. I would ask God why? Why this little innocent girl?"[39]

The church custodian detected Bush's presence each morning at 6:00 a.m. in the church and shared the information with the minister. The clergyman was responsive. "The minister then came every day. He didn't say anything. He just was there,"[40] Barbara said.

The Bushes also prayed together as they shared their day time and night time vigil at the hospital. Rather than despair, they tried to find something positive in their lives.

"We looked around and nobody had what we had," Barbara said.

"They either didn't believe in God, or they didn't love each other or they didn't have other children or they didn't have brothers and sisters. In a way it was good for us because we realized we had much more than anybody else."[41] They took comfort in what they had—love, faith, each other and their families—rather than agonizing over the one thing they did not have—a healthy daughter.

"Prayer had always been an important part of our lives, but never more so than during those six months. Barbara and I sustained each other; but in the end, it was our faith that truly sustained us. . . To this day, like every parent who has ever lost a child, we wonder why; yet we know that, whatever the reason, she is in God's loving arms,"[42] George said.

Helping Others

Volunteer work also helped Barbara Bush assuage the grief. After she had overheard her son, George W., explain to a friend that he had to stay with his mother, she threw herself into volunteer work. She began by starting a woman's exchange in Midland.

Barbara Bush was a lifelong volunteer. When her husband was the U. N. ambassador, from 1971 until 1973, she returned to the Memorial-Sloan Kettering Cancer Center where Robin was a patient, this time as a volunteer. Each Tuesday and Thursday morning, she provided whatever help was needed. She comforted patients who needed cheering up, but she was also not above emptying bedpans and doing some of the less glamorous jobs.

Renewed Hope

Life circumstances, including other children, competed with the couple's focus on their acute pain. Their son, Neil, was born fifteen months after Robin's death. Marvin followed just twenty–two months after his brother.

Barbara and George still suffered from chronic grief. Four years after Robin's death, twenty–four–year–old Otha Taylor served as their parttime babysitter for the four children. She recalled, "They were all still grieving." Every time the subject came up, she said, Mrs. Bush would say, "'What I'm going to do, I'm going to keep trying until I get another girl.'"[43]

Three years after Marvin's birth, and six years after Robin's death, Barbara got her wish. The couple's only living daughter, Dorothy—known as Doro—was born to complete their family.

For most couples, the death of a child results in the death of the marriage as well. George Bush wisely noted, "You know, the death of a child can be a family maker or breaker. As we shared our loss, Barbara and I grew stronger together."[44]

Barbara Bush added, that she does not dwell morbidly on her daughter's death. "I think of her now with much love and happiness."[45]

The Secret of Surviving Couples:
Remember the Past, Consider the Future, but Live in the Present

---

Politics aside, no one can disagree that George and Barbara Bush have had a wonderful marriage. What would their advice be for other couples? Barbara Bush answers easily, "I've often wondered how I could have been so lucky to have married George Bush. George is the least negative person I know, and he always has been. Nothing is impossible for George Bush. I'm not talking about the Presidency. I'm talking about how he'll say, `Let's get a group and have a picnic tonight.'"

"And I'll say, `Well, we can't ask the British ambassador tonight. I mean, it's too late.' And George will say, `Let's just try.' "That's his whole life, and of course you will end up by doing it. He's right, of course. Nothing's too much trouble for him—nothing ventured, nothing gained sort of approach—and he was very exciting to be around and still is."[46]

She adds a surprising disclosure about her husband.

"Well. . . he's very funny. And I always say to him, `Be funny so I can tell people some hysterically funny things you just did.' But George has good timing, and good timing is not repeatable, because it's his timing, not my timing. But he has fabulous timing, and he is funny."[47]

George Bush attributes their happy marriage to "give and take, respect for one another's opinions and giving each other elbow room in terms of not insisting on doing what *you* want. Barbara has her own array of interests," he said, "yet she never loses interest in the family or how I'm feeling about things. If I am down, she cares a lot."[48]

These bromides are good advice for any couple. However, the Bushes' lived experiences provide even more interesting advice. An examination of their behaviors and their communication illustrates that one of the foundations in the Bush marriage is the importance of time. For them, timing may be everything. Barbara Bush foreshadowed this notion when she discussed George's sense of humor.

Throughout their lives together, the Bushes have illustrated the importance of timing. Their time management has allowed them to have provided more time in service to country and to others than most other American couples. They also stress the importance of reserving time for themselves and their family, regardless of outside demands. Finally, and perhaps most important, they illustrate the importance of remembering the past, considering the future, but living in the precious present.

Timing is Everything

Throughout the story of the Bushes relationship is the importance of timing. For example, the couple met when they were home for the Christmas holiday from high schools in separate parts of the country. Timing was also important when, after they were introduced, the band changed tempo from the fox trot to the waltz. Since George did not do the waltz, they decided to spend time talking and getting to know each other.

Later when George was involved in flight training, he received seventeen days off. This event allowed him to invite Barbara to his family's home for an extended vacation. The event was critical: "They sailed, played tennis, rode bicycles, went on picnics, hung around with the large Bush family—and decided they would get married."[49]

Timing is important. This point was humorously illustrated by Arthur Goldberg who later served as the US ambassador to the United Nations (1965-1968) and chair of the US United Nations Association (1968-1970) when he served as President John F.

Kennedy's Secretary of Labor. In this post, he was congratulated by President Kennedy for averting a labor strike. "How did you do it, Arthur?" he asked. Goldberg smiled. "The trick is to be there when it's settled," he replied.[50] The Bushes, too, knew when to be there.

Organizing Time

A well known maxim suggests that "One always has time enough, if one will apply it well."[51] The Bushes serve as a prime example. The service that they have provided to others is superhuman. They have both spent hours in assistance to others—George in the public sphere and Barbara through volunteerism.

When they talk about their lives, it is clear that they are highly organized people. They each have priorities from which they do not deviate. Marvin Bush, the couple's fourth son discussed his father's schedule. "`A lot of candidates spend their time in their hotel room trying to regroup; he regroups on the airplane, where he has a chance to talk to people and get their advice.' When he lands he goes out for exercise. `It energizes him,' Marvin Bush says. `It makes him feel good.'"[52]

Barbara Bush has a clear vision of her time. She told a reporter that she spends "fifty percent of my time on volunteer projects, charitable causes and, of course, my fight for literacy; twenty-five percent handling organizational things about our house or our trips or my mail; selfishly maybe ten percent exercising or squeezing in one stolen game of tennis; and fifteen percent on my husband and children—unless they suddenly need more."[53]

Her daily routine confirms her division of time. "Mrs. Bush is usually up by six, walks Millie, plunges into a day of social appointments, official functions, planning of state dinners and family luncheons, time out for tennis, and ample time for the cause she is most deeply involved in: literacy and reading–motivation programs. As the Vice President's wife, she made hundreds of appearances related to literacy, and last winter she announced formation of the Barbara Bush Foundation for Family Literacy."[54]

Barbara Bush has spent a life time as a volunteer. She learned about volunteerism from her parents. "My mother and father did things for others. You know, it just never occurred to me everybody didn't do that."[55]

Her volunteerism has as much benefit for her as it does for others.

"After our little girl [Robin] died, I started a women's exchange in Midland. I put my head down and worked there for over a year. George was marvelously understanding. If I didn't work there I worked at home on a project and did the best I could with the children, and we were all right. But I needed that. It was very important to me. The pain was so extraordinary.I believe I have gotten at different times in my life extraordinarily much more out of [service projects] than I've given."[56]

The former first lady explains her interest in helping others. "There's the story—I think it's George's story I stole—of a child walking on the beach with his grandfather [amid] all the starfish. The child picks them up and throws them back into the ocean, and the grandfather says, `There are millions of them on the beach; you can't make a difference.' And the boy says, `Well, I can for this one.' And he throws it back in the water. That's sort of the way I feel. You've got to start someplace."[57]

When Barbara Bush became the First Lady, she had less time to do volunteer work than she had before. However, she still believed she could make a contribution. "I gave hours of time. And of course, money. Now what I can do best is highlight these programs."[58]

Barbara Bush is an appropriate symbol and lobbyist for the 80 million Americans who are volunteers. "Helping others has been a longtime theme for Barbara Bush. She serves on the national board of Reading Is Fundamental (RIF) and is a sponsor of Laubach Literacy international, a worldwide program committed to eradicating illiteracy. Project Head Start is another of her interests, as is the Chapter One Program, which assists children in deprived areas. She also serves as honorary chairwoman of the Leukemia Society of America. In addition, Mrs. Bush is particularly concerned with the problem of the homeless and the fact that one third of them now consist of families. She said that in Washington, D.C., alone, there are about 500 homeless families, with some 1,500 children."[59]

A sage observed that "Time is at once the most valuable and the most perishable of all our possessions."[60] Barbara Bush recognized this idea when she observed, "Everybody has something, whether you have time or money or know–how or space. Today you can no longer say, `The drug problem worries me' or `Illiteracy worries me.' If it worries you, then you've got to do something about it."[61]

Neal Sutherland, an oncologist in Hawaii, is an individual who has similarly devoted himself to the service of others. He said:

> ... I have chosen being with cancer patients because I felt that if I were with them enough, I could find the secret of living one day at a time and why some cancer patients are able to find such phenomenal inner peace through their disease. . . I think I now understand that inner peace and the transformation that leads to that inner peace. From my perspective it seems that it involves being willing to give up life as we normally perceive it and view life only as a moment by moment occurrence of opportunities to give love. In the giving of love, there is also the receiving of love, and this cycle grows endlessly and without bounds.[62]

Barbara Bush knows this secret. By providing so much help to others, she has received love in turn.

Time for the Family

The Bushes also find it essential to find time for their family. Barbara has no regrets about the amount of time she has devoted to her family. "Family life is important to me. And for what's important you pay the price. So . . . I never really resented the time I put in."[63]

In 1990, Barbara Bush was the commencement speaker at Wellesley College. The graduating class had selected novelist Alice Walker as their first choice, but she had refused their invitation. Barbara Bush was their second choice and some of the women protested believing that Barbara represented a woman who was only well–known because of her husband, not because of her own contributions.

Barbara used the opportunity to cue the young women, "But as important as your obligations as a doctor, a lawyer, a business leader will be, you are a human being first, and those human connections with spouses, with children, with friends are the most important investment you will ever make.[64]

She encouraged the young women to make "family and friends paramount, to cherish the human connections." She said, "Whatever the era, whatever the times, one thing will never change." She added, "Fathers and mothers, if you have children, they must come first. You must read to your children and you must hug your children and you must love your children. Your success as a family, our success as a society, depends not on what happens in the White House, but on what happens inside your house."[65]

Barbara Bush practiced what she preached. "My children have had only minor problems," she says sharply. "They don't forget, I'm right there with them every step. You'd better believe that I'm never to busy for my children. I absolutely have the time for them. And their father has, too. And all their brothers and sisters."[66]

Her oldest son, George W., attests to her presence. "Mom was unselfish with her time. I played a lot of Little League baseball, and I still have vivid memories of seeing her sitting at our games, keeping score. She bent over backward for me and my brothers, especially in our love of sports."[67]

Barbara's focus on her children is extended now to her grandchildren. As early as September of 1988, she discussed what she would do when she left the White House. High among her priorities was spending more time relaxing with her grandchildren.[68]

As important as Barbara Bush's children and grandchildren are, George Bush comes first. The couple has always arranged their lives to have time alone together. For example, they have had a lifetime habit of spending an hour in bed in the morning, reading the newspapers, having juice and coffee, and watching the TV news.

Biographer Pamela Kilian asked Barbara how her husband's love manifests itself. Barbara responded, "Mostly in the way he shares his life with me. He is thoughtful, he telephones me frequently and he asks what I want to do or where I want to go. He never refuses me what I want or need. . . for forty three years, he has taken the most wonderful care of me and the family."[69]

People in long and satisfying marriages learn to be unselfish in their giving to each other. They put each other first. Sometimes people in younger, newer marriages do not understand the importance of this behavior in their marital lives.

Barbara Bush put her husband first, but she always had time for all of the family members. Son George W. recalled that she "put her relationship with her husband above her relationship with us." He added that this did not cause resentment among the siblings because their mother "was so generous with her time for all family members."[70]

Apparently the Bush strategy worked. Pamela Kilian wrote, "None of the Bush children is estranged from each other or from their parents. Everyone in the family appears to like everyone else, and though the relationships are not perfect or problem free, the whole family pulls together in time of triumph and crisis—and often, just for fun."[71]

THE PRECIOUS PRESENT

The most important lesson about time provided by the Bushes is prophesied in the book, *The Precious Present*. The book tells the story of a boy who learned from an old man about "the precious present." The old man explained:

> "It is a present because
> it is a gift,"
> the contented man explained.
> "And it is precious because
> anyone who receives
> such a present
> is happy forever."

The little boy misunderstands the old man and interprets "present" to mean a gift rather than the current time. However, the youngster plays and works with enthusiasm and joy. The old man observes him and gains pleasure. As the young boy matures, he comes back time and again asking the old man what the precious present might be. The old man smiles and tells him that he already knew what it was when he was a child. The maturing man does not understand and asks still again and again. The old man explains, "The Precious Present is not something that someone gives you. It is a gift that you give yourself."

The younger man spends his lifetime searching for the precious present but only much later does he realize the wisdom of the older man who is now gone. One day, as he sat thinking, he discerned:

> The present is what is.
> It is valuable.
> Even if I do not know why.
> It is already just the way
> It is supposed to be.
> When I see the present,
> accept the present, and
> experience the present,
> I am well, and
> I am happy.

Pain is simply the difference
between
what is
and
what I want it to be.
When I feel guilty
over my imperfect past,
Or I am anxious
over my unknown future,
I do not live in the present.
I experience pain.
I make myself ill.
And I am unhappy.
My past was
the present.
And my future will be
the present.
The present moment is
the only reality
I ever experience.
As long as I
continue to stay
in the present,
I am happy forever:
because forever
is always
the present.
The present is simply who I am
just the way I am. . .
right now.
And it is precious.
I am precious.
I am The Precious Present.[72]

Another book explains the sentiment of this story quite simply.

We have been given everything we need to be happy now. To look directly at this instant is to be at peace. . . And we are unconcerned with what we said or did in the past, or whether someone we think mistreated us will get what he [sic] deserves. To be fully content within this moment is a state of mind so powerful in its ability to heal and extend peace that it cannot be even hinted at in words. Anxiety— the only alternative to trusting what is happening—is a state of immobilization caused by our focusing on what we believe cannot be changed: on what is over, or on what has not occurred.[73]

The author adds, "This instant is the only time there is."[74]

People often dwell on the past and dread the future. Yet as *The Precious Present* tells us, children intuitively understand how to live in the present. Gerald Jampolsky writes:

I have often thought that we have much to learn from infants. They have not yet adapted to the concept of linear time with a past, present and future. They relate only to the immediate present, to right *now*. It is my hunch that they do not see the world as fragmented. They feel that they are joined to everything in the world as part of a whole."[75]

We lose our ability to live in the moment as we grow older. The joys of each day are forfeited for the unpleasant memories of the past and the worries for the future. As adults we adopt the belief that the past predicts the future. We live in fear for what has been and for what is yet to come.

The idea that the future is dangerous might thus be more prevalent among people who have known problems than among those whose lives have been relatively trouble free. People who lose children, for example, might feel that their lives are doomed. They might lose hope for any future happiness. They might believe that any surviving children will similarly die. They might lose interest in their spouse and other family members. Their negative thoughts might create a self–fulfilling prophesy which allows them to spiral even deeper into despair and desolation.

Strangely enough, some people who have weathered the storms of unpredicted stress become even stronger. They learn from, and live in, the precious present. Their tragedies become positive—not negative—turning points. Their marriages are strengthened; their bonds with others are sustained.

The death of one's child or one's own potential death may provide the invaluable lesson of living in the present. One person described his own experience with cancer:

> Three years ago, I was graced with cancer. I looked my
> whole life for a teacher, and it wasn't until I got cancer that
> I really started to pay attention to the preciousness of each
> breath, to the momentum of each thought, till I saw that
> this moment is all. All my other teachers gave me ideas.
> This caused me to directly experience my life. When I got
> cancer, it was up to me to get born before I died.[76]

Barbara and George Bush have not forgotten their past and they
certainly have plans for the future. But, most important, they value
the present. When they speak about their past, they have no regrets.
Barbara Bush's biographer writes, "Barbara has never been the kind
of woman who spends much time on regrets. Life for her, whether
at the White House, in Maine, or in Texas, is always full speed ahead,
with as much fun and fellowship along the way as she can muster."[77]

The recollection of specific past events does not bring
recrimination or remorse to the surface. Barbara was asked about
never completing her college education at Smith College. She
responded quickly, "Why, I have had my own career as a
homemaker. I chose my life, and I have no regrets. I raised our
children and now George and I watch, with satisfaction, how they
bring up their children."[78]

She added, ". . . life's sole purpose is not just to gain the top. It's
to live a full, good life . . . success is not counted in a title but in the
joy you get and give in life."[79]

Barbara Bush offers a similar perspective. Her husband agrees.
In a letter to his only surviving daughter, Dorothy, he wrote, "When
I hear Sam say hi Ba Ba, Iran seems inconsequential, the White House
is blurred, the future seems not to matter; and so it will be tomorrow
or the next day when we have someone else to love, to laugh with,
to wonder at...This is life its ownself. This is our very heartbeat, this
is what matters most... "[80]

Ralph Waldo Emerson, in his oration, "The American Scholar,"
said, "The time, like all times, is a very good one, if we but know
what to do with it."[81]

How can the death of one's child possibly be construed as a good
time? While it may never be seen positively, couples honor their lost
children by learning from the tragedy and going on to live in the
present. When George Bush was asked about the death of Robin, he

stated, "We were heartbroken, but we tried to find comfort in God—to accept and learn from our sorrow."[82] George, like Barbara, understands the importance of accepting the past and not letting it destroy the present or the future.

Barbara Bush concludes, "Life has its bumps. We should enjoy ourselves during the good times and make the most of the bad times."[83]

Why do people live in the past and dwell on their hardships? The book, *Love is Letting Go of Fear*, provides a clue:

> The world we see that seems so insane may be the result of a belief system that isn't working. The belief system holds that the fearful past will extend into a fearful future, making the past and the future one. It is our memory of fear and pain that makes us feel so vulnerable. It is this feeling of vulnerability that makes us want to control and predict the future at all costs.[84]

Margaret Storm Jameson, the British novelist, observed:

> I believe that only one person in a thousand knows the trick of really living in the present. Most of us spend fifty-nine minutes of every hour living in the past, with regret for lost joys, or shame for things badly done (both utterly useless and weakening)—or in a future we either long for or dread. . . The only way to live is by accepting each minute as an unrepeatable miracle.[85]

When people live in the precious present, they recognize that the current time is the best time. Barbara was asked by a journalist about the best time of her life. She answered, "`Oh that's easy. It's now, right now. But then,' she adds, mischievously, `I would have said the exact same thing last year, and the year before that.'"[86]

By living in the present, Barbara Bush is probably less like her mother than her mother–in–law. She elaborated on how she was different from her mother, Pauline. "`She always thought the grass was going to be greener sometime, some other place,' Barbara has said. `I don't believe that. I believe life is right now.'[87]

When George Bush's mother celebrated her birthday in 1990, her son asked her about her best birthday. Although Dorothy Bush was very frail, she reached for her son's hand and responded, "I think this one is best. My son is President of the United States."[88] Although the moment was touching, the sentiment suggests that Dorothy Bush, like her son and daughter–in–law, also lived in the present.

Barbara's speech to the women of Wellesley similarly emphasized the importance of seizing the day. She also used an appropriate reference to a movie popular at the time among young people. "Find the joy in life," she said, "because as Ferris Bueller said on his day off: 'Life moves pretty fast and if you don't stop and look around once in a while you are going to miss it.'"[89]

Her advice is not unlike that provided in the book, *Why Me? Coping with Grief, Loss, and Change*. The authors write:

> Families go through so much unnecessary aggravation, so much torment, so many failures of communication that tear them apart, so many unfinished agendas. It would be so different if we could accept the wisdom of Maimonides, the great rabbi, physician, and philosopher, who said we should look at each day as if it were our last. That way we would have to open up completely, drop all pretenses, and be right there with and for one another.[90]

Bernie S. Siegel, in *Peace, Love, & Healing*, concurs: "I can help you create heaven on earth by getting you to live in the moment. . . That's the way each day should be lived, with the sense that it may be your last."[91]

Living in the moment does not suggest that we should have no concern for the future. In 1962, President John F. Kennedy, spoke to an audience at the University of California in Berkeley. He used a story that he repeated in many other speeches. While the attribution to Marshal Lyautey is unverified, the story makes an important point:

> . . . we must think and act not only for the moment but for our time. I am reminded of the great French Marshal Lyautey, who once asked his gardener to plant a tree. The gardener objected that the tree was slow–growing and would not reach maturity for a hundred years. The Marshall replied, "In that case, there is no time to lose, plant it this afternoon."[92]

Although we must plan for the future, we cannot reside there if we are to be happy and have lives filled with love.

Barbara Bush lives life in the present. She neither dwells in the past nor does she fear the future. She is also down to earth. As the First Lady of the land, she said, "The simple fact is, George is now in office. And when the time comes that he's out, we'll both be out. That's the way Washington works. George and I expect that, and we don't disdain it. We've been around too long. That's part of political life, and I'm prepared for it."[93]

George Bush provided a similar response to the future. When he was asked what he would do if he lost the most recent Presidential election, he said, "I don't intend to lose. But should that happen, Barbara will still be my first lady."[94]

The wisdom provided by George and Barbara Bush is unmistakable. People in happy marriages recall the past and they consider the future, but for the most part they live in the present. We can choose our own reality. We have free wills to live today.

None of us can escape danger or harm. We are all at risk to natural disaster, disease, and accidents. We might, like George and Barbara Bush, lose a child. All living beings—including people—live and die. Ralph Waldo Emerson wrote, "These times of ours are serious and full of calamity, but all times are essentially alike. As soon as there is life there is danger."[95]

We can live like robots and act like other people and the events around us govern our lives. On the other hand, we can recognize that our lives are our own. We can determine to see the events and people around us through the lens of love rather than the focus of fear.

One of the secrets of surviving couples is living life with love in the precious present. We, too, are free to choose this moment in which to live our lives or to doom ourselves by dwelling on the past or worrying about the future.

REFERENCES

1. Originally published in 1859. This is from the 1958 publication, p. 3.
2. Pamela Kilian, *Barbara Bush: A Biography* (New York: St. Martin's Press, 1992), p. 57.
3. Donnie Radcliffe, *Simply Barbara Bush* (New York: Warner Books, 1989), p. 73.
4. Kilian, p. 24.
5. "George and Barbara Bush," *McCall's*, September 1988, p. 84.
6. Cory SerVaas, "Our Healthy Veep & Family," *The Saturday Evening Post*, October 1988, p. 43.
7. George Bush with Victor Gold, *Looking Forward* (New York: Doubleday), p. 31.
8. Donnie Radcliffe, "Barbara and George: Their Love Story," *Good Housekeeping*, November 1989, p. 259. (Excerpted from Donnie Radcliffe, *Simply Barbara Bush*, Warner Books, Inc., 1989).
9. Kilian, p. 57.
10. Kilian, p. 35.
11. Bush with Gold, p. 31.
12. Radcliffe, "Barbara and George: Their Love Story," p. 260.
13. Joe Hyams, *Flight of the Avenger* (New York: Harcourt Brace Jovanovich, 1991), p. 55.
14. Bush with Gold, p. 41.
15. Radcliffe, "Barbara and George: Their Love Story," p. 260.
16. Radcliffe, "Barbara and George: Their Love Story," p. 260.
17. Jean Libman Block, "The Best Time of my Life is Now," *Good Housekeeping*, November 1989, p. 255.
18. Kilian, p. 56.
19. Bush with Gold, p. 68.
20. Kathy Lewis, "Hospital Visit Evokes Memories of Bushes' Tragedy," *Houston Post*, June 29, 1986, p. 1A.
21. Bush with Gold, p. 68.
22. Bush with Gold, pp. 68-69.
23. Radcliffe, "Barbara and George: Their Love Story," p. 262.
24. Radlicffe, "Barbara and George: Their Love Story," p. 262.
25. Radcliffe, "Barbara and George: Their Love Story," p. 262.
26. Bush with Gold, p. 69.
27. Bush with Gold, p. 69.
28. Bush with Gold, p. 69.
29. Kilian, p. 58.
30. Radcliffe, "Barbara and George: Their Love Story," p. 262.
31. Radcliffe, *Simply Barbara Bush*, p. 119.
32. Radcliffe, "Barbara and George: Their Love Story," p. 262.
33. Although Barbara Bush was a stalwart during this period of time, she did experience a physical change. Although she was only twenty–eight years old, Barbara became gray. She tried a variety of hair color treatments; none of which were successful. She finally gave up her attempts at changing her hair color during her husband's unsuccessful race for the U. S. Senate in 1964. Those who criticize the former first lady for looking older than her husband, principally because of her gray hair, might be more tolerant

when they understand the circumstances under which her hair changed color.

34. Kilian, p. 58.
35. Radcliffe, "Barbara and George: Their Love Story," p. 262.
36. Radcliffe, "George and Barbara: Their Love Story," p. 262.
37. Kilian, pp. 58-59.
38. Radcliffe, "Barbara and George: Their Love Story," p. 262.
39. Doug Wead, *George Bush, Man of Integrity* (Eugene, Oregon: Harvest House, 1988), pp. 46-47.
40. Kilian, p. 57.
41. Kilian, p. 58.
42. Bush with Gold, p. 69.
43. Kilian, p. 69.
44. "George and Barbara Bush," p. 84
45. "George and Barbara Bush," p. 84.
46. SerVaas, p. 45.
47. SerVaas, p. 45.
48. "A First Lady Who Cares," *Newsweek*, July 10, 1989, pp. 43-44.
49. Kilian, p. 41.
50. Reprinted in Clifton Fadiman, general editor, *The Little, Brown Book of Anecdotes* (Boston: Little, Brown and Company, 1985), p. 247.
51. Johann Wolfgang von Goethe, *The Autobiography of Johann Wolfgang Von Goethe*, trans. John Oxenford, vol. 2, book 10, 1974, p. 16.
52. SerVaas, p. 71.
53. Cindy Adams, "Barbara Bush First Lady, First Class,"*Ladies Home Journal*, November, 1990, p. 275.
54. Block, p. 257.
55. "The Good Fortune of Being Barbara Bush," *U. S. News and World Report*, May 28, 1990, p. 26.
56. "The Good Fortune of Being Barbara Bush," p. 26.
57. "The Good Fortune of Being Barbara Bush," pp. 26-27.
58. "A First Lady Who Cares," p. 43.
59. "George and Barbara Bush," p. 83.
60. John Randolph of Roanoke. In William Cabell Bruce, *John Randolph of Roanoke, 1773-1833*, vol. 2, chapter 7, (1922, reprinted 1970), p. 205. Randolph was a member of congress from 1799-1813, 1815-1817, and 1819-1829.
61. "A First Lady Who Cares," p. 44.
62. Cited in Bernie S. Siegel, *Communication and the Path to Self-Healing* (New York: HarperPerennial, 1990), p. 151.
63. Block, p. 257.
64. Kilian, p. 5.
65. Kilian, p. 13.
66. Adams, p. 276.
67. "George and Barbara Bush," p. 85.
68. "George and Barbara Bush," p. 82.
69. "George and Barbara Bush," p. 85.
70. Kilian, p. 69.
71. Kilian, p. 65.
72. Spencer Johnson, *The Precious Present* (New York: Doubleday & Company, 1981).

TO PLACE AN ORDER

Telephone

USA/Canada:	**1-800-228-0810**
International:	**1-319-589-1000**

Hours: 7:00 am - 6:00 pm, Monday - Friday

(Central Time)

Fax

USA/Canada:	1-800-772-9165
International:	1-319-589-1046

Hours: 24 hours a day / 7 days a week

(You may use the form on the next page.)

Mail

Kendall/Hunt Publishing Company
Kendall/Hunt Customer Service
4050 Westmark Drive, P.O. Box 1840
Dubuque, IA 52004-1840

(You may use the form on the next page.)

We fulfill all orders within twenty-four hours of entry. If no shipping instructions are given, we determine the most appropriate method and ship accordingly. For individual orders, shipping and handling charges are $3.50 for the first book and $.50 for each additional book.

All individual orders must be prepaid. We accept Master Card, Visa, or American Express. Sorry, no C.O.D.'s.

Orders being shipped to California, Iowa, Kentucky, Louisiana, and New York are subject to local sales tax unless a tax exemption certificate has been furnished to Kendall/Hunt.

ORDER FORM

To: Kendall/Hunt Publishing Company
Customer Service Department

Fax: 1-800-772-9165 (USA/Canada)
1-319-589-1046 (International)

From: _____

_____

Quantity	ISBN #	Author	Edition

Account number: _____ Purchase Order #: _____

Bill to:
Name: _____
Title: _____ Affiliation: _____
Address: _____
City: _____ State: _____ Zip Code: _____
Telephone Number: (_____) _____

Ship to: (only if different from "Bill to:")
Name: _____
Title: _____ Affiliation: _____
Address: _____
City: _____ State: _____ Zip Code: _____
Telephone Number: (_____) _____

Type of Credit Card: MASTER CARD   VISA   AMERICAN EXPRESS

Card Number: _____ Expiration Date: _____
Name (as it appears on card): _____
Signature: _____